SMALL BUSINESS CONSIDERATIONS, ECONOMICS AND RESEARCH

SMALL BUSINESS ADMINISTRATION INVESTMENT AND LOAN PROGRAMS

SMALL BUSINESS CONSIDERATIONS, ECONOMICS AND RESEARCH

Additional books in this series can be found on Nova's website under the Series tab.

Additional E-books in this series can be found on Nova's website under the E-book tab.

BUSINESS ISSUES, COMPETITION AND ENTREPRENEURSHIP

Additional books in this series can be found on Nova's website under the Series tab.

Additional E-books in this series can be found on Nova's website under the E-book tab.

SMALL BUSINESS CONSIDERATIONS, ECONOMICS AND RESEARCH

SMALL BUSINESS ADMINISTRATION INVESTMENT AND LOAN PROGRAMS

ALAN R. CONNOLY
EDITOR

nova publishers
New York

For permission to use material from this book please contact us:
Telephone 631-231-7269; Fax 631-231-8175
Web Site: http://www.novapublishers.com

Library of Congress Cataloging-in-Publication Data

ISBN: 978-1-62417-674-6

Published by Nova Science Publishers, Inc. † New York

Contents

PREFACE

The Small Business Administration's (SBA's) Small Business Investment Company (SBIC) Program is designed to enhance small business access to venture capital by stimulating and supplementing "the flow or private equity capital and long term loan funds which small business concerns need for the sound financing of their business operations and for their growth, expansion, and modernization, and which are not available in adequate supply." Facilitating the flow of capital to small businesses to stimulate the national economy was, and remains, the SBIC program's primary objective. This book examines small business administration investment and loan programs with a focus on the SBIC; SBA New Markets Venture Capital program; Small Business Administration 7(a) Loan Guaranty Program; the Small Business Administration 504/CDC Loan Guaranty Program; and the microloan program.

Chapter 1 – The Small Business Administration's (SBA's) Small Business Investment Company (SBIC) Program is designed to enhance small business access to venture capital by stimulating and supplementing "the flow of private equity capital and long term loan funds which small business concerns need for the sound financing of their business operations and for their growth, expansion, and modernization, and which are not available in adequate supply." Facilitating the flow of capital to small businesses to stimulate the national economy was, and remains, the SBIC program's primary objective. At the end of FY2011, there were 299 privately owned and managed SBICs licensed by the SBA participating in the SBIC program, providing financing to small businesses with private capital the SBIC has raised (called regulatory capital) and with funds the SBIC borrows at favorable rates (called leverage) because the SBA guarantees the debenture (loan obligation). SBICs pursue investments in a broad range of industries, geographic areas, and stages of investment. Some SBICs specialize in a particular field or industry, while others invest more generally. Most SBICs concentrate on a particular stage of investment (i.e., startup, expansion, or turnaround) and geographic area. The SBA is authorized to provide up to $3 billion in leverage to SBICs annually. The SBIC program has invested or committed about $17.1 billion in small businesses, with the SBA's share of capital at risk about $8.3 billion. In FY2011, the SBA guaranteed $1.8 billion in SBIC small business investments, and SBICs provided another $1.0 billion in investments from private capital, for a total of more than $2.8 billion in financing for 1,339 small businesses. Some Members of Congress and small business advocates have argued that the SBIC program should be expanded as a means to stimulate economic activity, create jobs, and assist in the national economic recovery. For example, S. 2136, a bill to increase the maximum amount of leverage permitted under title III of the Small Business Investment Act of 1958, would increase the program's authorization to $4 billion from $3 billion. Others worry about the potential risk an expanded SBIC program has for increasing the federal deficit. In their view, the best means to assist small business, promote economic growth, and create jobs is to reduce business taxes and exercise federal fiscal restraint. Some Members and small business advocates have also proposed that the program target additional assistance to startup and early stage small businesses, which are generally viewed as relatively risky investments but also as having a relatively high potential for job creation. The SBA, in an effort to target additional assistance to newer businesses, recently established, as part of the Administration's Startup America Initiative, a $1 billion early stage debenture SBIC initiative (up to $150 million in leverage in FY2012, and up to $200 million in leverage per fiscal year thereafter until the limit is reached). Early stage debenture SBICs are required to invest at least 50% of their investments in early stage small businesses, defined as small businesses that have never achieved positive cash flow from operations in any fiscal year. This report describes the SBIC program's structure and operations, including two recent SBA initiatives, one targeting early stage small businesses and one targeting underserved markets. It also examines legislative proposals to increase the leverage available to SBICs (e.g., H.R. 3219, the Small Business Investment Company Modernization Act of 2011) and to increase the SBIC program's authorization amount to $4 billion.

Chapter 2 – Authorized by P.L. 106-554, the Consolidated Appropriations Act, 2001 (Appendix H — the New Markets Venture Capital Program Act of 2000), the New Markets Venture Capital (NMVC) program is designed to promote economic development and the creation of wealth and job opportunities in low-income geographic areas by addressing the unmet equity investments needs of small businesses located in those areas. Modeled on the SBA's Small Business Investment Company (SBIC) program, SBA-selected, privately owned and managed NMVC companies provide funding and operational training assistance to small businesses using private capital the NMVC company has raised (called regulatory capital) and up to 150% of that amount (called leverage) from the sale of SBA-guaranteed 10-year debentures (loan obligations) to third parties, subject to the availability of funds. Because the SBA guarantees the debenture, the SBA is able to obtain favorable interest rates. NMVC companies are responsible for meeting the terms and conditions set forth in the debenture. At least 80% of the investments must be in small businesses located in a low-income area. Specialized Small Business Investment Companies (SSBICs) established under the SBIC program are also eligible for NMVC operational assistance training grants, which are awarded on a dollar-to-dollar matching basis. There are currently six NMVC companies participating in the program. The NMVC program was appropriated $21.952 million in FY2001 to support up to $150 million in SBA guaranteed debentures and $30 million for operational assistance training grants for FY2001 through FY2006. The funds were provided in a lump sum in FY2001 and were to remain available until expended. In 2003, the unobligated balances of $10.5 million for the NMVC debenture subsidies and $13.75 million for operational assistance grants were rescinded. The program continues to operate, with the number and amount of financing declining in recent years as the program's initial investments expire and NMVC companies engage only in additional follow-on financings with the small businesses in their portfolio. More than 30 bills have been introduced in recent Congresses to either expand or amend the NMVC program. Many of these bills would increase the program's funding. For example, during the 112th Congress, H.R. 2872, the Job Creation and

Urban Revitalization Act of 2011, was introduced on September 8, 2011. The bill would provide the NMVC program such subsidy budget authority as may be necessary to guarantee $75 million of debentures and $15 million for operational assistance training grants for FY2012 through FY2013. The bill was referred to the House Committee on Small Business on September 8, 2011, and is awaiting further action. This report examines the NMVC program's legislative origins and describes the program's eligibility and performance requirements for NMVC companies, eligibility requirements for small businesses seeking financing, and the definition of low-income areas. It also reviews regulations governing the SBA's financial assistance to NMVC companies and provides program statistics. The report concludes with an examination of (1) efforts to eliminate the program based on concerns that it duplicates other SBA programs and is relatively expensive, (2) the rescission of the program's unobligated funding in 2003, and (3) recent congressional efforts to provide the program additional funds.

Chapter 3 – The Small Business Administration (SBA) administers several programs to support small businesses, including loan guaranty programs designed to encourage lenders to provide loans to small businesses "that might not otherwise obtain financing on reasonable terms and conditions." The SBA's 7(a) loan guaranty program is considered the agency's flagship loan guaranty program. It is named from Section 7(a) of the Small Business Act of 1953 (P.L. 83-163, as amended), which authorized the SBA to provide business loans and loan guaranties to American small businesses. In FY2012, the SBA approved 44,377 7(a) loans amounting to more than $15.1 billion. Proceeds from 7(a) loans may be used to establish a new business or to assist in the operation, acquisition, or expansion of an existing business. Congressional interest in the 7(a) loan guaranty program has increased in recent years because of concerns that small businesses might be prevented from accessing sufficient capital to enable them to assist in the economic recovery. Some, including President Obama, argue that the SBA should be provided additional resources to assist small businesses in acquiring capital necessary to start, continue, or expand operations with the expectation that in so doing small businesses will create jobs. Others worry about the long-term adverse economic effects of spending programs that increase the federal deficit. They advocate business tax reduction, reform of financial credit market regulation, and federal fiscal restraint as the best means to assist small business economic growth and job creation. This report discusses the rationale provided for the 7(a) program; the program's borrower and lender eligibility standards and program requirements; and program statistics, including loan volume, loss rates, use of the proceeds, borrower satisfaction, and borrower demographics. It examines issues raised concerning the SBA's administration of the 7(a) program, including the oversight of 7(a) lenders and the program's lack of outcome-based performance measures. It also examines congressional action taken during the 111th Congress to help small businesses gain greater access to capital. For example, P.L. 111-5, the American Recovery and Reinvestment Act of 2009 (ARRA), provided $375 million to temporarily subsidize the 7(a) and 504/CDC loan guaranty programs' fees and to temporarily increase the 7(a) program's maximum loan guaranty percentage to 90%. P.L. 111-240, the Small Business Jobs Act of 2010, provided $505 million to extend the fee subsidies and 90% loan guaranty percentage through December 31, 2010; increased the 7(a) program's gross loan limit from $2 million to $5 million; and established an alternative size standard for the 7(a) and 504/CDC loan programs. P.L. 111-322, the Continuing Appropriations and Surface Transportation Extensions Act, 2011, authorized the SBA to continue the fee subsidies and 90% loan guaranty percentage through March 4, 2011, or until available funding was exhausted (which occurred on January 3, 2011). This report also examines three bills introduced during the 112th Congress that would affect the 7(a) program. S. 1828, a bill to increase small business lending, and for other purposes, would reinstate for a year following the date of its enactment ARRA's fee subsidies and 90% loan guaranty percentage for the 7(a) program. H.R. 2936, the Small Business Administration Express Loan Extension Act of 2011, would extend a one-year increase in the maximum loan amount for the SBAExpress program from $350,000 to $1 million for an additional year. That temporary increase expired on September 26, 2011. S. 532, the Patriot Express Authorization Act of 2011, would provide statutory authorization for the Patriot Express Pilot Program and increase its loan guaranty percentages and its maximum loan amount from $500,000 to $1 million. Information concerning the 7(a) program's SBAExpress, Patriot Express, Small Loan Advantage, and Community Advantage programs is also provided.

Chapter 4 – The Small Business Administration (SBA) administers programs to support small businesses, including several loan guaranty programs designed to encourage lenders to provide loans to small businesses "that might not otherwise obtain financing on reasonable terms and conditions." The SBA's 504 Certified Development Company (504/CDC) loan guaranty program is administered through non-profit Certified Development Companies (CDC). It provides long-term fixed rate financing for major fixed assets, such as land, buildings, equipment, and machinery. Of the total project costs, a third-party lender must provide at least 50% of the financing, the CDC provides up to 40% of the financing through a 100% SBA-guaranteed debenture, and the applicant provides at least 10% of the financing. It is named from Section 504 of the Small Business Investment Act of 1958 (P.L. 85-699, as amended), which authorized the program. In FY2012, the SBA approved 9,471 504/CDC loans amounting to about $6.7 billion. Congressional interest in the SBA's 504/CDC program has increased in recent years because of concern that small businesses might be prevented from accessing sufficient capital to assist in the economic recovery. During the 111th Congress, P.L. 111-240, the Small Business Jobs Act of 2010, increased the 504/CDC program's loan guaranty limits from $1.5 million to $5 million for "regular" borrowers, from $2 million to $5 million if the loan proceeds are directed toward one or more specified public policy goals, and from $4 million to $5.5 million for manufacturers. It also temporarily expanded, for two years, the types of projects eligible for 504/CDC program refinancing of existing debt, created an alternative 504/CDC size standard to increase the number of businesses eligible for assistance, and provided $510 million to extend temporary fee subsidies for the 504/CDC and 7(a) loan guaranty programs and a temporary increase in the 7(a) program's maximum loan guaranty percentage to 90%. The temporary fee subsidies and 90% loan guaranty percentage ended on January 3, 2011, and the temporary expansion of the projects eligible for 504/CDC program refinancing of existing debt expired on September 27, 2012. This report opens with a discussion of the rationale provided for the 504/CDC program, the program's borrower and lender eligibility standards, program requirements, and program statistics, including loan volume, loss rates, use of the proceeds, borrower satisfaction, and borrower demographics. It then examines congressional action taken during the 111th Congress to help small businesses gain greater access to capital, including the enactment of P.L. 111-5, the American Recovery and Reinvestment Act of 2009 (ARRA), and P.L. 111-240, the Small Business Jobs Act of 2010. It also discusses congressional efforts during the 112th Congress to extend the temporary expansion of the projects eligible for 504/CDC program refinancing of existing debt, which expired on September 27, 2012. For example, H.R. 2950, the Small Business Administration 504 Loan Refinancing Extension Act of 2011, would extend that expiration date another year and S. 3572, the Restoring Tax and Regulatory Certainty to Small Businesses Act of 2012, would extend that expiration date another year and a half. S. 1828, a bill to increase small business lending, and for other purposes, is also discussed. It would reinstate for a year following the date of its enactment the temporary fee subsidies for the 504/CDC and 7(a) programs and the 90% loan guaranty percentage for the 7(a) program, which ended on January 3, 2011. Issues raised concerning the SBA's administration of the program, including the oversight of 504/CDC lenders, are also discussed.

Chapter 5 – The Small Business Administration's (SBA's) Microloan program provides direct loans to qualified non-profit intermediary Microloan lenders who, in turn, provide "microloans" of up to $50,000 to small business owners, entrepreneurs, and non-profit child care centers. It also provides marketing, management, and technical assistance to Microloan borrowers and potential borrowers. The program was authorized in 1991 as a five-year demonstration project and became operational in 1992. It was made permanent, subject to reauthorization, in 1997. The SBA's Microloan program is designed to assist women, low-income, veteran, and minority entrepreneurs and small business owners and other individuals possessing the capability to operate successful business concerns by providing them small-scale loans for working capital or the acquisition of materials, supplies, or equipment. In FY2012, Microloan intermediaries provided 3,973 Microloans amounting to $44.7 million. The average Microloan was $11,254 and had a 8.18% interest rate. Critics of the SBA's Microloan program argue that it is expensive relative to alternative programs, duplicative of the SBA's 7(a) loan guaranty program, and subject to administrative shortfalls. The program's advocates argue that it provides assistance that reaches many who otherwise would not be served by the private sector and is an important source of capital and training assistance for low-income women and minority business owners. Congressional interest in the Microloan program has increased in recent years, primarily because microloans are viewed as a means to assist very small businesses, especially women- and minority-owned startups, to get loans that enable them to create and retain jobs. Job creation, always a congressional interest, has taken on increased importance given the nation's current economic difficulties. This report opens with a discussion of the rationale provided for having a Microloan program, describes the program's eligibility standards and operating requirements for lenders and borrowers, and examines the arguments presented by the program's critics and by its advocates. It concludes with an examination of changes to the program authorized by P.L. 111-240, the Small Business Jobs Act of 2010. The Small Business Jobs Act increased the Microloan program's loan limit for borrowers from $35,000 to $50,000, and for intermediaries after their first year of participation in the program from $3.5 million to $5 million. It also authorized the SBA to waive, in whole or in part through FY2012, the non-federal share requirement for loans to the Microloan program's intermediaries and for grants made to Microloan intermediaries for small business marketing, management, and technical assistance for up to a fiscal year.

In: Small Business Administration ...
Editor: Alan R. Connoly

ISBN: 978-1-62417-674-6

Chapter 1

SBA SMALL BUSINESS INVESTMENT COMPANY PROGRAM*

Robert Jay Dilger

SUMMARY

The Small Business Administration's (SBA's) Small Business Investment Company (SBIC) Program is designed to enhance small business access to venture capital by stimulating and supplementing "the flow of private equity capital and long term loan funds which small business concerns need for the sound financing of their business operations and for their growth, expansion, and modernization, and which are not available in adequate supply." Facilitating the flow of capital to small businesses to stimulate the national economy was, and remains, the SBIC program's primary objective.

At the end of FY2011, there were 299 privately owned and managed SBICs licensed by the SBA participating in the SBIC program, providing financing to small businesses with private capital the SBIC has raised (called regulatory capital) and with funds the SBIC borrows at favorable rates (called leverage) because the SBA guarantees the debenture (loan obligation). SBICs pursue investments in a broad range of industries, geographic areas, and stages of investment. Some SBICs specialize in a particular field or industry, while others invest more generally. Most SBICs concentrate on a particular stage of investment (i.e., startup, expansion, or turnaround) and geographic area.

The SBA is authorized to provide up to $3 billion in leverage to SBICs annually. The SBIC program has invested or committed about $17.1 billion in small businesses, with the SBA's share of capital at risk about $8.3 billion. In FY2011, the SBA guaranteed $1.8 billion in SBIC small business investments, and SBICs provided another $1.0 billion in investments from private capital, for a total of more than $2.8 billion in financing for 1,339 small businesses.

Some Members of Congress and small business advocates have argued that the SBIC program should be expanded as a means to stimulate economic activity, create jobs, and assist in the national economic recovery. For example, S. 2136, a bill to increase the maximum amount of leverage permitted under title III of the Small Business Investment

* This is an edited, reformatted and augmented version of a Congressional Research Service publication, CRS Report for Congress R41456, prepared for Members and Committees of Congress, from www.crs.gov, dated May 29, 2012.

Act of 1958, would increase the program's authorization to $4 billion from $3 billion. Others worry about the potential risk an expanded SBIC program has for increasing the federal deficit. In their view, the best means to assist small business, promote economic growth, and create jobs is to reduce business taxes and exercise federal fiscal restraint.

Some Members and small business advocates have also proposed that the program target additional assistance to startup and early stage small businesses, which are generally viewed as relatively risky investments but also as having a relatively high potential for job creation. The SBA, in an effort to target additional assistance to newer businesses, recently established, as part of the Administration's Startup America Initiative, a $1 billion early stage debenture SBIC initiative (up to $150 million in leverage in FY2012, and up to $200 million in leverage per fiscal year thereafter until the limit is reached). Early stage debenture SBICs are required to invest at least 50% of their investments in early stage small businesses, defined as small businesses that have never achieved positive cash flow from operations in any fiscal year.

This report describes the SBIC program's structure and operations, including two recent SBA initiatives, one targeting early stage small businesses and one targeting underserved markets. It also examines legislative proposals to increase the leverage available to SBICs (e.g., H.R. 3219, the Small Business Investment Company Modernization Act of 2011) and to increase the SBIC program's authorization amount to $4 billion.

SBIC PROGRAM OVERVIEW

The Small Business Administration (SBA) administers several programs to support small businesses, including loan guaranty programs to enhance small business access to capital; programs to increase small business opportunities in federal contracting; direct loans for businesses, homeowners, and renters to assist their recovery from natural disasters; and access to entrepreneurial education to assist with business formation and expansion.[1] It also administers the Small Business Investment Company (SBIC) Program.

Authorized by P.L. 85-699, the Small Business Investment Act of 1958, as amended, the SBIC program is designed to "improve and stimulate the national economy in general and the small business segment thereof in particular" by stimulating and supplementing "the flow of private equity capital and long term loan funds which small business concerns need for the sound financing of their business operations and for their growth, expansion, and modernization, and which are not available in adequate supply."[2]

The SBIC program was created to address concerns raised in a Federal Reserve Board report to Congress that concluded that a gap existed in the capital markets for long-term funding for growth-oriented small businesses. The report noted that the SBA's loan programs were "limited to providing short-term and intermediate-term credit when such loans are unavailable from private institutions," and the SBA "did not provide equity financing."[3] Equity financing (or equity capital) is money raised by a company in exchange for a share of ownership in the business. Ownership is represented by owning shares of stock outright or having the right to convert other financial instruments into stock. Equity financing allows a business to obtain funds without incurring debt, or without having to repay a specific amount of money at a particular time.

The Federal Reserve Board's report concluded that there was a need for a federal government program to "stimulate the availability of capital funds to small business" to assist them in gaining access to long-term financing and equity financing.[4] Facilitating the flow of capital to small businesses to stimulate the national economy was, and remains, the SBIC program's primary objective.

The SBA does not make direct investments in small businesses. It partners with privately owned and managed SBICs licensed by the SBA to provide financing to small businesses with private capital the SBIC has raised (called regulatory capital) and with funds (called leverage) the SBIC borrows at favorable rates because the SBA guarantees the debenture (loan obligation). At the end of FY2011, there were 299 licensed SBICs participating in the SBIC program.[5]

The SBA is authorized to provide up to $3 billion in leverage to SBICs annually. In FY2011, the SBA provided $1.8 billion in leverage to SBICs.[6]

Some Members of Congress and small business advocates have argued that the SBIC program should be expanded as a means to stimulate economic activity, create jobs, and assist in the national economic recovery. For example, S. 2136, a bill to increase the maximum amount of leverage permitted under title III of the Small Business Investment Act of 1958, would increase the program's authorization to $4 billion from $3 billion. The Obama Administration has also proposed that the SBIC program's authorization level be increased to $4 billion. Others worry about the potential risk an expanded SBIC program has for increasing the federal deficit. In their view, the best means to assist small business, promote economic growth, and create jobs is to reduce business taxes and exercise federal fiscal restraint.

Some Members and small business advocates have also proposed that the program target additional assistance to startup and early stage small businesses, which are generally viewed as relatively risky investments but also as having a relatively high potential for job creation. The SBA, in an effort to target additional assistance to newer businesses, recently established, as part of the Administration's Startup America Initiative, a $1 billion early stage debenture SBIC initiative (up to $150 million in leverage in FY2012, and up to $200 million in leverage per fiscal year thereafter until the limit is reached). Early stage debenture SBICs are required to invest at least 50% of their investments in early stage small businesses, defined as small businesses that have never achieved positive cash flow from operations in any fiscal year.

This report examines the structure and operation of the SBIC program, focusing on SBIC eligibility requirements, investment activity, and program statistics. It includes information concerning the SBIC program's debenture SBIC program, participating securities SBIC program, $1 billion early stage debenture SBIC initiative (targeting early stage small businesses), and $1 billion impact investment SBIC initiative (targeting underserved markets and communities facing barriers to access to credit and capital).

This report also examines proposals and legislation considered during the 111th and 112th Congresses, including H.R. 3854, the Small Business Financing and Investment Act of 2009; H.R. 5554, the Small Business Assistance and Relief Act of 2010; P.L. 111-240, the Small Business Jobs Act of 2010; H.R. 3219, the Small Business Investment Company Modernization Act of 2011; S.Amdt. 1833, the INVEST in America Act of 2012; S. 2136, a bill to increase the maximum amount of leverage permitted under title III of the Small Business Investment Act of 1958; and the Obama Administration's Startup America Initiative. These proposals and legislation address the targeting of additional assistance to startup and early stage small businesses and the SBIC program's financing levels.

SBIC Types

There are two types of SBICs. Investment companies licensed under Section 301(c) of the Small Business Investment Act of 1958, as amended, are referred to as original, or regular, SBICs. Investment companies licensed under Section 301(d) of the act, called Specialized Small Business Investment Companies (SSBICs), focus on providing financing to small business entrepreneurs "whose participation in the free enterprise system is hampered because of social or economic disadvantage."[7] Section 301(d) was repealed by P.L. 104-208, the Omnibus Consolidated Appropriations Act, 1997 (Title II of Division D, the Small Business Programs Improvement Act of 1996). As a result, no new SSBIC licenses have been issued since October 1, 1996. However, existing SSBICs were "grandfathered" and remain in operation.

With few exceptions, SBICs and SSBICs are subject to the same eligibility requirements and operating rules and regulations. Therefore, the SBIC name is usually used to refer to both SBICs and SSBICs simultaneously.

There are five types of regular SBICs. *Debenture* SBICs, *impact investment debenture* SBICs, and *early stage debenture* SBICs receive leverage through the issuance of debentures.[8] Debentures are debt obligations issued by SBICs and held or guaranteed by the SBA.[9] *Participating securities* SBICs receive leverage through the issuance of participating securities. Participating securities are redeemable, preferred, equity-type securities, often in the form of limited partnership interests, preferred stock, or debentures with interest payable only to the extent of earnings.[10] *Bank-owned, non-leveraged* SBICs do not receive leverage.[11] This report focuses on the four types of regular SBICs that receive leverage from the SBA.

SBIC Eligibility Requirements

An SBIC can be organized in any state, as either a corporation, limited partnership (LP), or a limited liability company (LLCs must be organized under Delaware law). Most SBICs are owned by relatively small groups of local investors, although many are partially owned, and some are wholly owned (46 of 299), by commercial banks. A few SBICs are corporations with publicly traded stock.[12]

One of the primary criteria for licensure as an SBIC is having qualified management. The SBA reviews and approves a prospective SBIC's management team based upon its professional capabilities and character. Specifically, the SBA examines the SBIC's management team looking for

- substantive and relevant principal investment experience;
- realized track record of superior returns, based on an overall evaluation of appropriate quantitative performance measures;
- evidence of a strong rate of business proposals and investment offers (deal flow) in the investment area proposed for the new fund;
- a cohesive management team, with complementary skills and history of working together;
- managerial, operational, or technical experience that can add value at the portfolio company level; and

- a demonstrated ability to manage cash flows so as to provide assurance the SBA will be repaid on a timely basis.[13]

SBIC Application Process

Applying for an SBIC debenture license is a multi-step process, beginning with the submission of the SBA Management Assessment Questionnaire (MAQ). It includes, among others, questions concerning

- the fund's legal name, and the name and addresses of its principals and control persons;[14]
- the fund's finances and expenses;
- the management team's professional experience;
- the fund's expected investing focus (e.g., will the fund be primarily a sole investor, lead investor, or co-investor; its anticipated percentage of investments in technology, life sciences, health care, manufacturing, distribution, service, consumer products and retail, or other industries; and its anticipated percentage of investments by business life cycle—seed, early stage, expansion, later stage, change of control, or turnaround);
- the geographic areas where the investments are expected to be made;
- the anticipated holding periods for investments;
- the types and characteristics of the securities that will be used to make investments; and
- the extent to which "special groups of businesses" will be targeted for investment, such as "ethnic groups, women, rural, inner city, etc."[15]

After receiving the firm's application, a member of the SBA's Program Development Office reviews the MAQ; assesses the investment company's proposal in light of the program's minimum requirements and management qualifications; performs initial due diligence, including making reference telephone calls; and prepares a written recommendation to the SBA's Investment Division's Investment Committee (composed of senior members of the division).

If, after reviewing the MAQ and the SBA's Program Development Office's evaluation, the Investment Committee concludes, by majority vote at a regularly scheduled meeting, that the investment company's management team may be qualified for a license, the investment company's management team is invited to the SBA's headquarters in Washington, DC, for an interview. If, following the interview, the Investment Committee votes to proceed, the investment team is provided a "Green Light" letter, formally inviting the investment team to file a license application, along with a filing fee of $10,000, plus an additional $5,000 for partnerships or LLC SBICs. If the license is approved, all SBIC principals must complete the SBA's SBIC Regulations training classes. On average, obtaining an SBIC license takes about six months from the time of the initial submission of the MAQ to issuance of the license.[16]

As will be discussed, new applications for the participating securities program are no longer being accepted. Impact investment debenture SBIC applicants are required to submit the same documents, follow the same process, and meet the same standards as applicants seeking a debenture SBIC license. However, impact investment debenture SBICs are provided an expedited review process.[17]

The application process for an early stage debenture SBIC license is similar to the application process for a SBIC debenture license. Two major differences are that the SBA only accepts applications to the early stage innovation program during specific time periods published “from time to time” in the *Federal Register* (expected to be annually) and places “particular emphasis on managers’ skills and experience in evaluating and investing in early stage companies.”[18] Also, early stage debenture SBIC applicants must pay a partnership licensee fee plus an additional $10,000, for a total application fee of $25,000.[19]

The eligibility requirements and application process for small businesses requesting financial assistance from an SBIC is provided in the *Appendix*.

SBIC Capital Investment Requirements

Debenture SBICs

P.L. 85-699, the Small Business Investment Act of 1958, authorized the SBA to select companies to participate in the SBIC program and to purchase debentures from those companies to provide them additional funds to invest in small businesses. Initially, debenture SBICs were required to have a private capital investment of at least $300,000 to participate in the SBIC program.

Debenture SBICs are now required to have a private capital investment of at least $5 million (called regulatory capital).[20] The SBA has discretion to license an applicant with regulatory capital of $3 million if the applicant has satisfied all licensing standards and requirements, has a viable business plan reasonably projecting profitable operations, and has a reasonable timetable for achieving regulatory capital of at least $5 million.[21] At least 30% of a debenture SBIC’s regulatory and leverageable capital must come from three people unaffiliated with the fund’s management and unaffiliated with each other.[22] Also, no more than 33% of a SBIC’s regulatory capital may come from state or local government entities.[23]

Participating Securities SBICs

P.L. 102-366, the Small Business Credit and Business Opportunity Enhancement Act of 1992 (Title IV, the Small Business Equity Enhancement Act of 1992), authorized the SBA to guarantee participating securities. Participating securities are redeemable, preferred, equity-type securities issued by SBICs in the form of limited partnership interests, preferred stock, or debentures with interest payable only to the extent of earnings.

In 1994, the SBA established the SBIC Participating Securities Program (SBIC PSP) to encourage the formation of participating securities SBICs that would make equity investments in startup and early stage small businesses. The SBA created the program to fill a perceived investment gap created by the SBIC debenture program’s focus on mid- and later-stage small businesses. The SBA stopped issuing new commitments for participation securities on October 1, 2004, beginning a process to end the program, which continues.[24]

The SBA stopped issuing new commitments for participating securities primarily because the program lost an estimated $2.7 billion during the early 2000s as investments in technology startup and early stage small businesses lost much of their stock value at that time. The SBA found that "the fees payable by SBICs for participating securities leverage are not sufficient to cover the projected net losses in the participating securities program."[25] The SBA continued to honor its existing commitments to participating securities SBICs and they were allowed to continue operations. However, they were required to comply with special rules concerning minimum capital, liquidity, non-SBA borrowing, and equity investing.[26] In recent years, some Members have expressed interest in either revising the program or starting a new program modeled on certain aspects of the SBIC PSP to assist startup and early stage small businesses has increased.[27]

Although the SBA is no longer issuing new commitments for participating securities, and each year several participating securities SBICs leave the program as their leverage commitments are retired, at the end of FY2011 there were still 97 participating securities SBICs in the SBIC program. To participate in the SBIC program, a participating securities SBICs must have regulatory capital of at least $10 million. The SBA has discretion to require less than $10 million in regulatory capital if the licensee can demonstrate that it can be financially viable over the long term with a lower amount. In this circumstance, the regulatory amount required may not be lower than $5 million.[28] At least 30% of a participating securities SBIC's regulatory and leverageable capital must come from three people unaffiliated with the fund's management and unaffiliated with each other.[29] Also, no more than 33% of a SBIC's regulatory capital can come from state or local government entities.[30]

Impact Investment Debenture SBICs

On April 7, 2011, the SBA announced that it was establishing a $1 billion impact investment SBIC initiative (up to $150 million in leverage in FY2012, and up to $200 million in leverage per fiscal year thereafter until the limit is reached). Under this initiative, SBA-licensed impact investment debenture SBICs are required to invest at least 50% of their financings, "which target areas of critical national priority including underserved markets and communities facing barriers to access to credit and capital."[31] Impact investment debenture SBICs are required to have a minimum private capital investment of at least $5 million, subject to the same conditions as debenture SBICs concerning the source of the funds.

Early Stage Debenture SBICs

On April 27, 2012, the SBA published a final rule in the *Federal Register* establishing a $1 billion early stage debenture SBIC initiative (up to $150 million in leverage in FY2012, and up to $200 million in leverage per fiscal year thereafter until the limit is reached).[32] Early stage debenture SBICs are required to invest at least 50% of their financings in early stage small businesses, defined as small businesses that have never achieved positive cash flow from operations in any fiscal year.[33]

In recognition of the higher risk associated with investments in early stage small businesses, the initiative includes "several new regulatory provisions intended to reduce the risk that an early stage SBIC would default on its leverage and to improve SBA's recovery prospects should a default occur."[34] For example, early stage debenture SBICs are required to raise more regulatory capital (at least $20 million) than debenture SBICs and impact investment debenture SBICs (at least $5 million) and participating securities SBICs (at least $10 million). They are also subject to special distribution rules to require pro rata repayment of SBA leverage when making distributions of profits to their investors. In addition, as will be discussed, early stage debenture SBICs are also provided less leverage (up to 100% of regulatory capital, $50 million maximum) than debenture SBICs and participating securities SBICs (up to 200% of regulatory capital, $150 million maximum per SBIC and $225 million for two or more SBICs under common control), and impact investment debenture SBICs (up to 200% of regulatory capital, $80 million maximum).

On May 1, 2012, the SBA published a notice in the *Federal Register* inviting venture capital fund managers to submit an application to become a licensed early stage debenture SBIC. The application deadline for applicants with signed commitments for at least $15 million in regulatory capital and evidence of their ability to raise the remaining $5 million in regulatory capital was set as July 30, 2012. The application deadline for all other applicants was set as May 15, 2013.[35] The SBA expects to award its first early stage debenture SBIC licenses in September 2012.[36]

Key Differences Among Regular SBIC Types

Table 1 provides a comparison of the key differences among the four types of regular SBICs that receive leverage from the SBA: debenture, participating securities, impact investment debenture, and early stage debenture SBICs.

SBIC Investments in Small Businesses

SBICs provide equity capital to small businesses in various ways, including by

- purchasing small business equity securities (e.g., stock, stock options, warrants, limited partnership interests, membership interests in a limited liability company, or joint venture interests);[37]
- making loans to small businesses, either independently or in cooperation with other private or public lenders, that have a maturity of no more than 20 years;[38]
- purchasing debt securities from small businesses, which may be convertible into, or have rights to purchase, equity in the small business;[39] and
- subject to limitations, providing small businesses a guarantee of their monetary obligations to creditors not associated with the SBIC.[40]

SBICs are subject to statutory and regulatory restrictions concerning the nature of their approved investments. For example, SBICs are not allowed to

Table 1. Key Differences Among SBA's Debenture, Participating Securities, Impact Investment Debenture, and Early Stage Debenture SBICs

Program Requirement	Debenture SBICs	Participating Security SBICs (no longer accepting new investments)	Impact Investment Debenture SBICs	Early Stage Debenture SBICs
Private Capital	$5 million minimum	$10 million minimum	$5 million minimum	$20 million minimum
SBA Leverage	200% of private capital up to $150 million per SBIC or $225 million for two or more SBICs under common control[a]	200% of private capital up to $150 million per SBIC or $225 million for two or more SBICs under common control	200% of private capital up to $80 million; limited to 100% of private capital during the first year	100% of private capital up to $50 million
Investments	Broad range of equity investments, but generally later stage and mezzanine	Broad range of equity investments	Broad range of equity investments, but generally later stage and mezzanine; at least 50% in underserved markets and communities facing barriers to access to credit and capital	Broad range of equity investments; at least 50% in early stage small businesses (no positive cash flow in any fiscal year prior to first financing)
Leverage Description	Interest and SBA annual charge payable semi-annually through maturity	SBA paid interest to bond holders; SBICs only owed and repaid SBA out of profits	Interest and SBA annual charge payable semi-annually through maturity	Standard: 5 years interest reserve required, interest and SBA annual charge payable quarterly through maturity OR Discounted: interest and SBA annual charge discounted for first 5 years plus the "stub" period; interest and SBA annual charge payable quarterly thereafter through maturity
Profit Participation	None	SBA typically received about 8% of any profits	None	None

Source: U.S. Small Business Administration, Office of Investment and Innovation, "Early Stage Small Business Investment Companies," Washington, DC, January 2012; and U.S. Small Business Administration, "Correspondence with the author," Washington, DC, May 2, 2012.

[a] A licensed debenture SBIC in good standing, with a demonstrated need for funds, may apply to the SBA for leverage of up to 300% of its private capital. However, the SBA has traditionally approved debenture SBICs for a maximum of 200% of their private capital. It is anticipated that the SBA will also limit impact investment debenture SBICs to a maximum of 200% of their private capital. Also, a debenture SBIC licensed on or after October 1, 2009, may elect to have a maximum leverage amount of $175 million per SBIC and $250 million for two or more licenses under common control if it has invested at least 50% of its financings in low-income geographic areas and certifies that at least 50% of its future investments will be in low-income geographic areas.

- directly or indirectly provide financing to any of their associates (e.g., officers, directors, and employees);[41]
- control, either directly or indirectly, any small business on a permanent basis;[42]
- invest, without SBA approval, more than specified percentages of its private (regulatory) capital in securities, commitments, or guarantees in any one small business (e.g., SBICs are not allowed to invest more than 30% of their private capital in any one small business if their investment plan includes two or more tiers of SBA leverage);[43]
- invest in farm land, unimproved land, or any small business classified under Major Group 65 (Real Estate) of the Standard Industrial Classification (SIC) Manual, with the exception of title abstract companies, real estate agents, brokers, and managers;[44]
- provide funds for small businesses whose primary business activity involves directly or indirectly providing funds to others, purchasing debt obligations, factoring, or leasing equipment on a long-term basis with no provision for maintenance or repair;[45] or
- provide funds to a small business if the funds will be used substantially for a foreign operation.[46]

The SBA also regulates the interest rates and fees SBICs are allowed to charge small businesses on loans, debt securities, and equity financing.[47]

In 1999, the SBA introduced the low and moderate income investments (LMI) initiative to encourage SBICs to invest in small businesses located in inner cities and rural areas "that have severe shortages of equity capital" because investments in those areas "often are of a type that will not have the potential for yielding returns that are high enough to justify the use of participating securities."[48] This ongoing initiative provides incentives to SBICs that invest in small businesses that have at least 50% of their employees or tangible assets located in a low-tomoderate income area (LMI Zone) or have at least 35% of their full-time employees with their primary residence in an LMI Zone.[49] For example, unlike regular SBIC debentures that typically have a 10-year maturity, LMI debentures are available in two maturities, for 5 years and 10 years, plus the stub period. The stub period is the time between the debenture's issuance date and the next March 1 or September 1. The stub period allows all LMI debentures to have common March 1 or September 1 maturity dates to simplify administration of the program.

In addition, LMI debentures are issued at a discount so that the proceeds that a SBIC receives for the sale of a debenture is reduced by (1) the debenture's interest costs for the first five years, plus the stub period; (2) the SBA's annual fee for the debenture's first five years, plus the stub period; and (3) the SBA's 2% leverage fee. As a result, these interest costs and fees are effectively deferred, freeing SBICs from the requirement to make interest payments on LMI debentures, or pay the SBA's annual fees on LMI debentures, for the first five years of a debenture, plus the stub period between the debenture's issuance date and the next March 1 or September 1.[50]

In FY2011, SBICs made 553 investments in small businesses located in a LMI Zone, totaling $687.1 million—about 24% of the total amount invested.[51]

LEVERAGE

Leverage Drawdown

A SBIC applies to the SBA for financial assistance (leverage) to secure the "SBA's conditional commitment to reserve a specific amount of leverage" for the SBIC's future use.[52] If the application is approved, a SBIC draws down the leverage as it makes financial commitments.

The SBA accepts draw applications from SBICs twice a month. When the draw is approved by the SBA, it issues a payment voucher to a SBIC (called an approval notice). The payment voucher has a term of approximately 60 days and provides a SBIC with the ability to draw funds on a daily basis.

A debenture is executed in conjunction with each draw and is held by an agent of a bank selected by the SBA (Federal Home Loan Bank of Chicago), which provides interim funding to the SBIC until a "SBIC's debenture(s) can be pooled with others and sold to the public, a process that occurs every six months [each March and September]."[53] During the interim period, the bank charges a SBIC the London Interbank Offered Rate (LIBOR), plus a 30 basis point premium.[54]

The SBA determines the size of the debenture pool two weeks prior to each scheduled pooling date. All of "the debentures scheduled to be pooled are purchased and pooled together by an entity called the Investment Trust which is managed by the Bank of New York Mellon" and, as the pooling occurs, "the SBA signs an agreement with the Trust to guarantee all the interest and principal payments due on each of the debentures in the pool."[55] The trust then securitizes the pool of debentures and issues new securities called trust certificates. Underwriters are hired to sell the trust certificates to investors in the public market. An offering circular is issued to notify investors of the trust certificates' availability, the terms of the securities, and information concerning how they can be purchased.[56]

The SBA operates the SBIC program on a zero-subsidy basis. To recoup its expenses should defaults occur, the SBA is authorized to charge SBICs a 3% origination fee for each debenture and for each participating security issued (1% at commitment and 2% at draw), an annual fee (not to exceed 1.38% for debentures and 1.46% for participating securities) on the leverage drawn, which is fixed at the time of the leverage commitment, and other administrative and underwriting fees which are adjusted annually.[57]

Debenture SBIC Leverage Requirements

A licensed debenture SBIC in good standing, with a demonstrated need for funds, may apply to the SBA for financial assistance (leverage) of up to 300% of its private capital. However, the SBA has traditionally approved debenture SBICs for a maximum of 200% of their private capital and no fund management team may exceed the allowable maximum amount of leverage of $150 million per SBIC and $225 million for two or more licenses under common control.[58] A SBIC licensed on or after October 1, 2009, may elect to have a maximum leverage amount of $175 million per SBIC and $250 million for two or more licenses under common control if it has invested at least 50% of its financings in low-income geographic areas and certifies that at least 50% of its future investments will be in low-income geographic areas.[59]

Debenture SBICs obtain leverage from the sale of SBA-guaranteed debenture participation trust certificates. SBA-guaranteed debenture participation trust certificates may have a term of up to 15 years, although only one outstanding SBA-guaranteed debenture participation trust certificate has a term exceeding 10 years and all recent public offerings have specified a term of 10 years.[60] Debenture SBICs are required to make semi-annual payments on the interest due on the debenture, semi-annual payments on the SBA's annual charge, and a lump sum principal payment to investors at maturity.[61] SBICs are allowed to prepay SBA-guaranteed debentures without penalty. However, a SBA-guaranteed debenture must be prepaid in whole and not in part, and can only be prepaid on a semi-annual payment date. The debenture's coupon (interest) rate is determined by market conditions and the interest rate of 10-year treasury securities at the time of the sale.[62] Also, as mentioned previously, LMI debentures are available in two maturities, for five years and 10 years (plus the stub period).

Because the SBA guarantees the debenture, investors are more likely to purchase a debenture participation trust certificate as opposed to others available on the market. They are also more likely to accept a lower coupon (interest) rate than what would be expected without the SBA's guarantee.[63] As a result, the SBIC program enhances a SBIC's access to venture capital, and reduces its cost of raising additional financial resources.

Because debenture SBICs are required to make semi-annual interest payments on the debenture and semi-annual payments on the SBA's annual charge, they tend to focus their investments on mid- and later-stage small businesses that have a positive cash flow. Businesses with a positive cash flow have resources available to make payments to the debenture SBIC, either in the form of interest payments or dividends. In many instances, small businesses with positive cash flow are seeking capital for expansion.[64]

Participating Securities SBIC Leverage Requirements

Although the SBA is no longer issuing new commitments for participating securities, the SBA is authorized to accept an application from a licensed participating securities SBIC for leverage of up to 200% of its private capital.[65] Also, no fund management team may exceed the allowable maximum amount of leverage of $150 million per SBIC and $225 million for two or more licenses under common control.

Participating securities SBICs obtained leverage by issuing SBA-guaranteed participating securities. The SBA pooled these participating securities and sold SBA-guaranteed participating securities certificates, representing an undivided interest in the pool, to investors through periodic public offerings. SBA participating securities may have a term of up to 15 years, but all recent public offerings had a specified a term of 10 years.

There were 35 public offerings of SBA-guaranteed participating securities certificates since the start of the participating securities program, amounting to just under $10.3 billion. The final SBA-guaranteed participating securities certificate, for $332 million, had a term of

10 years and was offered to investors on February 19, 2009, with delivery of the certificates on February 25, 2009.[66]

SBIC participating securities certificates provide for quarterly payments to investors from dividends on preferred stock, interest on an income bond, or a priority return on a preferred limited partnership equal to a specified interest rate on the principal amount and a lump sum principal payment at maturity. A participating securities SBIC is obligated to make these quarterly payments "only to the extent it has sufficient profits available to make such payments."[67] If a participating securities SBIC is unable to make any required payment, the SBA will make the payment on its behalf. Because startup and early stage small businesses often are not initially profitable, the SBA included language in its participating securities' offering circulars that it "anticipates that it will be called upon routinely to make such ... payments for the SBICs in the early years of the lives of such SBICs" and that it "expects to be reimbursed [by the SBIC] any amounts paid ... under its guarantee over the life of a participating security."[68]

Because the SBA guaranteed the certificate, investors were more likely to purchase a SBIC participating securities certificate as opposed to others available on the market. They were also more likely to accept a lower payment rate than what would be expected without the SBA's guarantee.[69]

In addition, participating securities SBICs are more likely than debenture SBICs to invest in startup and early stage small businesses because the SBA is willing to make a participating securities SBIC's required quarterly payments to investors, at least during the early years of the investment. Because participating securities SBICs are not required to make these quarterly payments, they are encouraged to focus on a small business's long-term prospects for growth and profitability, rather than on its prospects for having immediate, positive cash-flow.[70]

As of September 30, 2011, the SBA had a guarantee on an outstanding unpaid principal balance of $4.2 billion in SBIC debentures, $2.2 billion in SBIC participating securities, and $14.0 million in SSBIC financings.[71] The SBA also had an outstanding commitment on $1.8 billion in SBIC debentures and $61.1 million in outstanding SBIC participating securities.[72]

Impact Investment Debenture SBIC Leverage Requirements

On April 7, 2011, the SBA announced that it was establishing a $1 billion Impact Investment SBIC Initiative (up to $150 million in leverage in FY2012, and up to $200 million in leverage per fiscal year thereafter until the limit is reached). SBA licensed impact investment debenture SBICs are required to invest at least 50% of their investments, "which target areas of critical national priority including underserved markets and communities facing barriers to access to credit and capital."[73] On July 26, 2011, the SBA announced that the first impact investment debenture SBIC license was awarded to InvestMichigan! Mezzanine Fund.[74]

Licensed impact investment debenture SBICs may apply to the SBA for leverage of up to 300% of its private capital, limited to $80 million. In addition, they may receive leverage amounting to no more than 100% of their private capital during any fiscal year (subject to the

$80 million limit and the availability of impact investment initiative financing). It is anticipated that the SBA will limit impact investment debenture SBICs to a maximum of 200% of their private capital, up to $80 million.[75] Impact investment debenture SBICs obtain leverage in the same way that debenture SBICs obtain leverage — through the issuance of SBA-guaranteed debentures with a term of up to 10 years. They are also subject to the same terms and conditions as debenture SBICs, except they are provided an expedited application review process.

Early Stage Debenture SBIC Leverage Requirements

On April 27, 2012, the SBA published a final rule in the *Federal Register* establishing the $1 billion Early Stage Innovation SBIC Initiative (up to $150 million in SBA leverage in FY2012, and up to $200 million in SBA leverage per fiscal year thereafter until the limit is reached). A licensed early stage SBIC may apply to the SBA for leverage of up to 100% of its private capital, limited to $50 million. The SBA does not consider applications from an early stage SBIC applicant that is under common control with another early stage SBIC applicant or an existing early stage SBIC (unless the existing early stage SBIC has no outstanding leverage or leverage commitments and will not seek additional leverage in the future).[76]

Early stage debenture SBICs obtain leverage in the same way that debenture SBICs obtain leverage — through the issuance of SBA-guaranteed debentures with a term of up to 10 years. However, early stage debentures come in two forms: early stage standard debentures and early stage discounted debentures.

Early stage standard SBIC debentures are similar to standard SBIC debentures, but, instead of requiring semi-annual payments on the debenture's interest and on the SBA's annual charge, they require quarterly payments on the debenture's interest and on the SBA's annual charge. In addition, early stage SBICs must maintain a reserve sufficient to pay the interest on the debenture and on the SBA's annual charges for the first 21 payment dates following the date of issuance (five years plus the stub period —the length of time between the issue date and the next March 1, June 1, September 1, or December 1).[77] Because early stage standard debentures require early stage debenture SBICs to make quarterly payments, they are most appropriate for investments in small businesses that have established a positive cash flow that enables them to pay interest or dividends to the early stage debenture SBIC.

Early stage discounted debentures are issued at a discount (less than face value) equal to the first five years' of interest on the debenture and the first five years of annual SBA charges. The discount eliminates the need for early stage debenture SBICs to make interest payments on the debenture and to make payments on the SBA's annual charge for five years from the date of issuance, plus the stub period.[78] Early stage debenture SBICs make quarterly payments on the debenture's interest and on the SBA's annual charge during years six through 10. They are also responsible for paying the debenture's principal amount when the debenture reaches its maturity date.

Because early stage discounted debentures do not require interest payments or payments on the SBA's annual charge for five years, they are most appropriate for investments in small businesses that have not established a positive cash flow to pay interest or dividends to the early stage debenture SBIC. As a result, early stage discounted debentures are designed to encourage investments in early stage small businesses, which by definition have not established a positive cash flow.

Reporting Requirements

Once licensed, each SBIC is required to file with the SBA an annual financial report that includes an audit by an SBA-approved independent public accountant. SBICs are also subject to annual onsite regulatory compliance examinations.[79] SBICs are also required to provide the SBA:

- a portfolio financing report within 30 days of the closing date for each financing of a small business;[80]
- the value of its loans and investments within 90 days of the end of the fiscal year in the case of annual valuations, and within 30 days following the close of other reporting periods;[81]
- any material adverse changes in valuations at least quarterly (within 30 days following the close of the quarter);[82] and
- copies of reports provided to investors, documents filed with the Securities and Exchange Commission, and documents pertaining to litigation or other legal proceedings, including criminal charges against any person who was required by the SBA complete a personal history statement in connection with the SBIC's license.[83]

SBIC Program Statistics

At the end of FY2011, there were 299 licensed SBICs in operation (143 debenture SBICs, 97 participating securities SBICs, 46 bank-owned/non-leveraged SBICs, and 13 SSBICs).[84] In FY2011, 203 SBICs provided at least one new financing to a small business.[85]

The number of licensed SBICs has declined since FY2006, with most of the decline due to the planned phase-out of participating securities SBICs and SSBICs.[86] In FY2006, there were 396 licensed SBICs (132 debenture SBICs, 173 participating securities SBICs, 67 bank-owned/nonleveraged SBICs, and 24 SSBICs).[87] There were 369 licensed SBICs in FY2007, 348 in FY2008, 315 in FY2009, and 307 in FY2010. The SBA has made it a goal to increase the number of new SBIC licenses issued each year "to position the program for continued growth."[88]

Overall, SBICs pursue investments in a broad range of industries, geographic areas, and stage of investment. Some individual SBICs specialize in a particular field or industry in which their management has expertise, while others invest more generally. Most SBICs concentrate on a particular stage of investment (i.e., start-up, expansion, or turnaround) and identify a geographic area in which to focus.

Total Financing

Since its inception, the SBIC program has provided more than $61.0 billion in financial assistance and made more than 163,000 investments in small businesses.[89] As mentioned previously, as of September 30, 2011, the SBA had a guarantee on the outstanding unpaid principal balance of $4.2 billion in SBIC debentures, $2.2 billion in SBIC participating securities, and $14.0 million in SSBIC financings.[90] The SBA also had an outstanding commitment on $1.8 billion in SBIC debentures and $61.1 million in outstanding SBIC participating securities.[91] All together, the SBIC program currently has invested or committed about $17.1 billion in small businesses financings, with the SBA's share of capital at risk about $8.3 billion.[92]

In FY2011, SBICs made 2,270 financings (including 46 financings by SSBICs). The average financing amount was $1,248,181 ($1,272,538 for debenture SBICs, $382,514 for participating securities SBICs, $372,330 for bank-owned/non-leveraged SBICs, and $70,575 for SSBICs).[93] The funds were used primarily for acquiring an existing business (45.9%). Other uses were for operating capital (25.8%), refinancing or refunding debt (18.1%), purchasing equipment (2.0%), research and development (1.7%), a new building or plant construction (1.1%), marketing activities (0.4%), plant modernization (0.2%), and other uses (4.8%).[94]

As shown in *Table 2*, total SBIC financing fell from just under $2.9 billion in FY2005 and FY2006 to just under $1.9 billion in FY2009. Since then, total SBIC financing has increased, exceeding $2.8 billion in FY2011. In addition, with the exception of FY2008 to FY2009, the amount of SBA leverage has increased each fiscal year and, with the exception of FY2010 to FY2011, the amount of private-sector investments has decreased. As a result, the SBA's leverage now accounts for a larger share of the SBIC program's total financings than in previous years. For example, the SBA's leverage accounted for 12.3% of total financings in FY2005, compared with 64.5% in FY2011.

The SBA has had congressional authorization to issue up to $3.0 billion in SBIC leverage each year since 2005. For comparative purposes, private venture capital firms invested $19.8 billion in 3,066 companies in 2009, $23.2 billion in 3,526 companies in 2010, and $28.5 billion in 3,696 companies in 2011.[95]

The SBA has indicated that one of its goals is "to enhance program acceptance in the marketplace and increase the number of funds licensed and the amount of leverage issued so as to improve capital access for small businesses."[96]

In 2008, the Urban Institute released an analysis comparing debenture SBIC investments made from 1997 to 2005 to private-sector venture capital investments made during that time period in second stage business loans, third stage business loans, and bridge loans "because these investments are likely to be of the same character (debt with equity features) as those made by debenture SBICs."[97] The Urban Institute found that debenture SBIC investments accounted for more than 62% of all venture capital financings in second stage business loans, third stage business loans, and bridge loans in the United States during that time period. However, because the average amount of an SBIC debenture investment was much smaller than the industry average, SBIC debenture investments accounted for "only 8% of total dollars invested."[98]

Table 2. SBIC Financing, FY2005-FY2011

Year	*SBA*	($ in millions)		*# of Small*
		Private-Sector		*Businesses*
	Leverage/Guarantee	*Investment*	*Total Financing*	*Financed*
FY2011	$1,828	$1,005	$2,833	1,339
FY2010	$1,165	$882	$2,047	1,331
FY2009	$788	$1,068	$1,856	1,481
FY2008	$1,029	$1,398	$2,427	1,905
FY2007	$708	$1,940	$2,648	2,057
FY2006	$477	$2,420	$2,897	2,121
FY2005	$355	$2,540	$2,895	2,298

Source: U.S. Small Business Administration, "Performance and Financial Highlights, FY2007," Washington, DC, February 4, 2008, p. 4; U.S. Small Business Administration, "FY2008 Budget Request and Performance Plan," Washington, DC, 2007, p. 23; U.S. Small Business Administration, Investment Division, "SBIC Program Overview," Washington, DC, January 23, 2009; U.S. Small Business Administration, "SBIC Program Overview: Program Achievements & Success Stories," Washington, DC, at http://www.sba.gov/content/sbic-programoverview-2; and U.S. Small Business Administration, Investment Division, "SBIC Program Overview," Washington, DC, September 30, 2011.

Financing to Specific Demographic Groups

As shown in *Table 3*, in FY2011, SBICs made 114 financings (5.0% of all financings) amounting to $45.1 million (1.6% of the total amount of financings) to minority-owned and -controlled small businesses.

Table 3. SBIC Financing, Minority-Owned Small Businesses, FY2011

Small Business Ownership Demographic	# of Financings	% of Financings	$ Amount of Financings	% of Total $ Amount of Financings
Black-Owned	24	1.1%	$16,648,532	0.6%
Subcontinent Asian-Owned	44	1.9%	$4,060,511	0.1%
Hispanic-Owned	29	1.3%	$9,972,122	0.4%
Asian Pacific-Owned	17	0.7%	$14,382,700	0.5%
Native American-Owned	0	0.0%	$0	0.0%
Subtotal	114	5.0%	$45,063,865	1.6%
Other (non-minority)	2,156	95.0%	$2,788,307,184	98.4%
Total—All Financings	2,270	100.0%	$2,833,371,046	100.0%

Source: U.S. Small Business Administration, "SBIC Program Licensees Financing to Small Businesses Reported Between October 2010 and September 2011," Washington, DC.

Notes: Ownership is defined as owning at least 50% of the small business.

In addition, in FY2011, SBICs made 47 financings (2.1% of all financings) amounting to $18.8 million (0.7% of the total amount of financings) to women-owned small businesses, and 14 financings (0.6% of all financings) amounting to $21.4 million (0.8% of the total amount of financings) to veteran-owned small businesses.[99]

Research concerning private venture capital investment in minority-owned or women-owned small businesses is limited. As a result, it is difficult to find the data necessary to compare the SBIC program's investment in minority-owned or women-owned small businesses to the private sector's investment in these firms.[100]

In 2007, the SBA acknowledged at a congressional hearing on the SBA's investment programs that "women and minority representation in [the SBIC program] is low" and has been low for many years.[101] The SBA reported at that time that it did not control the investments made by SBICs, but it has tried to increase women and minority representation in the SBIC program by reaching out to venture capital firms, trade organizations, and others to better understand why women and minority representation in the SBIC program is low, and by "finding debenture firms with minority representation on their investment committees and in senior management."[102] However, despite these efforts, in 2009, the Small Business Investor Alliance (then called the National Association of Small Business Investment Companies) asserted at a congressional hearing on the SBA's capital access programs that the SBA's SBIC licensing process "has done an abysmal job at attracting and licensing funds led by women and minorities."[103]

During the 111th Congress, S. 1831, the Small Business Venture Capital Act of 2009, was introduced on October 21, 2009, and referred to the Senate Committee on Small Business and Entrepreneurship. No further action was taken on the bill.

It would have encouraged SBIC investments in women-owned small businesses and socially and economically disadvantaged small business concerns by increasing the amount of leverage available to SBICs that invest at least 50% of their financings in small business concerns owned and controlled by women or socially and economically disadvantaged small business concerns.

Financing by State

As shown in *Table 4,* in FY2011, SBICs provided financing to small businesses located in 45 states and the District of Columbia, with the most financings taking place in New York (405 financings amounting to $253.1 million), California (332 financings amounting to $399.3 million), and Texas (181 financings amounting to $297.9 million).

The previously mentioned 2008 Urban Institute comparative analysis of debenture SBIC financing from 1997 to 2005 found that the dollar volume of investments from debenture SBICs was more evenly distributed across the nation than from comparable private venture capital funds. For example, the Urban Institute found that California (45.8%) and Massachusetts (12.9%) received the largest share of the total dollar volume invested by private venture capital funds from 1997 to 2005. The two states accounted for more than half (58.7%) of the total dollar volume invested by private venture capital funds. In contrast, New York (18.7%) and California (11.1%) received the largest share of the total dollar volume invested by debenture SBICs from 1997 to 2005. The two states accounted for less than one-third (29.8%) of the total dollar volume invested by debenture SBICs. Also, the top 10 states in terms of their share of the total dollar volume invested accounted nearly 84% of the total invested by private venture capital funds, compared with 64% for debenture SBICs.[104]

Table 4. SBIC Financing, by State, FY2011
($ in millions)

State	# of Financings	Amount of Financings	State	# of Financings	Amount of Financings
Alabama	4	$12.2	Montana	1	$0.2
Alaska	0	$0.0	Nebraska	1	$8.8
Arizona	34	$57.2	Nevada	8	$33.0
Arkansas	13	$12.2	New Hampshire	9	$1.3
California	332	$399.3	New Jersey	147	$97.0
Colorado	58	$100.0	New Mexico	16	$1.7
Connecticut	23	$85.8	New York	325	$253.1
Delaware	6	$7.9	North Carolina	52	$113.9
District of Columbia	2	$0.5	North Dakota	0	$0.0
Florida	99	$163.7	Ohio	41	$88.4
Georgia	42	$95.9	Oklahoma	5	$27.9
Hawaii	0	$0.0	Oregon	11	$3.2
Idaho	0	$0.0	Pennsylvania	71	$121.7
Illinois	112	$131.4	Puerto Rico	0	$0.0
Indiana	21	$32.5	Rhode Island	9	$40.2
Iowa	7	$3.6	South Carolina	15	$37.3
Kansas	22	$9.6	South Dakota	1	$2.6
Kentucky	16	$18.5	Tennessee	19	$38.5
Louisiana	6	$22.3	Texas	181	$297.9
Maine	1	$5.6	Utah	90	$29.7
Maryland	20	$62.7	Vermont	11	$4.2
Massachusetts	166	$156.8	Virginia	60	$40.0
Michigan	21	$44.8	Washington	41	$16.3
Minnesota	34	$40.0	West Virginia	1	$9.2
Mississippi	3	$0.6	Wisconsin	12	$44.4
Missouri	21	$59.6	Wyoming	0	$0.0
Total				2,270	$2,833.4

Source: U.S. Small Business Administration, "SBIC Program Licensees Financing to Small Businesses Reported Between October 2010 and September 2011," Washington, DC.

A comparison of the state-by-state distribution of private-sector venture capital fund investments and SBIC financings in FY2011 (see *Table 4*) suggest that the Urban Institute's finding that SBICs investments were more evenly distributed across the nation than private-sector venture capital fund investments from 1997 to 2005 continue to be the case today.[105] For example, California (51.1%), Massachusetts (10.4%), New York (7.9%), and Texas (5.2%) received the largest share of the total dollar volume invested by private venture capital funds during FY2011. The four states accounted for about three-quarters (74.6%) of the total dollar volume invested by private venture capital funds. In contrast, the four states with the largest share of the total volume invested by SBICs in FY2011 (California at 14.1%, Texas at 10.5%, New York at 8.9%, and Florida at 5.7%) accounted for 39.2% of the total dollar volume invested by SBICs.

Financing by Industry

As shown on *Table 5*, in FY2011, SBIC financings were made in a variety of industries, led by investments in manufacturing; transportation and warehousing; information; and professional, scientific, and technical services.

The previously mentioned 2008 Urban Institute comparative analysis of SBIC financings from 1997 to 2005 found that "SBIC financing is less concentrated by industry than financing from private venture capital firms" and "total financings by SBICs are much less likely to be in high-tech industries" than comparable private-sector venture capital investment firms.[106] The Urban Institute found that unlike SBICs, "the value of investments by private venture capital firms is predominately directed towards information and finance," with computer and Internet firms receiving roughly half of all private-sector investments.[107]

Table 5. SBIC Financing, by Industry, FY2011

Industry	# of Financings	% of Financings	$ Amount of Financings	% of $ Amount of Financings
Manufacturing	547	24.1%	$741,973,599	26.2%
Transportation and Warehousing	437	19.2%	$232,201,658	8.2%
Information	331	14.6%	$347,510,980	12.3%
Professional, Scientific, and Technical	324	14.3%	$474,124,718	16.7%
Services				
Retail Trade	136	6.0%	$151,863,211	5.4%
Administrative and Support and	88	3.9%	$166,550,231	5.9%
Waste Management				
Wholesale Trade	83	3.7%	$205,233,195	7.2%
Accommodation and Food Services	75	3.3%	$59,182,253	2.1%
Health Care and Social Assistance	56	2.5%	$127,650,907	4.5%
Real Estate and Rental Leasing	34	1.5%	$40,466,297	1.4%
Construction	37	1.6%	$60,558,603	2.1%
Finance and Insurance	32	1.4%	$49,071,806	1.7%
Educational Services	26	1.1%	$26,410,089	0.9%
Arts, Entertainment and Recreation	15	0.7%	$26,390,833	0.9%
Mining	15	0.7%	$66,185,000	2.3%
Other Industries	34	1.5%	$57,997,666	2.1%
Total	2,270	100.0%	$2,833,371046	100.0%

Source: U.S. Small Business Administration, "SBIC Program Licensees Financing to Small Businesses Reported Between October 2010 and September 2011," Washington, DC.

Legislative Activity

P.L. 111-5, the American Recovery and Reinvestment Act of 2009 (ARRA), included provisions designed to increase the amount of leverage issued under the SBIC program by increasing the maximum amount of leverage available to an individual SBIC to 300% of its private capital, or $150 million, whichever is less; and by increasing the maximum amount of leverage available for two or more licenses under common control to $225 million.[108] It also encouraged SBIC investment in smaller enterprises by requiring SBICs licensed on or after the date of its enactment (February 17, 2009) to certify that at least 25% of all future financing dollars are invested in smaller enterprises. ARRA defined smaller enterprises as firms having either a net worth of no more than $6 million and average after-tax net income for the preceding two years of no more than $2 million, or meeting the SBA's size standard for its industry classification.[109]

ARRA also encouraged SBIC investments in low-income areas by allowing a SBIC licensed on or after October 1, 2009, to elect to have a maximum leverage amount of $175 million, and $250 million for two or more licenses under common control, if the SBIC has invested at least 50% of its financings in low-income geographic areas and certified that at least 50% of its future investments will be in low-income geographic areas.110

Several bills were introduced during the 111th Congress, and two bills (H.R. 3219, the Small Business Investment Company Modernization Act of 2011, and S. 2136, a bill to increase the maximum amount of leverage permitted under title III of the Small Business Investment Act of 1958) have been introduced during the 112th Congress to address the targeting of additional assistance to startup and early stage small businesses and the SBIC program's financing levels. In addition, as part of its Startup America Initiative, the Obama Administration has recommended that the SBIC program's annual authorization be increased to $4 billion from $3 billion and that the amount of SBA leverage available to licensees under common control be increased to $350 million from $225 million.[111]

Legislation to Target Additional Assistance to Startup and Early Stage Small Businesses

As mentioned previously, some Members and small business advocates have proposed that the SBIC program target additional assistance to startup and early stage small businesses, which are generally viewed as relatively risky investments but also as having a relatively high potential for job creation. Advocates of targeting additional assistance to startup and early stage small businesses argue that the SBA's participating securities program was created to fill a perceived investment gap resulting from the SBA's debenture program's focus on mid- and later-stage small businesses. Because the SBA is no longer providing new licenses or leverage for participating securities SBICs, several Members have introduced legislation to create a new SBA program that would focus on the investment needs of startup and early stage small businesses.

For example, during the 111th Congress the House passed, by a vote of 241-182, H.R. 5297, the Small Business Jobs and Credit Act of 2010.[112] Among its provisions, as passed by the House, H.R. 5297 would have authorized a $1 billion Small Business Early Stage Investment Program. The proposed program would have provided equity investment financing of up to $100 million in matching funds to each participating investment company. It would have required participating investment companies to invest in small businesses, with at least 50% of the financing in early stage small businesses, defined as those small businesses not having "gross annual sales revenues exceeding $15 million in any of the previous three years."[113] The proposed program emphasized venture capital investments in startup companies operating in nine targeted industries.[114]

H.R. 5297, as subsequently enacted by Congress and signed into law by President Obama on September 27, 2010 (P.L. 111-240, the Small Business Jobs Act of 2010) did not include legislative language authorizing a Small Business Early Stage Investment Program.[115] However, it authorized a three-year Intermediary Lending Pilot Program to provide direct loans to not more than 20 eligible nonprofit lending intermediaries each year, totaling not more than $20 million and $1 million per intermediary. The intermediaries, in turn, may make loans to new or growing small businesses, not to exceed $200,000 per business.[116] On August 4, 2011, the SBA announced the selection of the first 20 lenders to participate in the program.[117]

Discussion

Advocates of efforts to encourage capital investment in startup and early stage small businesses, including Members of Congress who have served on the House or Senate Small Business Committees, have argued that the SBA's elimination of the SBIC participating securities program has created a gap "in the SBA's existing array of capital access programs, particularly in the provision of capital to early stage small businesses in capital-intensive industries."[118] As Representative Nydia Velázquez argued on the House floor during congressional consideration of H.R. 5297

> This legislation, Mr. Chairman, also recognizes that capital markets are changing dramatically. Credit standards are stricter, and small businesses are now looking not only to loans and to credit cards to finance their operations, but they are also looking to equity investment to turn their ideas into reality. This has become even more pronounced as asset values have declined, leaving entrepreneurs with less collateral to borrow against. Unfortunately, small firms' access to venture capital and to equity investment has declined. Last year, such investments plummeted from $28 billion in 2008 to only $17 billion last year. This is due, in part, to the previous administration's decision to terminate the SBA's largest pure equity financing program—the Small Business Investment Company Participating Securities program. This has left many entrepreneurs who need equity investment to fulfill their business plans without a source of such financing.[119]

Opponents of efforts to encourage capital investment in startup and early stage small businesses have argued that such efforts could "pile unnecessary risk or costs onto taxpayers at a time when we're dealing with record debt and unsustainable deficit spending."[120] During consideration of the proposed Small Business Early Stage Investment Program, opponents argued that it was untested, would likely encourage risky investments, and the legislation required "only 50% of the funding ... to be invested" in early stage small businesses.[121]

Legislation to Increase SBIC Financing Levels

In 2009, the Small Business Investor Alliance characterized the SBIC program as "dramatically underused."[122] It argued that the program's financing levels would increase if (1) the SBA further improved its licensing processing procedures to make them more timely and objective, (2) the percentage of SBIC regulatory capital allowed from state or local government entities was increased from its present maximum of 33%, and (3) the SBIC program's family of funds limit ($225 million for two or more licenses under common control) was increased to allow SBICs to have a series of investment funds in place, where, for example, "one fund could be winding down, another could be at peak, and another could just be ramping up."[123]

During the 111th Congress, H.R. 3854, the Small Business Financing and Investment Act of 2009, which was passed by the House on October 29, 2009, and H.R. 5554, the Small Business Assistance and Relief Act of 2010, which was not reported after being referred to five committees for consideration, proposed to encourage greater use of the SBIC program by increasing the maximum percentage of SBIC regulatory capital allowed from state or local government entities to 45% from 33%.[124] Both measures would have also increased the SBIC program's family of funds limit to $350 million from $225 million; increased the SBIC program's limit of $250 million to $400 million for multiple funds under common control that were licensed after September 30, 2009, and invested 50% of their dollars in low-income geographic areas; and increased the SBIC program's authorization level from to $5.5 billion from $3 billion in FY2011.[125]

The Obama Administration has also recommended, as part of its Startup America Initiative (which included the SBA's $1 billion early stage debenture SBIC initiative and $1 billion impact investment SBIC initiative), that the 112th Congress adopt legislation to increase the SBIC program's annual authorization to $4 billion from $3 billion. The Administration recommended as well that the 112th Congress adopt legislation to increase the amount of SBA leverage available to licensees under common control to $350 million from $225 million.[126]

H.R. 3219, the Small Business Investment Company Modernization Act of 2011, was introduced on October 14, 2011, and referred to the House Committee on Small Business. No further action has, so far, taken place on the bill. It proposes to encourage greater utilization of the SBIC program by increasing the maximum amount of outstanding SBA leverage available to any single licensed SBIC from the lesser of 300% of its private capital or $150 million, to the lesser of 300% of its private capital or $200 million if a majority of the managers of the company are experienced in managing one or more SBIC licensed companies. It would also increase the maximum amount of outstanding SBA leverage available to two or more licenses under common control to $350 million from $225 million.

S. 2136, a bill to increase the maximum amount of leverage permitted under title III of the Small Business Investment Act of 1958, was introduced on February 28, 2012, and referred to the Senate Committee on Small Business and Entrepreneurship. No further action has yet taken place on the bill. It proposes to encourage greater use of the SBIC program by increasing the maximum amount of outstanding SBA leverage available to two or more licenses under common control to $350 million from $225 million. It would also increase the SBIC program's authorization level to $4 billion from $3 billion.

On March 15, 2012, S.Amdt. 1833, the INVEST in America Act of 2012, was offered on the Senate floor as an amendment in the nature of a substitute to H.R. 3606, the Jumpstart Our Business Startups Act, which had previously passed the House.

Two of the provisions in the amendment proposed to encourage greater use of the SBIC program by (1) increasing the maximum amount of outstanding SBA leverage available to two or more licenses under common control to $350 million from $225 million and (2) increasing the SBIC program's authorization level to $4 billion from $3 billion. The Senate later passed H.R. 3606 with amendments, which did not address the SBIC program. The House accepted the Senate amendments and passed the bill, which President Obama signed into law (P.L. 112-106).

Discussion

In 2010, the SBA announced that one of its goals for the SBIC program was to increase its "acceptance in the marketplace and increase the number of funds licensed and the amount of leverage issued so as to improve capital access for small businesses."[127]

The SBA asserted that ARRA's changes to the SBIC program would help it to achieve this goal. ARRA increased the maximum leverage available to SBICs to up "to three times the private capital raised by the SBIC, or $150 million, whichever is less, and $225 million for multiple licensees under common control" and increased "the maximum leverage amounts to $175 million for single funds and $250 million for multiple funds under common control who are licensed after September 30, 2009, and invest 50% of their dollars in low income geographic areas."[128]

As mentioned previously, advocates of increasing the SBIC program's leverage limits still further and to increase the SBIC program's authorization level to $4 billion from $3 billion have argued that these actions are necessary to help fill a perceived gap in the SBA's "array of capital access programs."[129] In addition, they argue that the demise of the SBIC participating securities program and the current "underutilization" of the SBIC debentures program is preventing many small firms from accessing the capital necessary to fully realize their economic potential and assist in the national economic recovery.[130]

On the other hand, others worry about the potential risk that an expanded SBIC program has for the taxpayer, especially if investments are targeted at startup and early stage small businesses which, by definition, have a more limited credit history and a higher risk for default than businesses that have established positive cash flow.

CONCLUSION

Some, including President Obama, as most recently evidenced by his Startup America Initiative, have agued that current economic conditions make it imperative that the SBA be provided additional resources to assist small businesses in acquiring capital necessary to start, continue, or expand operations and create jobs.[131] In their view, encouraging greater utilization of the SBIC program will increase small business access to capital, result in higher levels of job creation and retention, and promote economic growth. For example, on March 19, 2012, during Senate consideration of S.Amdt. 1833, the INVEST in America Act of 2012, Senator Olympia Snowe argued

> The amendment [S.Amdt. 1833] I and Senator Landrieu introduced would also help small companies access capital by modifying the Small Business Investment Company, SBIC, Program to raise the amount of SBIC debt the Small Business Administration, SBA, can guarantee from $3 billion to $4 billion. It would also increase the amount of SBA guaranteed debt a team of SBIC fund managers who operate multiple funds can borrow. The SBIC provisions in this amendment have bipartisan support, are

noncontroversial, come at no cost to taxpayers and will create jobs. We do not get many bills of this kind in the Senate anymore.

One of the most difficult challenges facing new small businesses today is access to capital. The SBIC Program has helped companies like Apple, FedEx, Callaway Golf, and Outback Steakhouse become household names. As entrepreneurs and other aspiring small business owners well know, it takes money to make money. This legislation ensures that our entrepreneurs and high-growth companies have access to the resources they need so they can continue to drive America's economic growth and job creation in these challenging times. There is no reason why Congress should not approve this amendment to ensure capital is getting into the hands of America's job creators.

This amendment will spur investment in capital-starved startup small businesses, which will play a critical role in leading the Nation of the devastating economic down turn from which we have yet to emerge. For those who may be unfamiliar, despite significant entrepreneurial demand for small amounts of capital, because of their substantial size, most private investment funds cannot dedicate resources to transactions below $5 million. The Nation's SBICs are working to fill that gap, especially even during these challenging times.[132]

Others worry about the potential risk an expanded SBIC program may have for increasing the federal deficit. In their view, the best means to assist small business, promote economic growth, and create jobs is to reduce business taxes and exercise federal fiscal restraint.[133] For example, Representative Sam Graves, chair of the House Committee on Small Business, indicated in the Small Business Committee's FY2013 "views and estimates" letter to the House Budget Committee that the House Small Business Committee supported an increase in the SBIC program's authorization to $4 billion from $3 billion. However, he indicated that the committee opposed funding for the SBA's early stage debenture SBIC initiative and impact investment SBIC initiative because of their potential to generate losses that could lead to higher SBIC fees, or for the need to provide federal funds to subsidize the SBIC program. Representative Graves wrote in the FY2013 views and estimates letter that

The debenture SBIC program is designed to provide equity injections to small businesses that have been operational and have a track record of cash-flow and profits. ... The program is financially sound because the structure of repayments ensures that the government will not suffer significant losses. Thus, no changes are needed to the program and it operates on a zero subsidy basis without an appropriation. The SBA budget is fully supportive of this program and we concur in that recommendation, including raising the program level from $3 billion to $4 billion.

Presumably, some of the additional program level (which will cost the federal government no money) will be used to support two new variations in the Debenture SBIC Program [the early stage debenture SBIC initiative and the impact investment SBIC initiative] ... Neither initiative has received authority from Congress nor had its operational principles assessed by the Committee prior to implementation. The Committee reiterates its recommendation from last year's views and estimates – no funds should be allocated from the additional debenture program levels for these two programs. The Committee on the Budget also should provide further protection to the existing debenture SBIC program by requiring any modifications to the program, whether a pilot program or not, be based on a new subsidy calculation that ensures the current debenture

> program will operate at zero subsidy without any increase in fees due to losses stemming from the Impact and Early Stage Innovation programs.[134]

As these quotations attest, congressional debate concerning the SBIC program has primarily involved assessments of the ability of small businesses to access capital from the private sector and evaluations of the program's risk, the effect of proposed changes on the program's risk, and the potential impact of the program's risk on the federal deficit. Empirical analysis of economic data can help inform debate concerning the ability of small businesses to access capital from the private sector and the extent of the program's risk, the affect of proposed changes on the program's risk, and the potential impact of the program's risk on the federal deficit. Additional data concerning SBIC investment impact on recipient job creation and firm survival might also prove useful.

Appendix. Small Business Eligibility Requirements and Application Process

Small Business Eligibility Requirements

Only businesses that meet the SBA's definition of "small" may participate in the SBIC program. They must meet either the SBA's size standard for the industry in which they are primarily engaged, or a separate financial size standard that has been established for the SBIC program. SBICs use the size standard that is most likely to qualify the company, typically the financial size standard for the SBIC program. The SBIC alternative size standard is currently set as a maximum net worth of no more than $18 million and average after-tax net income for the preceding two years of not more than $6 million.[135] All of a company's subsidiaries, parent companies, and affiliates are considered in determining if it meets the size standard.

In addition, since 1997, the SBA has required SBICs to set aside a specified percentage of their financing for "businesses at the lower end of the permitted size range," primarily because "the financial size standards applicable to the SBIC program are considerably higher than those used in other SBA programs."[136] Indeed, P.L. 111-5, the American Recovery and Reinvestment Act of 2009 (ARRA), requires SBICs licensed on or after the date of its enactment (February 17, 2009) to certify that at least 25% of their future financing is invested in smaller enterprises. A smaller enterprise is a company that, together with any affiliates, either has net worth of no more than $6 million and average after-tax net income for the preceding two years of no more than $2 million, or meets the SBA's size standard in the industry in which the applicant is primarily engaged.[137]

A SBIC licensed before February 17, 2009, that has not received any SBA leverage commitments after February 17, 2009, must have at least 20% of its aggregate financing dollars (plus 100% for leverage commitments over $90 million) invested in smaller enterprises.

A SBIC licensed before February 17, 2009, that has received an SBA leverage commitment after February 17, 2009, must meet the 20% threshold (plus 100% for leverage commitments over $90 million) for financing provided before the date of the first leverage commitment issued after February 17, 2009, and the 25% threshold for financing made on or after such date.[138]

SBICs are not allowed to invest in the following: other SBICs; finance and investment companies or finance-type leasing companies; unimproved real estate; companies with less than 51% of their assets and employees in the United States; passive or casual businesses (those not engaged in a regular and continuous business operation); or companies that will use the proceeds to acquire farmland.[139] In addition, SBICs may not provide funds for a small business whose primary business activity is deemed contrary to the public interest or if the funds will be used substantially for a foreign operation.[140]

Small Business Application Process

Small business owners interested in receiving SBIC financing can search for active SBICs using the SBA's SBIC directory.[141] The directory provides contact information for all licensed SBICs, sorted by state. It also includes the SBIC's preferred minimum and maximum financing size range, the type of capital provided (e.g., equity, mezzanine, subordinated debt, 1st and 2nd lien secured term, or preferred stock), funding stage preference (e.g., early stage, growing and expansion stage, or later stage), industry preference (e.g., business services, manufacturing, environmental services, or distribution), geographic preference (e.g., national, regional, or specific state or states), and a description of the firm's focus (e.g., equity capital to later stage companies for expansion and acquisition, or targeting companies with revenues of at least $5 million and profitability at the time of financing).[142]

After locating a suitable SBIC, the small business owner presents the SBIC a business plan that addresses the business's operations, management, financial condition, and funding requirements. The typical business plan includes the following information:

- the name of the business as it appears on the official records of the state or community in which it operates;
- the city, county, and state of the principal location and any branch offices or facilities;
- the form of business organization and, if a corporation, the date and state of incorporation;
- a description of the business, including the principal products sold or services rendered;
- a history of the general development of the products or services during the past five years (or since inception);
- information about the relative importance of each principal product or service to the volume of the business and to its profits;
- a description of business's real and physical property and adaptability to other business ventures;
- a description of technical attributes of its products and facilities;
- detailed information about the business's customer base, including potential customers;
- a marketing survey or economic feasibility study;

- a description of the distribution system for the business's products or services;
- a descriptive summary of the competitive conditions in the industry in which the business is engaged, including its competitive position relative to its largest and smallest competitors;
- a full explanation and summary of the business's pricing polices;
- brief resumes of the business's management personnel and principal owners, including their ages, education, and business experience;
- banking, business, and personal references for each member of management and for the principal owners;
- balance sheets and profit and loss statements for the last three fiscal years (or from inception);
- detailed projections of revenues, expenses, and net earnings for the coming year;
- a statement of the amount of funding requested and the time requirements for the funds;
- the reasons for the request for funds and a description of the proposed uses; and
- a description of the benefits the business expects to gain from the financing (e.g., expansion, improvement in financial position, expense reduction, or increase in efficiency).[143]

Because SBICs typically receive hundreds of business plans per year, the SBA recommends that small business owners seek a personal referral or introduction to the particular SBIC fund manager being targeted to increase "the likelihood that the business plan will be carefully considered."[144] According to the Small Business Investor Alliance, "a thorough study an SBIC must undertake before it can make a final decision could take several weeks or longer."[145]

End Notes

[1] U.S. Small Business Administration, "Fiscal Year 2011 Congressional Budget Justification and FY2009 Annual Performance Report," Washington, DC, 2010, p. 1.

[2] 15 U.S.C. §661.

[3] U.S. Congress, House Committee on Banking and Currency, Small Business Investment Act of 1958, report to accompany S.3651, 85th Cong., 2nd sess., June 30, 1958, H.Rept. 85-2060 (Washington: GPO, 1958), pp. 4, 5.

[4] Ibid., p. 5.

[5] U.S. Small Business Administration, "SBIC Program Statistics & Administrative Performance," Washington, DC, at http://www.sba.gov/content/program-statistics-administ rative-performance#LicTimes.

[6] U.S. Small Business Administration, Investment Division, "SBIC Program Overview," Washington, DC, at http://www.sba.gov/content/sbic-program-overview-0.

[7] P.L. 92-595, the Small Business Investment Act Amendments of 1972.

[8] A debenture SBIC may issue and have outstanding both guaranteed debentures and participating securities, provided that the total amount of participating securities outstanding does not exceed 200% of its private capital. See 13 CFR §107.1170. The SBA stopped issuing new commitments for participating securities on October 1, 2004.

[9] 13 CFR §107.50.

[10] Ibid.

[11] Commercial banks may invest up to 5% of their capital and surplus to partially or wholly own an SBIC. Bank investments in an SBIC are presumed by federal regulatory agencies to be a "qualified investment" for Community Reinvestment Act purposes. See P.L. 90-104, the Small Business Act Amendments of 1967; The

Board of Governors of the Federal Reserve Board, "Small Business Investment Companies," 33 Federal Register 6967, May 9, 1968; and U.S. Small Business Administration, "Small Business Investment Companies (SBICs)," Small Business Notes, Washington, DC, 2009, at http://www.smallbusinessnotes.com /financing/sbic.html.

12 U.S. Small Business Administration, "For SBIC Applicants: Phase II: Licensing Review," Washington, DC, at http://www.sba.gov/content/phase-ii-licensing-review.

13 U.S. Small Business Administration, "For SBIC Applicants: Pre-Screening," Washington, DC, at http://www.sba.gov/content/pre-screening.

14 A control person is generally defined as someone with the power to direct corporate management and policies.

15 U.S. Small Business Administration, "SBIC Management Assessment Questionnaire and License Application: Form 2181," Washington, DC, p. 21, at http://www.sba.gov/sites/ default/files/SBA%20Form%202181.pdf.

16 U.S. Small Business Administration, "SBIC Program Statistics & Administrative Performance," Washington, DC, at http://www.sba.gov/content/program-statistics-administ rative-performance#LicTimes; and U.S. Small Business Administration, Office of Congressional and Legislative Affairs, "Correspondence with the author," September 21, 2010.

17 U.S. Small Business Administration, "Impact Investment Initiative," Washington, DC, at http://www.sba.gov/ content/small-business-investment-company-sbic-impact-investment-initiative-2.

18 U.S. Small Business Administration, "Small Business Investment Companies - Early Stage SBICs," 77 Federal Register 25052, April 27, 2012.

19 Ibid.

20 13 CFR §107.210.

21 Ibid.

22 13 CFR §107.150.

23 13 CFR §107.230.

24 U.S. Congress, House Committee on Small Business, Private Equity for Small Firms: The Importance of the Participating Securities Program, 109th Cong., 1st sess., April 13, 2005, Serial No. 109-10 (Washington: GPO, 2005), p. 5, 33; and U.S. Small Business Administration, "SBIC Program: FAQs 7. What is the status of the Participating Securities Program?," Washington, DC, at http://www.sba.gov/content/faqs.

25 U.S. Small Business Administration, "Offering Circular, Guaranteed 4.727% Participating Securities Participation Certificates, Series SBIC-PS 2009-10 A," Washington, DC, at http://www.sba.gov/content/sbic-ps-2009-10-cusip831641-ep6.

26 13 CFR §107.1500. A SBIC that wishes to be eligible to issue participating securities must have regulatory capital of at least $10 million unless it can demonstrate to the SBA's satisfaction that it can be financially viable over the longterm with a lower amount, but not less than $5 million. See 13 CFR §107.210. It must also maintain sufficient liquidity to avoid a condition of "Liquidity Impairment," defined as a liquidity ratio (total current funds available divided by total current funds required) of less than 1.2. See 13 CFR §107.1505. The only type of debt, other than leverage, than a SBIC that has applied to issue participating securities or have outstanding participating securities is permitted to incur is temporary debt. Temporary debt is defined as short-term borrowings from a regulated financial institution, a regulated credit company, or a non-regulated lender approved by the SBA for the purpose of maintaining the SBIC's operating liquidity or providing funds for a particular financing of a small business. The total outstanding borrowings, not including leverage, may not exceed 50% of a SBIC's leveraged capital and all such borrowings must be fully paid off for at least 30 consecutive days during a SBIC's fiscal year so that it has no outstanding third-party debt for 30 days. See 13 CFR §107.570. A SBIC issuing participating securities is required to invest an amount equal to the original issue price of such securities solely in equity capital investments (e.g., common or preferred stock, limited partnership interests, options, warrants, or similar equity instruments). See 13 CFR §107.1505.

27 U.S. Congress, House Committee on Small Business, Subcommittee Markup of Legislation Affecting the SBA Capital Access Programs, 111th Cong., 1st sess., October 8, 2009, House Small Business Committee Document No. 111-050 (Washington: GPO, 2009), pp. 7, 10, 11, 187-194; U.S. Congress, House Committee on Small Business, Full Committee Hearing on Increasing Capital for Small Business, 111th Cong., 1st sess., October 14, 2009, House Small Business Committee Document No. 111-051 (Washington: GPO, 2009), pp. 1, 2, 40, 98; and U.S. Congress, House Committee on Small Business, Small Business Financing and Investment Act of 2009, report to accompany H.R. 3854, 111th Cong., 1st sess., October 26, 2009, H.Rept. 111-315 (Washington: GPO, 2009), pp. 3, 4, 10-12.

28 13 CFR §107.210.

29 13 CFR §107.150.

[30] 13 CFR §107.230.

[31] U.S. Small Business Administration, "Impact Investment Initiative," Washington, DC, at http://www.sba.gov/content/small-business-investment-company-sbic-impact-investment-initiative-2. To receive an investment, a small business must meet at least one of the following criteria: (a) it must be located in, or have at least 35% of its full-time employees, at the time of the initial investment, residing in a low or moderate income area as defined in 13 CFR §107.50; or be located in an economically distressed area as defined by Section 3011 of the Public Works and Economic Development Act of 1965, as amended [per capita income of 80% or less of the national average or an unemployment rate that is, for the most recent 24-month period for which data are available, at least 1% greater than the national average unemployment rate]; or (b) be in an industrial sector that the SBA has identified as a national priority (currently clean energy and education). The SBA has announced that additional industrial sectors will be added over time in partnership with other mission-driven agencies.

[32] U.S. Small Business Administration, "Small Business Investment Companies - Early Stage SBICs," 77 Federal Register 25043, 25050, April 27, 2012.

[33] Ibid., pp. 25051-25053.

[34] Ibid., p. 25043.

[35] U.S. Small Business Administration, "Small Business Investment Companies - Early Stage SBICs," 77 Federal Register 25775-25779, May 1, 2012.

[36] Ibid., p. 25775.

[37] 13 CFR §107.800. A SBIC is not allowed to become a general partner in any unincorporated business or become jointly or severally liable for any obligations of an unincorporated business.

[38] 13 CFR §107.810; and 13 CFR §107.840.

[39] 13 CFR §107.815. Debt securities are instruments evidencing a loan with an option or any other right to acquire equity securities in a small business or its affiliates, or a loan which by its terms is convertible into an equity position, or a loan with a right to receive royalties that are excluded from the cost of money.

[40] 13 CFR §107.820.

[41] 13 CFR §107.730.

[42] 13 CFR §107.865. The period of time that a SBIC may exercise control over a small business for purposes connected with its investment through ownership of voting securities, management agreements, voting trusts, majority representation on the board of directors, or otherwise, is "limited to the seventh anniversary of the date on which such control was initially acquired, or any earlier date specified by the terms of any investment agreement." With the SBA's prior written approval, an SBIC "may retain control for such additional period as may be reasonably necessary to complete divestiture of control or to ensure the financial stability of the portfolio company."

[43] A tier of SBA leverage equals the amount of a SBIC's private (regulatory) capital. A SBIC approved for less than two tiers of SBA leverage must not invest more than 20% of its private capital in any one small business if the SBIC's plan contemplates one tier of leverage and no more than 25% of its private capital if its plan contemplates 1.5 tiers of leverage. See 13 CFR §107.740; and U.S. Small Business Administration, "American Recovery and Reinvestment Act of 2009: Implementation of SBIC Program Changes," letter from Harry Haskins, Acting Associate Administrator for Investment, to All Small Business Investment Companies (SBICs) and Applicants, Washington, DC, May 4, 2009, p. 2, at http://archive.sba.gov/idc/groups/public/documents/sba_program_office/ inv_rcvry_ act_sbic_changes.pdf.

[44] 13 CFR §107.720.

[45] Ibid.

[46] Ibid. A SBIC may provide venture capital financing to "disadvantaged concerns" engaged in relending or reinvesting activities (except agricultural credit companies and banking and savings and loan institutions not insured by a federal agency). Without SBA approval, these financings, at the end of the fiscal year, may not exceed a SBIC's regulatory capital. A disadvantaged concern is defined as a small business that is at least 50% owned, controlled, and managed, on a day-to-day basis, by a person or persons whose participation in the free enterprise system is hampered because of social or economic disadvantages.

[47] The SBA has a general interest rate ceiling of 19% for a loan and 14% for a debt security, with provisions for a higher interest rate under specified circumstances. See 13 CFR §107.855. A SBIC is allowed to collect a nonrefundable application fee of no more than 1% of the amount of financing requested from a small business to review its financing application, a closing fee of no more than 2% of the amount of financing requested from a small business concern for a loan, charged no earlier than the date of the first disbursement, and a closing fee of no more than 4% of the amount of financing requested from a small business concern for a debt

security or equity security financing, charged no earlier than the date of the first disbursement. A SBIC is also allowed to charge a small business for reasonable out-of-pocket expenses, other than management expenses incurred to process the small business's financing application. See 13 CFR §107.860.

[48] U.S. Small Business Administration, "Small Business Investment Companies," 64 Federal Register 52645, September 30, 1999.

[49] U.S. Small Business Administration, "Small Business Investment Companies," 64 Federal Register 52641-52646, September 30, 1999. LMI Zones are areas located in a HUBZone; an Urban Empowerment Zone or Urban Enterprise Community designated by the Secretary of the U.S. Department of Housing and Urban Development; a Rural Empowerment Zone or Rural Enterprise Community as designated by the Secretary of the U.S. Department of Agriculture; an area of low income or moderate income as recognized by the Federal Financial Institutions Examination Council; or a county with persistent poverty as classified by the U.S. Department of Agriculture's Economic Research Service. See 13 CFR §107.50.

[50] U.S. Small Business Administration, "For SBICs: Background Information on Low or Moderate Income (LMI) Debentures," Washington, DC, at http://www.sba.gov/content/low-or-moderate-income-lmi-debentures.

[51] U.S. Small Business Administration, "SBIC Program Licensees Financing to Small Businesses Reported Between October 2010 and September 2011," Washington, DC.

[52] 13 CFR §107.1100.

[53] U.S. Small Business Administration, "Funding the SBIC Program: An Overview," Washington, DC, at http://www.sba.gov/content/funding-sbic-program-overview. The SBA is required by statute to issue guarantees "at periodic intervals of not less than every 12 months and shall do so at such shorter intervals as it deems appropriate, taking into consideration the amount and number of such guarantees or trust certificates." See 15 U.S.C. §687m.

[54] U.S. Small Business Administration, "Funding the SBIC Program: An Overview," Washington, DC, at http://www.sba.gov/content/funding-sbic-program-overview.

[55] Ibid.

[56] To view recent SBIC debenture offering circulars see U.S. Small Business Administration, "SBIC Debentures Offering Circulars," Washington, DC, at http://www.sba.gov/category /lender-navigation/sba-loan-programs/sbicprogram/program-data-performance/information-tru-1.

[57] 13 CFR §107.1130; and 13 CFR §107.1210.

[58] 13 CFR §107.1120; 13 CFR §107.1150; and U.S. Small Business Administration, "American Recovery and Reinvestment Act of 2009: Implementation of SBIC Program Changes," letter from Harry Haskins, Acting Associate Administrator for Investment, to All Small Business Investment Companies (SBICs) and Applicants, Washington, DC, May 4, 2009, p. 1, at http://archive.sba.gov/idc/ groups/public/ documents/sba_program_office/ inv_rcvry_act _sbic_changes.pdf.

[59] 13 CFR §107.1150. A low-income area is (1) any population census tract that has a poverty rate that is not less than 20% or (a) if located within a metropolitan area, 50% or more of the households in that census tract have an income equal to less than 60% of the area median gross income; or (b) if not located within a metropolitan area, the median household income in that census tract does not exceed 80% of the statewide median household income; or (c) has been determined by the SBA Administrator to contain a substantial population of low-income individuals in residence, an inadequate access to investment capital, or other indications of economic distress; or (2) any area located within (i) a Historically Underutilized Business Zone; (ii) an Urban Empowerment Zone or Urban Enterprise Community (as designated by the Secretary of the United States Department of Housing and Urban Development); or (iii) a Rural Empowerment Zone or Rural Enterprise Community (as designated by the Secretary of the United States Department of Agriculture). See 13 CFR §108.50.

[60] U.S. Small Business Administration, "Offering Circular, Guaranteed 4.727% Participating Securities Participation Certificates, Series SBIC-PS 2009-10 A," Washington, DC, p. 11, at http:// www.sba.gov/content/sbic-ps-2009-10- cusip-831641-ep6.

[61] U.S. Small Business Administration, "Small Business Investment Companies (SBICs)," Small Business Notes, Washington, DC, 2009, http://www.smallbusinessnotes.com/business-finances/small-business-investment-companiessbics.html; and U.S. Small Business Administration, "For SBIC Applicants: Financing Options Explained," Washington, DC, at http://www.sba.gov/content/financing-options-explained.

[62] Ibid.; 13 CFR §107.50; and 13 CFR §107.1150.

[63] The coupon (interest) rate on SBA debentures is based on the 10-year Treasury rate (adjusted to the nearest 1/8th of one percent) plus a market-driven spread, currently about 70-90 basis points. See 13 CFR §107.50; and U.S. Small Business Administration, "Trust Certificate Rates: SBIC Debenture Pools," Washington, DC, at

http://www.sba.gov/ content/trust-certificate-rates-sbic-debenture-poolsat http://archive.sba.gov/aboutsba/ sbaprograms/ inv/ faq/index.html. The coupon rate for the most recent sale of a SBA debenture participating certificate, which took place on March 14, 2012, was 2.766%. U.S. Small Business Administration, "Guaranteed 2.766% Debenture Participation Certificates, Series SBIC 2012-10 A," Washington, DC, at http://www.sba.gov/content/sbic-2012-10-cusip-831641-ew1.

[64] U.S. Congress, House Committee on Small Business, Small Business Financing and Investment Act of 2009, report to accompany H.R. 3854, 111th Cong., 1st sess., October 26, 2009, H.Rept. 111-315 (Washington: GPO, 2009), p. 11; and U.S. Small Business Administration, "SBIC Program: FAQs: 8. What investment styles and fund types fit best with the SBIC Program?," Washington, DC, http://www.sba.gov/content/faqs.

[65] 13 CFR §107.1170.

[66] 13 CFR §107.1500; and U.S. Small Business Administration, "Offering Circular, Guaranteed 4.727% Participating Securities Participation Certificates, Series SBIC-PS 2009-10 A," Washington, DC, p. 7, 14, at http://www.sba.gov/ content/sbic-ps-2009-10-cusip-831641-ep6.

[67] U.S. Small Business Administration, "Offering Circular, Guaranteed 4.727% Participating Securities Participation Certificates, Series SBIC-PS 2009-10 A," Washington, DC, p. 2, at http://www.sba.gov/ content/sbic-ps-2009-10-cusip831641-ep6.

[68] Ibid., pp. 2, 3. Also, see U.S. Congress, House Committee on Small Business, Private Equity for Small Firms: The Importance of the Participating Securities Program, 109th Cong., 1st sess., April 13, 2005, Serial No. 109-10 (Washington: GPO, 2005), p. 5.

[69] The coupon rate for most recent sale of a SBA guaranteed participating securities participation certificate, which took place on February 25, 2010, was 4.727%. U.S. Small Business Administration, "Offering Circular, Guaranteed 4.727% Participating Securities Participation Certificates, Series SBIC-PS 2009-10 A," Washington, DC, p. 1, at http://www.sba.gov/content/sbic-ps-2009-10-cusip-831641-ep6.

[70] U.S. Congress, House Committee on Small Business, Small Business Financing and Investment Act of 2009, report to accompany H.R. 3854, 111th Cong., 1st sess., October 26, 2009, H.Rept. 111-315 (Washington: GPO, 2009), p. 11; and U.S. Small Business Administration, "SBIC Program: FAQs 7. What is the status of the Participating Securities Program?," Washington, DC, at http://www.sba.gov/content/faqs.

[71] U.S. Small Business Administration, Investment Division, "SBIC Program Overview," Washington, DC, September 30, 2011.

[72] Ibid.

[73] U.S. Small Business Administration, "Impact Investment Initiative," Washington, DC, at http://www.sba.gov/ content/small-business-investment-company-sbic-impact-investment-initiative-2.

[74] U.S. Small Business Administration, "SBA Licenses First Impact Investment Fund in Michigan," Washington, DC, July 26, 2011, at http://www.sba.gov/content/sba-licenses-first-impact-investment-fund-michigan. Mezzanine financing is a hybrid of debt and equity financing and is typically used to finance the expansion of an existing business. It provides the lender the right to convert to an ownership or equity interest in the company if the loan is not paid back in time and in full. It is generally subordinated to debt provided by senior lenders such as banks and venture capital companies.

[75] U.S. Small Business Administration, "Impact Investment Initiative," Washington, DC, at http://www.sba.gov/ content/small-business-investment-company-sbic-impact-investment-initiative-2.

[76] U.S. Small Business Administration, "Small Business Investment Companies - Early Stage SBICs," 77 Federal Register 25052, April 27, 2012.

[77] 13 CFR §107.1181. The required reserve is reduced on each payment date upon payment of the required interest and charges.

[78] U.S. Small Business Administration, Office of Congressional and Legislative Affairs, "Correspondence with the author," Washington, DC, May 2, 2012.

[79] 13 CFR §107.630; and 13 CFR §107.690.

[80] 13 CFR §107.640.

[81] 13 CFR §107.650.

[82] Ibid.

[83] 13 CFR §107.660.

[84] U.S. Small Business Administration, Investment Division, "SBIC Program Statistics and Administrative Performance," Washington, DC, at http://www.sba.gov/content/program-statistics-administrative-performance.

[85] U.S. Small Business Administration, "SBIC Program Licensees Financing to Small Businesses Reported Between October 2010 and September 2011," Washington, DC.

[86] U.S. Small Business Administration, Investment Division, "SBIC Program Overview," Washington, DC, September 29, 2010; and U.S. Small Business Administration, Investment Division, "SBIC Program Overview," Washington, DC, September 30, 2011.

[87] U.S. Small Business Administration, Investment Division, "SBIC Program Overview," Washington, DC, September 29, 2010.

[88] U.S. Small Business Administration, "FY 2012 Congressional Budget Justification and FY 2010 Annual Performance Report," Washington, DC, p. 60, at http://www.sba. gov/sites/default/files/ FINAL%20FY%202012%20CBJ%20FY%202010%20APR_0.pdf. In FY2008, the SBA issued six new SBIC licenses (five to debenture SBICs and one to a bank-owned/non-leveraged SBIC). In FY2009, the SBA issued 11 new SBIC licenses (eight to debenture SBICs and three to bank-owned/non-leveraged SBICs). In FY2010, the SBA issued 23 new SBIC licenses (21 to debenture SBICs and 2 to bank-owned/non-leveraged SBICs).

[89] U.S. Small Business Administration, "Offering Circular, Guaranteed 2.766% Debenture Participation Certificates, Series SBIC 2012-10 A," Washington, DC, at http://www.sba. gov/content/sbic-2012-10-cusip-831641-ewl. The SBA has a selected list of firms that have received SBIC financing, including Apple Computer, Compaq Computer, Costco Wholesale Corporation, FedEx, Intel, Jenny Craig, Inc., Outback Steakhouse, Sports Authority, Staples, and Sun Microsystems, on its website. See U.S. Small Business Administration, "Investment Division," Washington, DC, at http://archive.sba.gov/aboutsba/sbaprograms/ inv/INV_SUCCESS_STORIES.html.

[90] U.S. Small Business Administration, Investment Division, "SBIC Program Overview," Washington, DC, September 30, 2011.

[91] Ibid.

[92] Ibid.

[93] U.S. Small Business Administration, "SBIC Program Licensees Financing to Small Businesses Reported Between October 2010 and September 2011," Washington, DC.

[94] Ibid.

[95] National Venture Capital Association, "Corporate VC Stats as of 12/31/2011 by Year," Arlington, VA, at http://www.nvca.org/index.php?option=com_ docman&task=cat_view &gid=99&Itemid=317.

[96] U.S. Small Business Administration, "Fiscal Year 2011 Congressional Budget Justification and FY2009 Annual Performance Report," Washington, DC, 2010, p. 52.

[97] Kenneth Temkin and Brett Theodos, with Kerstin Gentsch, "The Debenture Small Business Investment Company Program: A Comparative Analysis of Investment Patterns with Private Venture Capital Equity," Washington, DC: The Urban Institute, January 2008, p. 3, at http://www.urban.org/ UploadedPDF/411601_ sbic_gap_analysis.pdf.

[98] Ibid., p. 1.

[99] U.S. Small Business Administration, "SBIC Program Licensees Financing to Small Businesses Reported Between October 2010 and September 2011," Washington, DC.

[100] Kenneth Temkin and Brett Theodos, with Kerstin Gentsch, "The Debenture Small Business Investment Company Program: A Comparative Analysis of Investment Patterns with Private Venture Capital Equity," Washington, DC: The Urban Institute, January 2008, pp. 2, 26, at http://www.urban.org/ UploadedPDF/411601_sbic_gap_analysis.pdf.

[101] U.S. Congress, House Committee on Small Business, Full Committee Hearing on Legislation Updating and Improving the SBA's Investment and Surety Bond Programs, 110th Cong., 1st sess., September 6, 2007, Serial Number 110-44 (Washington: GPO, 2007), p. 15.

[102] Ibid.

[103] U.S. Congress, House Committee on Small Business, Full Committee Hearing On Increasing Capital For Small Business, 111th Cong., 1st sess., October 14, 2009, House Small Business Committee Document No. 111-051 (Washington: GPO, 2009), p. 89.

[104] Kenneth Temkin and Brett Theodos, with Kerstin Gentsch, "The Debenture Small Business Investment Company Program: A Comparative Analysis of Investment Patterns with Private Venture Capital Equity," Washington, DC: The Urban Institute, January 2008, pp. 3, 18-24, at http://www.urban.org/ UploadedPDF/411601_sbic_gap_analysis.pdf.

[105] National Venture Capital Association, "Venture Capital Investments Q1-2012 – MoneyTree Results, Regional Data," Arlington, VA, at http://www.nvca.org/.

[106] Kenneth Temkin and Brett Theodos, with Kerstin Gentsch, "The Debenture Small Business Investment Company Program: A Comparative Analysis of Investment Patterns with Private Venture Capital Equity,"

Washington, DC: The Urban Institute, January 2008, pp. 3, 11-17, at http://www.urban.org/UploadedPDF/411601_sbic_gap_analysis.pdf.

[107] Ibid., p. 11.

[108] 13 CFR §107.1120; 13 CFR §107.1150; and U.S. Small Business Administration, "American Recovery and Reinvestment Act of 2009: Implementation of SBIC Program Changes," letter from Harry Haskins, Acting Associate Administrator for Investment, to All Small Business Investment Companies (SBICs) and Applicants, Washington, DC, May 4, 2009, p. 1, at http://archive.sba.gov/idc/groups/public/documents/sba_program_office/ inv_rcvry_act _sbic_changes.pdf. Previously, " ... the total principal amount of outstanding debentures and participating securities guaranteed by SBA and issued by any SBIC or group of commonly controlled SBICs may not, in general, exceed at any one time an amount equal to three times such SBIC's Private Capital or $130.6 million, whichever is less, of which no more than two times the SBIC's Private Capital may be represented by participating securities. Such dollar limit has been adjusted annually to reflect increases in the Consumer Price Index since March 31, 1993." See U.S. Small Business Administration, "Offering Circular, Guaranteed 5.725% Debenture Participation Certificates, Series SBIC 2008-10 B," Washington, DC, September 18, 2008, at http://www.sba.gov/content/sbic-2008-10-b-cusip831641-en1.

[109] 13 CFR §107.1150; and 13 CFR §107.710.

[110] 13 CFR §107.1150.

[111] The White House, "Startup America Legislative Agenda," Washington, DC, at http://www.whitehouse.gov/sites/default/files/uploads/startup_america_legislative_agenda.pdf.

[112] Representative Edward Perlmutter, "Providing for Further Consideration of H.R. 5297, Small Business Jobs and Credit Act of 2010, Roll No. 368," Congressional Record, daily edition, vol. 156, no. 91 (June 17, 2010), pp. H4608, H4609.

[113] H.R. 5297, the Small Business Lending Fund Act of 2010, Section 399L. Definitions.

[114] Ibid. The nine targeted industries are: agricultural technology, energy technology, environmental technology, life science, information technology, digital media, clean Business Early Stage Investment Program was included in H.R. 3854, the Small Business Financing and Investment Act of 2009, which was passed by the House on October 29, 2009, by a vote of 389-32. It is awaiting action in the Senate.

[115] Senator Al Franken, "Small Business Lending Fund Act of 2010," Rollcall Vote No. 237 Leg., Congressional Record, daily edition, vol. 156, part 125 (September 16, 2010), p. S7158.

[116] P.L. 111-240, the Small Business Jobs Act of 2010, Section 1131. Small Business Intermediary Lending Pilot Program.

[117] U.S. Small Business Administration, "Small Businesses Have New Non-Profit Sources for SBA-financed Loans," Washington, DC, August 4, 2011, at http://www.sba.gov/content/ intermediary-lending-pilot-program-0.

[118] U.S. Congress, House Committee on Small Business, Small Business Financing and Investment Act of 2009, report to accompany H.R. 3854, 111th Cong., 1st sess., October 26, 2009, H.Rept. 111-315, p. 2. For the arguments presented by various organizations advocating programs to assist early stage small businesses and startups see U.S. Congress, House Committee on Small Business, Subcommittee on Finance and Tax Hearing on Legislative Proposals to Reform the SBA's Capital Access Programs, 111th Cong., 1st sess., July 23, 2009, House Small Business Committee Document No. 111-039 (Washington: GPO, 2009), pp. 10-12, 60-67; and U.S. Congress, House Committee on Small Business, Full Committee Hearing on Increasing Access to Capital for Small Business, 111th Cong., 1st sess., October 14, 2009, House Small Business Committee Document No. 111-051 (Washington: GPO, 2009), pp. 33-35, 50-54, 63-69, 86-99.

[119] Representative Nydia Velázquez, "Small Business Jobs and Credit Act of 2010," House debate, Congressional Record, daily edition, vol. 156, no. 90 (June 16, 2010), p. H4516.

[120] Representative Sam Graves, "Small Business Jobs and Credit Act of 2010," House debate, Congressional Record, vol. 156, no. 90 (June 16, 2010), p. H4516.

[121] Ibid; and Representative Jeff Flake, "Small Business Early Stage Investment Act of 2009," House debate, Congressional Record, vol. 155, no. 171 (November 18, 2009), p. H13083. Note: H.R. 3738, the Small Business Early-Stage Investment Act of 2009, was one of eight bills merged into H.R. 3854, the Small Business Financing and Investment Act of 2009, and was later added to H.R. 5297, Small Business Jobs and Credit Act of 2010, by H.Res. 1436.

[122] U.S. Congress, House Committee on Small Business, Full Committee Hearing On Increasing Capital For Small Business, 111th Cong., 1st sess., October 14, 2009, House Small Business Committee Document No. 111-051 (Washington: GPO, 2009), pp. 32, 87.

[123] Ibid., pp. 88, 89.

[124] H.R. 3854, the Small Business Financing and Investment Act of 2009, Section 401. Increased Investment from States; and H.R. 5554, the Small Business Assistance and Relief Act of 2010, Section 591. Increased Investment from States.

[125] H.R. 3854, the Small Business Financing and Investment Act of 2009, Section 401. Increased Investment From States, Section 403. Revised Leverage Limitations For Successful SBICs, and Section 408. Program Levels; and H.R. 5554, the Small Business Assistance and Relief Act of 2010, Section 591. Increased Investment from States, Section 593. Revised Leverage Limitations for Successful SBICs, and Section 598. Program Levels.

[126] The White House, "Startup America Legislative Agenda," Washington, DC, at http://www.whitehouse.gov/sites/default/files/uploads/startup_america_legislative_agenda.pdf.

[127] U.S. Small Business Administration, "Fiscal Year 2011 Congressional Budget Justification and FY2009 Annual Performance Report," Washington, DC, 2010, p. 52.

[128] U.S. Small Business Administration, "SBA Project Plan, Section 505: SBIC Program Changes," Washington, DC, June 16, 2010, at http://archive.sba.gov/idc/groups/public/ documents/sba_homepage/sba_sbic_plan.pdf.

[129] U.S. Congress, House Committee on Small Business, Small Business Financing and Investment Act of 2009, report to accompany H.R. 3854, 111th Cong., 1st sess., October 26, 2009, H.Rept. 111-315 (Washington: GPO, 2009), p. 3.

[130] U.S. Congress, House Committee on Small Business, Full Committee Hearing on Increasing Capital for Small Business, 111th Cong., 1st sess., October 14, 2009, House Small Business Committee Document No. 111-051 (Washington: GPO, 2009), pp. 88-91; and Representative Nydia Velázquez, "Small Business Jobs and Credit Act of 2010," House debate, Congressional Record, daily edition, vol. 156, no. 90 (June 16, 2010), p. H4516.

[131] Representative Nydia Velázquez, "Small Business Financing and Investment Act of 2009," House debate, Congressional Record, daily edition, vol. 155, no. 159 (October 29, 2009), pp. H12074, H12075; Senator Mary Landrieu, "Statements on Introduced Bills and Joint Resolutions," remarks in the Senate, Congressional Record, daily edition, vol. 155, no. 185 (December 10, 2009), p. S12910; The White House, "Remarks by the President on Job Creation and Economic Growth," Washington, DC, December 8, 2009, at http://www.whitehouse.gov/the-press-office/ remarks-president-job-creation-and-economic-growth; and The White House, "Startup America Legislative Agenda," Washington, DC, at http://www.whitehouse.gov/sites/default/files/uploads/startup_america_legislative_agenda.pdf.

[132] Senator Olympia Snowe, "Jumpstart Our Business Startups Act," remarks in the Senate, Congressional Record, vol. 158, no. 45 (March 19, 2012), p. S15845.

[133] National Federation of Independent Business, "Payroll Tax Holiday," Washington, DC, at http://www.nfib.com/issues-elections/issues-elections-item/cmsid/49039/; and NFIB, "Government Spending," Washington, DC, at http://www.nfib.com/issues-elections/issues-elections-item/cmsid/49051/.

[134] Representative Sam Graves, "Views and Estimates of the Committee on Small Business on Matters to be set forth in the Concurrent Resolution on the Budget for Fiscal Year 2013," Washington, DC, pp. 4, 5, at http://smbiz.house.gov/ UploadedFiles/Views_and_ Estimates_FY_2013.pdf. Also, see Representative Sam Graves, "Views and Estimates of the Committee on Small Business on Matters to be set forth in the Concurrent Resolution on the Budget for Fiscal Year 2012," Washington, DC, pp. 4, 5, at http://smbiz.house.gov/UploadedFiles/ March_17_Views_and_Estimates_Letter.pdf.

[135] 13 CFR §107.700; 13 CFR §107.710; 13 CFR §301(c)(2); and 13 CFR §301(c)(1).

[136] U.S. Small Business Administration, "Small Business Investment Companies — Leverage Eligibility and Portfolio Diversification Requirements," 74 Federal Register 33912, July 14, 2009.

[137] 13 CFR §107.710.

138 U.S. Small Business Administration, "Small Business Investment Companies — Leverage Eligibility and Portfolio Diversification Requirements," 74 Federal Register 33912, July 14, 2009.

[139] 13 CFR §107.720.

[140] Ibid.

[141] U.S. Small Business Administration, "All SBIC Licensees By State," Washington, DC, at http://www.sba.gov/content/all-sbic-licensees-state.

[142] Ibid.

[143] National Association of Small Business Investment Companies, "SBIC Financing: Step-by-Step," Washington, DC, at http://www.nasbic.org/?page=SBIC_financing.

[144] U.S. Small Business Administration, "SBIC Program," Washington, DC, at http://www. sba. gov/content/sbic-program-0.

[145] Small Business Investor Alliance (formerly the National Association of Small Business Investment Companies), "SBIC Financing: Step-by-Step," Washington, DC, at http:// www. nasbic.org/?page=SBIC_financing.

In: Small Business Administration ...
Editor: Alan R. Connoly

ISBN: 978-1-62417-674-6

Chapter 2

SBA NEW MARKETS VENTURE CAPITAL PROGRAM*

Robert Jay Dilger

SUMMARY

Authorized by P.L. 106-554, the Consolidated Appropriations Act, 2001 (Appendix H — the New Markets Venture Capital Program Act of 2000), the New Markets Venture Capital (NMVC) program is designed to promote economic development and the creation of wealth and job opportunities in low-income geographic areas by addressing the unmet equity investments needs of small businesses located in those areas. Modeled on the SBA's Small Business Investment Company (SBIC) program, SBA-selected, privately owned and managed NMVC companies provide funding and operational training assistance to small businesses using private capital the NMVC company has raised (called regulatory capital) and up to 150% of that amount (called leverage) from the sale of SBA-guaranteed 10-year debentures (loan obligations) to third parties, subject to the availability of funds. Because the SBA guarantees the debenture, the SBA is able to obtain favorable interest rates. NMVC companies are responsible for meeting the terms and conditions set forth in the debenture. At least 80% of the investments must be in small businesses located in a low-income area.

Specialized Small Business Investment Companies (SSBICs) established under the SBIC program are also eligible for NMVC operational assistance training grants, which are awarded on a dollar-to-dollar matching basis. There are currently six NMVC companies participating in the program.

The NMVC program was appropriated $21.952 million in FY2001 to support up to $150 million in SBA guaranteed debentures and $30 million for operational assistance training grants for FY2001 through FY2006. The funds were provided in a lump sum in FY2001 and were to remain available until expended. In 2003, the unobligated balances of $10.5 million for the NMVC debenture subsidies and $13.75 million for operational assistance grants were rescinded. The program continues to operate, with the number and amount of financing declining in recent years as the program's initial investments expire

* This is an edited, reformatted and augmented version of a Congressional Research Service publication, CRS Report for Congress R42565, prepared for Members and Committees of Congress, from www.crs.gov, dated June 12, 2012.

and NMVC companies engage only in additional follow-on financings with the small businesses in their portfolio.

More than 30 bills have been introduced in recent Congresses to either expand or amend the NMVC program. Many of these bills would increase the program's funding. For example, during the 112th Congress, H.R. 2872, the Job Creation and Urban Revitalization Act of 2011, was introduced on September 8, 2011. The bill would provide the NMVC program such subsidy budget authority as may be necessary to guarantee $75 million of debentures and $15 million for operational assistance training grants for FY2012 through FY2013. The bill was referred to the House Committee on Small Business on September 8, 2011, and is awaiting further action.

This report examines the NMVC program's legislative origins and describes the program's eligibility and performance requirements for NMVC companies, eligibility requirements for small businesses seeking financing, and the definition of low-income areas. It also reviews regulations governing the SBA's financial assistance to NMVC companies and provides program statistics. The report concludes with an examination of (1) efforts to eliminate the program based on concerns that it duplicates other SBA programs and is relatively expensive, (2) the rescission of the program's unobligated funding in 2003, and (3) recent congressional efforts to provide the program additional funds.

New Markets Venture Capital Program Overview

The Small Business Administration (SBA) administers several programs to support small businesses, including loan guaranty programs to enhance small business access to capital; programs to increase small business opportunities in federal contracting; direct loans for businesses, homeowners, and renters to assist their recovery from natural disasters; and access to entrepreneurial education to assist with business formation and expansion.1 It also administers the New Markets Venture Capital (NMVC) Program.

Authorized by P.L. 106-554, the Consolidated Appropriations Act, 2001 (Appendix H — the New Markets Venture Capital Program Act of 2000), the NMVC program is designed to

- promote economic development and the creation of wealth and job opportunities in low-income geographic areas and among individuals living in such areas by encouraging developmental venture capital investments in smaller enterprises primarily located in such areas; and
- address the unmet equity investment needs of small enterprises located in low-income geographic areas.[2]

Modeled on the SBA's Small Business Investment Company (SBIC) program, SBA-selected, privately owned and managed NMVC companies provide funding and operational training assistance to small businesses using private capital the NMVC company has raised (called regulatory capital) and up to 150% of that amount (called leverage) from the sale of SBA-guaranteed 10-year debentures (loan obligations) to third parties, subject to the availability of funds.[3] Because the SBA guarantees the debenture, the SBA is able obtain favorable interest rates. NMVC companies are responsible for meeting the terms and conditions set forth in the debenture. At least 80% of the investments must be in small businesses located in a low-income area, as defined in the statute.

Specialized Small Business Investment Companies (SSBICs) established under the SBIC program are also eligible for NMVC operational assistance training grants, which are awarded on a dollar-to-dollar matching basis. There are currently six NMVC companies participating in the program.

The NMVC program was appropriated $21.952 million in FY2001 to support up to $150 million in SBA guaranteed debentures and up to $30 million for operational assistance training grants for FY2001 through FY2006.[4] The funds were provided in a lump sum in FY2001 and were to remain available until expended. The SBA subsequently provided $72.0 million in leverage to NMVC companies in FY2002 and FY2003 ($12.5 million in FY2002 and $59.5 million in FY2003) and $14.4 million for operational assistance grants ($3.75 million in FY2002 and $10.65 million in FY2003).[5] In 2003, the unobligated balances of $10.5 million for the NMVC debenture subsidies and $13.75 million for operational assistance grants were rescinded.[6] The program continues to operate, with the number and amount of financing declining in recent years as the program's initial investments expire and NMVC companies engage only in additional follow-on financings with the small businesses in their portfolio.

As will be discussed, more than 30 bills have been introduced in recent Congresses to amend the NMVC program. Many of these bills would provide the program additional funding (a list and summary of bills introduced, by Congress, to provide the program additional funding is provided in the *Appendix*). For example, during the 112th Congress, H.R. 2872, the Job Creation and Urban Revitalization Act of 2011, was introduced on September 8, 2011. The bill would provide the NMVC program such subsidy budget authority as may be necessary to guarantee $75 million of debentures and $15 million for operational assistance training grants for FY2012 through FY2013. The bill was referred to the House Committee on Small Business on September 8, 2011, and is awaiting further action.

This report examines the NMVC program's legislative origins and describes the program's eligibility and performance requirements for NMVC companies, eligibility requirements for small businesses seeking financing, and the definition of low-income areas. It also reviews regulations governing the SBA's financial assistance to NMVC companies and provides program statistics. The report concludes with an examination of (1) efforts to eliminate the program based on concerns that it duplicates other SBA programs and is relatively expensive, (2) the rescission of the program's unobligated funding in 2003, and (3) recent congressional efforts to provide the program additional funds.

LEGISLATIVE ORIGINS

105th Congress

On September 15, 1998, the Senate Committee on Small Business conducted a markup of several bills pending before the committee, including H.R. 3412, the Small Business Investment Company Technical Corrections Act of 1998, which the House had passed.[7] Senator Christopher Bond, chair of the Senate Committee on Small Business, proposed an amendment in the nature of a substitute to H.R. 3412 incorporating the full texts of S. 2372, the Year 2000 Readiness Act; and S. 2407, the Small Business Programs Restructuring and Reform Act of 1998; and provisions from S. 2448, the Small Business Loan Enhancement Act.[8] The committee also debated and approved by unanimous voice votes seven amendments to the substitute amendment. One of the seven approved amendments was a precursor of the NMVC program.

The Community Development Venture Capital Demonstration Program

The amendment, offered by Senator Paul Wellstone, would have authorized a $20 million, four-year technical assistance program—the Community Development Venture Capital Demonstration Program—to provide grants, on a matching dollar-to-dollar basis, to experienced community development venture capital (CDVC) firms that invest in small businesses located in economically distressed areas, such as inner cities and poor rural counties. The grants would be used to provide technical expertise and operating assistance to new, emerging, less experienced CDVC organizations.[9] The program's stated purpose was "to develop and expand a new but growing field of organizations that use the tools of venture capital to create good jobs, productive wealth, and entrepreneurial capacity that benefit disadvantaged people and economically distressed communities."[10] The program's advocates argued that despite difficulties associated with making investments in economically distressed areas some successful CDVCs had produced "a 'double bottom line' of not only financial returns, but also social benefits in the form of good jobs and healthier communities."[11]

On September 15, 1998, the committee reported H.R. 3412, as amended, by a vote of 18-0. On September 30, 1998, the Senate passed the bill, with an amendment, by unanimous consent. The House did not act on the bill.

106th Congress

On January 19, 1999, President Bill Clinton announced during his State of the Union Address support for what was later called the "New Markets Investment Initiative."12 The proposed initiative was comprised of several programs, including a New Markets Tax Credit program and a New Markets Venture Capital program, to encourage economic development in economically distressed areas.[13] President Clinton subsequently drew attention to the initiative by taking three separate trips to "underserved" inner city and rural communities, visiting the Pine Ridge Indian Reservation in South Dakota and Phoenix, AZ, on July 7, 1999, and Los Angeles, CA, and Anaheim, CA, on July 8, 1999 (trip 1); Newark, NJ, and Hartford, CT, on November 4, 1999 (trip 2); and Hermitage, AR, and Chicago, IL, on November 5, 1999 (trip 3).14 During his remarks in Chicago, President Clinton announced that he had reached an agreement with House Speaker Dennis Hastert (who was present) to develop a bipartisan legislative initiative on developing new market investments as a means to revitalize impoverished communities.[15]

SBA's LMI Initiative

In a related development, on February 9, 1999, the SBA proposed several incentives to encourage companies participating in its SBIC program to "expand their investment activity into economically distressed inner cities and rural areas."[16] After receiving public comments on several proposed incentives, the SBA issued a final rule, on September 30, 1999, implementing the SBIC low and moderate investments (LMI) initiative.[17]

The ongoing LMI initiative is designed to encourage SBICs to invest in small businesses located in inner cities and rural areas "that have severe shortages of equity capital" because investments in those areas "often are of a type that will not have the potential for yielding returns that are high enough to justify the use of participating securities."[18] SBICs that invest in small businesses that have at least 50% of their employees or tangible assets located in a low-to-moderate income area (LMI Zone), or have at least 35% of their full-time employees with their primary residence in an LMI Zone are eligible for the incentives.[19]

For example, unlike regular SBIC debentures that typically have a 10-year maturity, LMI debentures are available in two maturities, 5 years and 10 years, plus the stub period. The stub period is the time between the debenture's issuance date and the next March 1 or September 1. The stub period allows all LMI debentures to have common March 1 or September 1 maturity dates to simplify administration of the program.

In addition, LMI debentures are issued at a discount so that the proceeds that an SBIC receives for the sale of a debenture are reduced by (1) the debenture's interest costs for the first five years, plus the stub period; (2) the SBA's annual fee for the debenture's first five years, plus the stub period; and (3) the SBA's 2% leverage fee. As a result, these interest costs and fees are effectively deferred, freeing SBICs from the requirement to make interest payments on LMI debentures, or pay the SBA's annual fees on LMI debentures, for the first five years of a debenture, plus the stub period between the debenture's issuance date and the next March 1 or September 1.[20]

The Community Development and Venture Capital Act of 2000

On September 16, 1999, Senator John Kerry introduced S. 1594, the Community Development and Venture Capital Act of 2000.[21] The bill included several provisions in President Clinton's New Markets Investment Initiative. The bill had three main parts: a New Markets Venture Capital Program, very similar to the present program, to encourage investment in economically distressed communities; a Community Development Venture Capital Assistance Program to expand the number of community development venture capital firms and professionals devoted to investing in economically distressed communities; and BusinessLINC, a mentoring program to link established, successful businesses with small business owners in economically stagnant or deteriorating communities to facilitate the development of small businesses in those communities.[22]

After conducting two hearings and sponsoring a roundtable discussion on the Community Development and Venture Capital Act of 2000, the Senate Committee on Small Business reported the bill, as amended, by a vote of 16-1, on July 26, 2000.

In the report accompanying the bill, Senator Christopher Bond, chair of the Senate Committee on Small Business, argued that the SBIC program had "proven to be an extremely successful public-private sector partnership with the government" and mentioned the SBA's LMI initiative as a new means to encourage SBICs to make investments in low-to-moderate income areas.[23] However, he argued that "as successful as the SBIC program is, it does not sufficiently reach areas of our country that need economic development the most."[24]

He added that SBICs invested $771 million in low-to-moderate income areas in 1999, but "the vast majority of those investments were very large and not at all comparable to the type of investments [NMVC] funds would make."[25] Senator Bond argued that the committee was approving the bill because it was necessary

> to expand the number of smaller investments being made to small businesses in the poorest areas, low-income geographic areas, and to fill another gap in access to capital that small businesses face. Investments for NMVC funds typically will range from $50,000 to $300,000 versus the $300,000 to $5 million range found in the Agency's SBIC program."[26]

The Senate did not take further action on the bill.

The New Markets Venture Capital Program Act of 2000

On December 14, 2000, Representative (later Senator) Jim Talent, chair of the House Committee on Small Business, introduced H.R. 5663, the New Markets Venture Capital Program Act of 2000.[27] The bill had two parts: the current New Markets Venture Capital Program and BusinessLINC. The next day, the bill was incorporated by reference in the conference report accompanying H.R. 4577, the Consolidated Appropriations Act, 2001, which became law (P.L. 106-554) on December 21, 2000.[28]

On January 22, 2001, the SBA published an interim final rule in the *Federal Register* to establish the NMVC program. Comments on the proposed rule were due by March 23, 2001. The SBA also published a notice in the *Federal Register* on January 22, 2001, inviting applications from venture capital firms and Specialized Small Business Investment Companies (SSBICs) established under the SBIC program to participate in the program.[29] The SBA published a final rule formally establishing the NMVC program on May 23, 2001.[30]

NMVC Company Eligibility and Performance Requirements

P.L. 106-554 specified that venture capital companies interested in participating in the program must submit

- a detailed application to the SBA that includes, among other items, a business plan describing how the company intends to make successful developmental venture capital investments in identified low-income geographic areas, and
- information regarding the community development finance or relevant venture capital qualifications and general reputation of the company's management.[31]

In addition, an NMVC company must

- be a newly formed for-profit entity or a newly formed for-profit subsidiary of an existing entity;
- be organized under state law solely for the purpose of performing the functions and conducting the activities contemplated under the act;

- be organized either as a corporation, a limited partnership, or a limited liability company;
- show, to the SBA's satisfaction, that its current or proposed management team is qualified and has the knowledge, experience, and capability in community development finance or relevant venture capital finance necessary for investing in the types of businesses contemplated by the act; and
- have a primary objective of economic development of low-income areas.[32]

On January 22, 2001, the SBA solicited applications from venture capital companies and SSBICs to participate in the NMVC program. The SBA had planned to offer another round of applications for the program during the first quarter of 2003.

However, the second round of applications was canceled because, as mentioned previously, P.L. 108-7, the Consolidated Appropriations Resolution, 2003, which became law on February 20, 2003, rescinded the program's unobligated funding.[33]

The SBA received 23 applicants during its initial solicitation from companies interested in participating in the NMVC program, and conditionally approved 7 of them.[34] Final approval is subject to the applicant meeting several conditions. For example, applicants are required to raise, within 18 months of being conditionally approved, at least $5 million in private capital or in binding capital commitments from one or more investors (other than federal agencies or departments) who meet criteria established by the administrator (the private funds are called regulatory capital). Applicants also must have in place binding commitments from sources other than the SBA that are payable or available over a multiyear period not to exceed 10 years that amount to not less than 30% of the total amount of regulatory capital and commitments raised (30% of $5 million = $1.5 million).[35] This additional funding is required to guarantee the applicant's ability to meet the required dollar-to-dollar matching contribution for operational assistance training grants.[36] Six of the seven companies granted conditional approval subsequently met all of the program requirements (one in April 2002, three in March 2003, one in April 2003, and one in August 2003) and were accepted into the program after signing a formal participation agreement with the SBA.[37] The six NMVC companies, which continue to participate in the program, initially raised $48 million in private capital and were subsequently provided $72 million in leverage.[38]

The companies are

- Adena Ventures, L.P., Athens, OH, approved on April 24, 2002, with targeted low-income areas in Ohio, West Virginia, and Maryland;
- New Markets Venture Partners, College Park, MD, approved on March 5, 2003, with targeted low-income areas in Maryland, Virginia, and the District of Columbia;
- CEI Community Ventures Fund, LLC, Portland, ME, approved on March 21, 2003, with targeted low-income areas in Maine, New Hampshire, and Vermont;
- Murex Investments I, L.P., Philadelphia, PA, approved on March 31, 2003, with targeted low-income areas in Pennsylvania, New Jersey, and Delaware;
- Penn Venture Partners, LP, Harrisburg, PA, approved on April 23, 2003, with targeted low-income areas in Pennsylvania;

- Southern Appalachian Fund, L.P., London, KY, approved on August 8, 2003, with targeted low-income areas in Kentucky, Tennessee, Georgia, Alabama, and Mississippi.[39]

NMVC companies are subject to various reporting requirements. For example, for each fiscal year, NMVC companies must file an annual financial statement with the SBA that has been audited by an independent public accountant acceptable to the SBA.[40] The annual financial statement must include an assessment of the social, economic, or community development impact of each financing; the number of fulltime equivalent jobs created as a result of the financing; the impact on the revenues and profits of the business being financed; the impact on the taxes paid by the business being financed and by its employees; and a listing of the number and percentage of the business's employees that reside in a low-income area.[41] NMVC companies are also required to submit to the SBA a portfolio financing report for each financing made within 30 days of the closing date.[42]

ELIGIBILITY OF SMALL BUSINESSES AND LOW-INCOME GEOGRAPHIC AREAS

NMVC companies are required to provide financial assistance and operational assistance training only to small businesses as defined under the SBA's SBIC program. The business must meet either the SBA's size standard for the industry in which it is primarily engaged or have a maximum net worth of no more than $18 million and average after-tax net income for the preceding two years of not more than $6 million.[43] All of the company's subsidiaries, parent companies, and affiliates are considered in the size standard determination.[44] In addition, at the close of each NMVC company's fiscal year, at least 80% of the company's total financings (in total dollars) and 80% of the total number of concerns in that company's portfolio must be small businesses that, at the time of the financing, had their principal offices located in a low-income area (low-income enterprises).[45] NMVC companies that fail to reach these required percentages at the end of any fiscal year must be in compliance by the end of the following fiscal year. They are not eligible for additional leverage from the SBA until such time as they reach the required percentages.[46] A low-income area is defined in the act as any census tract, or equivalent county division as defined by the Bureau of the Census, that meets any of the following criteria:

- a poverty rate of 20% or more;
- if located in a metropolitan area, at least 50% of its households have an income that is below 60% of the area median gross income;
- if not located in a metropolitan area, has a median household income that does not exceed 80% of the statewide median household income;
- is located within a HUBZone;
- is located in an urban empowerment zone or urban enterprise community as designated by the Department of Housing and Urban Development; or
- is located in a rural empowerment zone or rural enterprise community as designated by the Department of Agriculture.

NMVC LEVERAGE

NMVC companies invest funds that they have raised themselves (regulatory capital) in small businesses and, in addition, can receive up to 150% of that amount from the SBA, subject to the availability of funds. NMVC companies follow essentially the same process for obtaining SBA funding as prescribed under the SBIC program. The SBA's funding (leverage) comes from the sale of 10-year securities (debentures) to third parties which are backed by the full faith and credit of the United States.[47] Because the SBA guarantees the timely payment of the principal and interest due on the securities, the SBA is able to obtain favorable interest rates. NMVC companies are responsible for meeting the terms and conditions set forth in the debenture.

NMVC debentures are deferred interest debentures issued at a discount (less than face value) equal to the first five years' interest to eliminate the need for NMVC companies to make interest payments during that period. As a result, NMVC companies make no payments on the debenture for five years from the date of issuance, plus the length of time between the issue date and the next March 1 or September 1, whichever comes first.[48] The SBA refers to this period of time as the "stub" period and employs its use so that all NMVC debentures have common prepayment and maturity dates of either March 1 or September 1.[49] NMVC companies make semi-annual interest payment on the face amount of the debenture during years 6 to 10, and are responsible for paying the debenture's principal amount when the debenture reaches its maturity date.

NMVC companies receive funding (leverage) from the SBA in a two-step process. First, they submit a request to the SBA for a conditional commitment to reserve a specific amount of leverage for future use.[50] This request authorizes the SBA to sell the requested debenture amount to a third party at an interest rate approved by the SBA or to pool the requested debenture amount with other requests, providing each request with the same maturity date, interest rates, and conditions. The NMVC companies then apply to the SBA to draw against the SBA's leverage commitment. These requests may come at any time during the term of the SBA's leverage commitment.[51]

Although the SBA is authorized to pool NMVC debentures, the Federal Home Loan Bank of Chicago (FHLB) has an agreement with the SBA to purchase all NMVC debentures and hold them until maturity. The interest rate on the debentures is determined by FHLB using a spread over the FHLB's cost of funds as determined on each draw date.[52]

The SBA does not allow NMVC companies to prepay their draws for a period of 12 months (plus the stub period) after issuance. Prepayments are allowed after that waiting period, but only on March 1 or September 1 of each year. The cost of prepayment is the present value of the NMVC debenture on the semi-annual date chosen for prepayment.[53]

After receiving funds, NMVC companies make equity investments in small businesses of their choice. Equity investments typically are in the form of common or preferred stock, and sometimes in subordinated debt with equity features (provided that the debt is not amortized and provides for interest payments contingent upon and limited to the extent of earnings) or in limited partnership interests, options, warrants, and similar equity investment instruments.[54]

Operational Assistance Training Grants

The SBA awards grants to NMVC companies and to SSBICs to provide free operational assistance training to small businesses financed, or expected to be financed, under the program.[55] The grants have a dollar-to-dollar matching requirement and cannot be used for general and administrative expenses, including overhead.[56]

Matching resources may be in the form of (1) cash; (2) in-kind contributions; (3) binding commitments for cash or in-kind contributions that are payable or available over a multiyear period acceptable to the SBA, but not to exceed 10 years; or (4) an annuity, purchased with funds other than regulatory capital, from an insurance company acceptable to the SBA that may be payable over a multiyear period acceptable to the SBA, but not to exceed 10 years.[57]

NMVC companies and SSBICs are eligible for an operational assistance training grant award equal to the amount of matching resources the company has raised, subject to the availability of funds.[58]

NMVC companies must use at least 80% of both the grant funds awarded by the SBA and its matching resources to provide free operational assistance training to small businesses located in a low-income area. SSBICs must use both the grant funds awarded by the SBA and its matching resources to provide free operational assistance training to small businesses "in connection with a low-income investment made by the SSBIC with regulatory capital raised after September 21, 2000."[59] Operational assistance includes management, marketing, and other technical assistance training that assists a small business with its development.[60]

Table 1. New Markets Venture Capital Program Statistics, FY2002-FY2012

Fiscal Year	Operational Assistance Training Grant Awards	NMVC Financings	Number of Small Businesses Financed
2002	$3,750,000	$500,000	1
2003	$10,650,000	$2,694,164	6
2004	$0	$9,667,145	19
2005	$0	$8,603,678	22
2006	$0	$16,279,591	35
2007	$0	$14,015,821	32
2008	$0	$13,351,779	36
2009	$0	$4,241,016	24
2010	$0	$3,424,407	16
2011	$0	$2,506,576	18
2012 (to June 5)	$0	$368,472	5
Total	$14,400,000	$75,652,649	67[a]

Source: U.S. Small Business Administration, Congressional Budget Justification, Washington, DC, various years; U.S. Small Business Administration, Performance and Accountability Report, Washington, DC, various years; U.S. Small Business Administration, Office of Congressional and Legislative Affairs, "Correspondence with the author," Washington, DC, June 5, 2012.

[a] The total number of small businesses financed is fewer than the sum of small businesses financed each year because NMVC companies may make multiple financings into any one of their "portfolio companies" over the life of the fund.

PROGRAM STATISTICS

As shown in *Table 1*, NMVC companies received operational assistance training grant awards in FY2002 and FY2003, and started making equity investments in small businesses in FY2002. As mentioned previously, the six NMVC companies, which continue to participate in the program, initially raised $48 million in private capital and were subsequently provided $72 million in leverage.[61] Since the program's inception through June 5, 2012, NMVC companies have invested more than $75.6 million in 67 different small businesses.

The program reached its peak, in terms of the amount of financings, in FY2007, investing nearly $16.3 million in 35 different small businesses that year. Since then, the amount of financings has declined as the program's initial investments expire and NMVC companies engage only in additional follow-on financings with the small businesses in their portfolios.

CONGRESSIONAL ISSUES

As mentioned previously, the NMVC program has not received any additional funding since 2001. Opposition to the program within Congress began to gain momentum when President George W. Bush recommended in his FY2002 budget request that the NMVC program be eliminated, arguing that the program is relatively expensive and duplicative of other federal programs.[62]

> The Administration supports the objectives of the New Markets Venture Capital (NMVC) program but believes those objectives can be achieved more efficiently and at a lower cost through other existing programs. Several vehicles and incentives to direct investment into economically distressed communities already exist. Communities targeted by NMVC have access to a wide range of private for-profit and economic development programs, including the federally supported community development financial institutions administered through the Department of Treasury. In addition, SBA's SBIC program, which has 412 licensed venture capital companies with total capital resources amounting to $17.7 billion, is implementing incentives to encourage investment in economically distressed areas.
>
> The NMVC program is also expensive relative to the impact that it is expected to have. The total cost of the program in FY2001 is $52 million, not including administrative cost of running the program. Since the program is expected to generate $150-$200 million of investment activity, it will yield only $3.00-$4.00 of investment for every taxpayer dollar spent. In comparison, under the Small Business Investment Company (SBIC) program, there is no cost associated with the debenture portion of the program.[63]

Others argued that the NMVC program's targeted clientele of small businesses located in economically distressed areas is inherently too risky for government involvement. In their view, NMVC companies are "designed and chartered to operate (as profit-making firms) in a market niche that mainstream venture capital firms will not touch."[64]

The program's advocates argued that the NMVC program is necessary precisely because mainstream venture capital firms generally avoided investments in small businesses located in economically distressed areas. In their view, the NMVC program is an essential part of a larger federal effort, which includes tax incentives, to fill a market niche in private sector venture capital investments and, in the process, help to revitalize areas experiencing long-term economic difficulties. They also objected to the Bush Administration's argument that the program is duplicative of other federal programs. In their view, the NMVC program is targeted at a clientele that is not being adequately served by other federal programs.[65]

The Bush Administration continued to recommend the program's elimination in each of its subsequent budget requests. As mentioned previously, during congressional consideration of the FY2003 budget the unobligated balances of $10.5 million for NMVC debenture subsidies and $13.75 million for operational assistance training grants were rescinded.[66]

Since then, more than 30 bills have been introduced to amend the NMVC program, including bills to

- reduce the amount of capital NMVC companies must raise to become eligible for operational assistance training grants,
- eliminate the matching requirement for operational assistance training grants,
- create an Office of New Markets Venture Capital within the SBA,
- require the SBA to provide conditionally approved NMVC companies a full two years to meet all program requirements,
- provide increased financing to small manufacturers, and
- amend the program's definition for low-income area to correspond with the definition used by the New Market Tax Credits program (§45D(e) of the Internal Revenue Code of 1986) (26 U.S.C. 45D(e)).

Many of these bills also include provisions to provide the NMVC program additional funding.[67]

LEGISLATIVE EFFORTS TO PROVIDE ADDITIONAL NMVC FUNDING

As shown in *Table A-1* in the *Appendix*, during the 108th Congress, two bills were introduced, one in the House and one in the Senate, to provide the NMVC program "such subsidy budget authority as may be necessary to guarantee $75 million of debentures" and $15 million for operational assistance training grants over FY2004 and FY2005.[68] Neither bill was enacted.[69]

During the 109th Congress, an amendment was offered during the House during floor debate on H.R. 2862, the Science, State, Justice, Commerce, and Related Agencies Appropriations Act, 2006, to provide "$30 million in debenture guarantees and $5 million for operational assistance grants to fund the creation of a fresh round of New Market Venture Capital companies ... paid for by using funds from the Small Business Administration's salary and expense account."[70] The amendment failed by voice vote.[71] Also, a bill introduced in the House would have authorized an expansion of the NMVC program to include the selection of an NMVC company whose primary objective was the economic development of small businesses located in Hurricane Katrina-affected areas. The bill would have authorized "such subsidy budget authority as may be necessary to guarantee ... $50 million of debentures issued by the Gulf Region New Markets Venture Capital Company ... and $10 million for grants to the Gulf Region New Markets Venture Capital Company."[72] Another House bill would have provided the NMVC program "such subsidy budget authority as may be necessary to guarantee $100 million of debentures and $25 million for operational assistance training grants for FY2006 through FY2008."[73] Neither bill was enacted.[74]

During the 110th Congress, four bills were introduced, two in the House and two in the Senate, to provide the NMVC program additional funding. One of the House bills would have provided the NMVC program such subsidy budget authority as may be necessary to guarantee $100 million of debentures and $25 million for operational assistance training grants for FY2007 through FY2009.[75] The other House bill would have provided the NMVC program such subsidy budget authority as may be necessary to guarantee $30 million of debentures and $5 million for operational assistance training grants for FY2008 through FY2010.[76] The two Senate bills would have provided the NMVC program $20 million for operational assistance training grants.[77] None of these bills was enacted.

During the 111th Congress, two bills were introduced in the House to provide the NMVC program additional funding. One of the bills would have provided the NMVC program such subsidy budget authority as may be necessary to guarantee $100 million of debentures and $25 million for operational assistance training grants for FY2009 through FY2011.[78] The other bill would have provided the NMVC program such subsidy budget authority as may be necessary to guarantee $100 million of debentures and $20 million for operational assistance training grants for FY2010 through FY2011.[79]

During the 112th Congress, one bill, to date, has been introduced to provide additional funding for the NMVC program. H.R. 2872, the Job Creation and Urban Revitalization Act of 2011, was introduced by Representative Nydia Velázquez on September 8, 2011. The bill would provide the NMVC program such subsidy budget authority as may be necessary to guarantee $75 million of debentures and $15 million for operational assistance training grants for FY2012 through FY2013. The bill was referred to the House Committee on Small Business on September 8, 2011, and is awaiting further action.

Related SBIC Program Developments

P.L. 111-5, the American Recovery and Reinvestment Act of 2009 (ARRA), included provisions designed to encourage SBIC investments in low-income areas.

The act allows an SBIC licensed on or after October 1, 2009, to elect to have a maximum leverage amount of $175 million, instead of $150 million, if the SBIC has invested at least 50% of its financings in low-income geographic areas, as defined under the NMVC program, and certified that at least 50% of its future investments will be in low-income geographic areas.[80] ARRA also increased the maximum amount of leverage available for two or more licenses under common control to $250 million from $225 million if these requirements are met.

In addition, on April 7, 2011, the SBA announced a $1 billion impact investment SBIC initiative (up to $150 million in leverage in FY2012, and up to $200 million in leverage per fiscal year thereafter until the limit is reached). Under this initiative, SBA-licensed impact investment debenture SBICs are required to invest at least 50% of their financings "which target areas of critical national priority including underserved markets and communities facing barriers to access to credit and capital."[81]

To receive an impact investment, a small business must meet at least one of the following criteria: (1) it must be located in, or have at least 35% of its full-time employees, at the time of the initial investment, residing in a low or moderate income area as defined in 13 CFR Section 107.50;[82] or be located in an economically distressed area as defined by Section 3011 of the Public Works and Economic Development Act of 1965, as amended (per capita income of 80% or less of the national average or an unemployment rate that is, for the most recent 24-month period for which data are available, at least 1% greater than the national average unemployment rate); or (2) be in an industrial sector that the SBA has identified as a national priority (currently clean energy and education).

CONCLUSION

The NMVC program continues to operate, but the amount and number of its financings remain lower than anticipated by its original sponsors and below levels desired by its advocates. In recent years, the amount of SBIC program investments in low-to-moderate income areas has increased—from $372.7 million in FY2009 (20.1% of total SBIC financing), to $444.5 million in FY2010 (21.1% of total SBIC financing), and to $687.1 million in FY2011 (24.3% of total SBIC financing).[83] In addition, the SBA's LMI and impact investment initiatives are designed to encourage SBIC investments in low-to-moderate income areas. It could be argued that the increased levels of SBIC investments in low-to-moderate income areas in recent years, coupled with the SBA's efforts to encourage SBIC investments in low-to-moderate income areas, may diminish the need for the NMVC program. NMVC advocates disagree. In FY2011, SBICs provided 553 financings amounting to $687.1 million to small businesses located in a low-tomoderate income area, an average investment of $1.24 million.[84] NMVC advocates argue, as Senator Bond did when the NMVC program was proposed, that the NMVC program targets small businesses seeking much smaller investments.[85]

The debate over the NMVC program's future, particularly whether the program should be provided additional funding, is, in many ways, reflective of broader disagreements about the role of government, and the SBA, in private enterprise. Some believe that the federal government, and the SBA, should take an active role in assisting small businesses to access capital—through the provision of loan guarantees, equity financing, and management training—to assist the economic recovery. In their view, the SBA's programs fill a market niche by providing loans to small businesses unable to get credit elsewhere, equity financings to small businesses often overlooked by private investors, and training for new and aspiring entrepreneurs unable to find affordable training elsewhere. They assert that increasing funding for the NMVC program is an investment that will create jobs by making capital available to entrepreneurs unable to find it in the private marketplace.

Others worry about the long-term adverse economic effects of the federal deficit. Instead of advocating increased funding for federal spending programs, they advocate business tax reduction, reform of financial credit market regulation, and federal fiscal restraint as the best means to assist small businesses, generate economic growth, and create jobs. They are particularly interested in achieving greater government efficiency by eliminating federal spending programs, such as the NMVC program, which they perceive are duplicative of others.

APPENDIX. LEGISLATIVE EFFORTS TO PROVIDE ADDITIONAL FUNDING FOR THE NMVC PROGRAM

Table A-1. Legislative Efforts to Provide Additional NMVC Funding

Congress	*Legislation and Sponsor*	*Funding Necessary to Support NMVC Debenture Guarantee of*	*Funding for Operational Assistance Training Grants*	*Legislative Action*
108th	H.R. 2802, the Small Business Reauthorization and Manufacturing Revitalization Act of 2003 (Representative Donald Manzullo) S. 1886, the MADE in America Act (by Senator Tom Daschle on behalf of Senator John Kerry)	$75 million $75 million	$15 million $15 million	Introduced on July 21, 2003, and referred to the House Committee on Small Business; reported by the House Committee on Small Business on October 21, 2003; and placed on the Union Calendar on March 8, 2004. No further action. Introduced on November 18, 2003, and referred to the Senate Committee on Small Business and Entrepreneurship. No further action.
109th	H.Amdt. 268, to H.R. 2862, the Science, State, Justice, Commerce, and Related Agencies Appropriations Act, 2006, to provide the NMVC program $30 million in debenture guarantees and $5 million for operational assistance (Representative Gwen Moore)	$30 million	$5 million	Offered on June 15, 2005. Failed by voice vote.
	H.R. 4234, the Small Business Gulf Coast Revitalization Act of 2005 (Representative Nydia Velázquez)	$50 million	$10 million	Introduced on November 5, 2005, and referred to the House Committee on Small Business. No further action.

Table A-1. (Continued)

Congress	*Legislation and Sponsor*	*Funding Necessary to Support NMVC Debenture Guarantee of*	*Funding for Operational Assistance Training Grants*	*Legislative Action*
	H.R. 4303, the Securing Equity for the Economic Development of Low Income Areas Act of 2005 (Representative Gwen Moore)	$100 million	$25 million	Introduced on November 10, 2005, and referred to the House Committee on Small Business. No further action.
110th	H.R. 1719, the Securing Equity for the Economic Development of Low Income Areas Act of 2007 (Representative Gwen Moore)	$100 million	$25 million	Introduced on March 27, 2007, and referred to the House Committee on Small Business. No further action.
	H.R. 3567, the Small Business Investment Expansion Act of 2007 (Representative Jason Altmire)	$30 million	$5 million	Introduced on September 18, 2007, and referred to the House Committee on Small Business; reported by the House Committee on Small Business on September 25, 2007;
				passed by the House on September 27, 2007, by a vote of 325-72; received in the Senate on September 28, 2007, and referred to the Senate Committee on Small Business and Entrepreneurship. No further action.
	S. 1663, the Securing Equity for the Economic Development of Low Income Areas Act of 2007 (Senator John Kerry)	NA	$20 million	Introduced on June 19, 2007, and referred to the Senate Committee on Small Business and Entrepreneurship; incorporated into S. 1662, the Small Business Venture Capital Act of 2007, which addressed the Small Business Administration's SBIC program; that bill, as amended, was reported by the Senate Committee on Small Business and Entrepreneurship on October 16, 2007. No further action.

Congress	*Legislation and Sponsor*	*Funding Necessary to Support NMVC Debenture Guarantee of*	*Funding for Operational Assistance Training Grants*	*Legislative Action*
	S. 2920, the SBA Reauthorization and Improvement Act of 2008 (Senator John Kerry)	NA	$20 million	Introduced on April 24, 2008, and placed on the Senate Legislative Calendar under General Orders under Read the First Time on September 24, 2008; placed on the Senate Legislative Calendar under General Orders under Read the Second Time on September 28, 2008. No further action.
111th	H.R. 1491, the Securing Equity for the Economic Development of Low Income Areas Act of 2009 (Representative Gwen Moore)	$100 million	$25 million	Introduced on March 12, 2009, and referred to the House Committee on Small Business. No further action.
111th	H.R. 3722, the Enhanced New Markets and Expanded Investment in Renewable Energy for Small Manufacturers Act of 2009 (Representative Ann Kirkpatrick)	$100 million	$20 million	Introduced on October 6, 2009, and referred to the House Committee on Small Business; incorporated into H.R. 3854, the Small Business Financing and Investment Act of 2009, introduced by Representative Kurt Schrader on October 20, 2009; that bill was reported by the House Committee on Small Business on October 26, 2009, and passed by the House, by a
				vote of 389-32, on October 29, 2009; received in the Senate and referred to the Senate Committee on Small Business and Entrepreneurship on November 2, 2009. No further action.
112th	H.R. 2872, the Job Creation and Urban Revitalization Act of 2011 (Representative Nydia Velázquez)	$75 million	$15 million	Introduced on September 8, 2011, and referred to the House Committee on Small Business. No further action to date.

Source: Legislative Information Service database, CRS.

End Notes

[1] U.S. Small Business Administration, "Fiscal Year 2013 Congressional Budget Justification and FY2011 Annual Performance Report," Washington, DC, 2012, p. 1.

[2] 15 U.S.C. §689(a).

[3] For further information and analysis concerning the SBA's Small Business Investment Company program, see CRS Report R41456, SBA Small Business Investment Company Program, by Robert Jay Dilger. The SBA is authorized to issue debentures with a term of up to 15 years. The SBA has opted to limit the term for NMVC debentures to 10 years.

[4] Because the SBA's NMVC debentures are discounted to guarantee the payment of interest during the first five years of the debenture, the funding provided was estimated to be sufficient to raise about $100 million in available capital for investment. Also, the appropriation was for FY2001 through FY2006, but was provided as a lump sum payment in FY2001.

[5] U.S. Small Business Administration, Office of Congressional and Legislative Affairs, "Correspondence with the author," Washington, DC, June 5, 2012.

[6] P.L. 108-7, the Consolidated Appropriations Resolution, 2003; and U.S. Congress, Committee of Conference, Making Further Continuing Appropriations for the Fiscal Year 2003, and for Other Purposes, report to accompany H.J.Res. 2, 108th Cong., 1st sess., February 13, 2003, H.Rept. 108-10 (Washington: GPO, 2003), p. 787.

[7] H.R. 3412, the Small Business Investment Company Technical Corrections Act of 1998, was introduced by Representative (later Senator) Jim Talent, chair of the House Committee on Small Business, on March 10, 1998. The bill would have authorized several technical corrections to the Small Business Administration's SBIC program. The House Committee on Small Business reported the bill on March 17, 1998, and the House passed it (on motion to suspend the rules and pass the bill, as amended), 407-0, on March 24, 1998.

[8] U.S. Congress, Senate Committee on Small Business, Year 2000 Readiness and Small Business Programs Restructuring and Reform Act of 1998, 105th Cong., 2nd sess., September 25, 1998, S.Rept. 105-347 (Washington: GPO, 1998).

[9] Ibid., pp. 18, 23; and Pherabe Kolb, "Senate Small Business Markup: Year 2000 Assistance, Drug-Free Workplace," CQ Markup and Vote Coverage, Washington, DC, September 15, 1998, http://www.cq.com/doc/committeesCOMM159517?print=true.

[10] U.S. Congress, Senate Committee on Small Business, Year 2000 Readiness and Small Business Programs Restructuring and Reform Act of 1998, 105th Cong., 2nd sess., September 25, 1998, S.Rept. 105-347 (Washington: GPO, 1998), p. 18.

[11] Ibid.

[12] U.S. President (Clinton), "Address Before a Joint Session of the Congress on the State of the Union," Weekly Compilation of Presidential Documents, vol. 35 (January 19, 1999), p. 83.

[13] U.S. President (Clinton), "Remarks on the New Markets Initiative," Weekly Compilation of Presidential Documents, vol. 35 (May 11, 1999), pp. 860-861.

[14] U.S. President (Clinton), "Remarks to the Community at Pine Ridge Indian Reservation, South Dakota," Weekly Compilation of Presidential Documents, vol. 35 (July 7, 1999), pp. 1298-1302; U.S. President (Clinton), "Remarks in a Roundtable Discussion on Small Business Development in Phoenix, Arizona," Weekly Compilation of Presidential Documents, vol. 35 (July 7, 1999), pp. 1303-1308; U.S. President (Clinton), "Remarks in a Discussion on Youth Opportunities in Los Angeles, California," Weekly Compilation of Presidential Documents, vol. 35 (July 8, 1999), pp. 1318-1321; U.S. President (Clinton), "Remarks to the National Academy Foundation Conference in Anaheim, California," Weekly Compilation of Presidential Documents, vol. 35 (July 8, 1999), pp. 1322-1327; U.S. President (Clinton), "Remarks to the Community in Newark," Weekly Compilation of Presidential Documents, vol. 35 (November 4, 1999), pp. 2246-2249; U.S. President (Clinton), "Remarks to the North End Community in Hartford, Connecticut," Weekly Compilation of Presidential Documents, vol. 35 (November 4, 1999), pp. 2257-2259; The White House, Office of the Press Secretary, "Remarks by the President to the people of Bradley County: Hermitage Tomato Cooperative, Hermitage, Arkansas," Washington, DC, November 5, 1999, at http://clinton3.nara.gov/WH/New/New_Markets_Nov/remarks/1105-1045a.html; and U.S. President (Clinton)," Remarks to the Englewood Community in Chicago, Illinois," Weekly Compilation of Presidential Documents, vol. 35 (November 4, 1999), pp. 2271-2275.

[15] U.S. President (Clinton)," Remarks to the Englewood Community in Chicago, Illinois," Weekly Compilation of Presidential Documents, vol. 35 (November 4, 1999), pp. 2273.

[16] U.S. Small Business Administration, "Small Business Investment Companies," 64 Federal Register 6256, February 9, 1999.

[17] U.S. Small Business Administration, "Small Business Investment Companies," 64 Federal Register 52641-52646, September 30, 1999.

[18] U.S. Small Business Administration, "Small Business Investment Companies," 64 Federal Register 52645, September 30, 1999.

[19] U.S. Small Business Administration, "Small Business Investment Companies," 64 Federal Register 52641-52646, September 30, 1999. LMI Zones are areas located in a HUBZone; an Urban Empowerment Zone or Urban Enterprise Community designated by the Secretary of the U.S. Department of Housing and Urban Development; a Rural Empowerment Zone or Rural Enterprise Community as designated by the Secretary of the U.S. Department of Agriculture; an area of low income or moderate income as recognized by the Federal Financial Institutions Examination Council; or a county with persistent poverty as classified by the U.S. Department of Agriculture's Economic Research Service. See 13 CFR §107.50.

[20] U.S. Small Business Administration, "For SBICs: Background Information on Low or Moderate Income (LMI) Debentures," Washington, DC, at http://www.sba.gov/content/low-or-moderate-income-lmi-debentures. In FY2011, SBICs made 553 investments in small businesses located in a LMI Zone, totaling $687.1 million—about 24% of the total amount invested. See U.S. Small Business Administration, "SBIC Program Licensees Financing to Small Businesses Reported Between October 2010 and September 2011," Washington, DC.

[21] The bill's five original co-sponsors were Senators Jeff Bingaman, Max Cleland, Carl Levin, Paul Sarbanes, and Paul Wellstone.

[22] U.S. Congress, Senate Committee on Small Business, Community Development and Venture Capital Act of 1999, report to accompany S. 1594, 106th Cong., 2nd sess., August 25, 2000, S.Rept. 106-383 (Washington: GPO, 2000), p. 4.

[23] Ibid., p. 3.

[24] Ibid.

[25] Ibid.

[26] Ibid.

[27] The bill was co-sponsored by Representative Nydia Velázquez.

[28] U.S. Congress, Committee of Conference, Making Omnibus Consolidated and Emergency Supplemental Appropriations for Fiscal Year 2001, report to accompany H.R. 4577, 106th Cong., 2nd sess., December 15, 2000, H.Rept. 106-1033 (Washington: GPO, 2000), pp. 1041-1054.

[29] U.S. Small Business Administration, "13 CFR Part 108: New Markets Venture Capital Program, Interim Final Rule" 66 Federal Register 7218-7246, January 22, 2001; and U.S. Small Business Administration, "New Markets Venture Capital Program; Notice of Funds Availability (NOFA) Inviting Applications for the New Markets Venture Capital Program," 66 Federal Register 7247, January 22, 2001.

[30] U.S. Small Business Administration, "New Markets Venture Capital Program: Final Rule," 66 Federal Register 28601-28632, May 23, 2001.

[31] In addition to these two items, NMVC applicants must also submit a description of how the company intends to work with community organizations and to seek to address the unmet capital needs of the communities served; a proposal describing how the company intends to use the grant funds provided under this part to provide operational assistance to smaller enterprises financed by the company, including information regarding whether the company intends to use licensed professionals, when necessary, on the company's staff or from an outside entity; with respect to binding commitments to be made to the company under this part, an estimate of the ratio of cash to in kind contributions; a description of the criteria to be used to evaluate whether and to what extent the company meets the objectives of the program established under this part; information regarding the management and financial strength of any parent firm, affiliated firm, or any other firm essential to the success of the company's business plan; and such other information as the Administrator may require. See U.S. Congress, Committee of Conference, Making Omnibus Consolidated and Emergency Supplemental Appropriations for Fiscal Year 2001, report to accompany H.R. 4577, 106th Cong., 2nd sess., December 15, 2000, H.Rept. 106-1033 (Washington: GPO, 2000), p. 1044.

[32] 13 C.F.R. §108.100; 13 C.F.R. §108.110; and 13 C.F.R. §108.120.

[33] P.L. 108-7, the Consolidated Appropriations Resolution, 2003; and U.S. Congress, Committee of Conference, Making Further Continuing Appropriations for the Fiscal Year 2003, and for Other Purposes, report to accompany H.J.Res. 2, 108th Cong., 1st sess., February 13, 2003, H.Rept. 108-10 (Washington: GPO, 2003), p.787.

[34] The initial application deadline was April 19, 2001, and was later extended twice: first, to May 21, 2001; and second, to May 29, 2001. See U.S. Small Business Administration, "New Markets Venture Capital Program; Extension of Application Deadline," 66 Federal Register 18993, April 12, 2001; and U.S. Small Business Administration, "New Markets Venture Capital Program; Extension of Application Deadline," 66 Federal Register 27721, May 18, 2001.

[35] The SBA may accept binding commitments for operational assistance matching resources equal to at least 20% of the required minimum if the company has a viable plan to raise the balance. In no case, however, will the SBA disburse grant funds for operational assistance in excess of the amount actually raised, including in-kind contributions. See 13 C.F.R. §108.380.

[36] P.L. 106-554 authorized the SBA to provide conditionally approved applicants a period of time, not to exceed two years, to satisfy all program requirements necessary to participate in the program. The SBA provided applicants 18 months. See U.S. Small Business Administration, Off ice of New Markets Venture Capital, "New Markets Venture Capital (MNVC) Program, FAQs: How much time does a conditionally approved NMVCC have to raise its capital and grant matching resources?" Washington, DC, at http://www.sba.gov/content/how-much-time-does-conditionallyapproved-nmvcc-have-raise-its-capital-and-grant-matching-resources.

[37] U.S. Small Business Administration, Off ice of New Markets Venture Capital, "New Markets Venture Capital (MNVC) Program," Washington, DC, June 2010, p. 13, at http://www.slideshare.net/Freddy56/new-markets-venturecapital-nmvc-program; and U.S. Small Business Administration, "NMVC Companies," Washington, DC, at http://www.sba.gov/content/nmvc-companies.

[38] The Community Development Venture Capital Alliance, "The New Markets Venture Capital Program," Washington, DC, pp. 6, 18, at http://www.community-wealth.org/_pdfs/articles-publications/cdfis/paper-cdvca.pdf; and U.S. Small Business Administration, Office of Congressional and Legislative Affairs, "Correspondence with the author," Washington, DC, June 5, 2012.

[39] U.S. Small Business Administration, "NMVC Companies," Washington, DC, at http://www.sba.gov/ content/nmvc companies.

[40] 13 C.F.R. §108.630.

[41] Ibid.

[42] 13 C.F.R. §108.640.

[43] When the NMVC program started, to be deemed small, a business had to meet either the SBA's size standard for the industry in which it was primarily engaged, or had a maximum net worth of no more than $6 million and average after-tax net income for the preceding two years of not more than $2 million.

[44] 13 C.F.R. §121.301(c)(1) and 13 C.F.R. §121.301(c)(2). NMVC companies are not permitted to invest in passive businesses or real estate businesses, or to invest in project financings, farm land purchases, the financing of NMVC companies or SBICs, or projects that will be used substantially for a foreign operation or when more than 49% of the employees or tangible assets of the small business are located outside of the United States. See 13 C.F.R. §108.720.

[45] 13 C.F.R. §108.710.

[46] Ibid.

[47] P.L. 106-554 authorizes the SBA to sale debentures with a maturity of up to 15 years. The SBA has opted to sell debentures with a maturity of up to 10 years.

[48] The SBA does not charge a fee for the issuance of debentures by a NMVC company. See 13 C.F.R. §108.1130. In contrast, the SBA is authorized to charge SBICs a 3% origination fee for each debenture and participating security issued (1% at commitment and 2% at draw), an annual fee (not to exceed 1.38% for debentures and 1.46% for participating securities) on the leverage drawn which is fixed at the time of the leverage commitment, and other administrative and underwriting fees which are adjusted annually. See 13 CFR §107.1130; and 13 CFR §107.1210.

[49] U.S. Small Business Administration, "Debenture Calculator," Washington, DC, at http:// www.sba.gov/content/ debenture-calculator.

[50] 13 C.F.R. §108.1230; and 13 C.F.R. §108.1240.

[51] 13 C.F.R. §108.1230.

[52] U.S. Small Business Administration, "Debenture Calculator," Washington, DC, at http://www. sba.gov/content/ debenture-calculator; and Federal Home Loan Bank of Chicago, "New Markets Debenture Calculator," Chicago, Illinois, at http://www.fhlbc.com/sba/ newmarketcalculatorpage.htm. The interest rate was 5.494% on June 6, 2012.

[53] U.S. Small Business Administration, "Debenture Calculator," Washington, DC, at http://www. sba.gov/content/ debenture-calculator; and 13 C.F.R. §108.1610.

[54] Subordinated debt (also known as subordinated debenture or junior debt) ranks after other debts should a company fall into liquidation or bankruptcy. Because subordinated debt is repayable after other debts have been paid, they are considered to carry a higher level of risk to the lender.

[55] The SBA disbursed operational assistance training grants over a 4.5 year period. See U.S. Small Business Administration, Off ice of New Markets Venture Capital, "New Markets Venture Capital (MNVC) Program," Washington, DC, June 2010, p. 7, at http://www. slideshare.net/Freddy56/new-markets-venture-capital-nmvc-program.

[56] 13 C.F.R. §108.2010; and 13 C.F.R. §108.2030.

[57] 13 C.F.R. §108.2040.

[58] 13 C.F.R. §108.2030.

[59] 13 C.F.R. §108.2010.

[60] 13 C.F.R. §108.10. Some examples of operational assistance training include writing or assisting in the preparation of a business plan, legal assistance relating to business formation or reorganization (but not litigation), recruitment of executives, creation of Internet capability, engineering or other technical services to create or enhance production or distribution of products or services, creation of marketing materials, creation of customized accounting or information systems, and active participation in negotiation with financial institutions (debt). See Adena Ventures, L.P., "Operational Assistance," Athens, Ohio, at http://www.adenaventures.com/serviceprograms/opsassist.aspx.

[61] The Community Development Venture Capital Alliance, "The New Markets Venture Capital Program," Washington, DC, pp. 6, 18, at http://www.community-wealth.org/_pdfs/articles-publications/cdfis/paper-cdvca.pdf; and U.S. Small Business Administration, Office of Congressional and Legislative Affairs, "Correspondence with the author," Washington, DC, June 5, 2012.

[62] U.S. Small Business Administration, "FY 2002 Budget Request and Performance Plan," Washington, DC, p. 15, at http://archive.sba.gov/idc/groups/public/documents/ sba_ homepage/serv_abt_budget_5.pdf.

[63] U.S. Congress, Senate Committee on Small Business and Entrepreneurship, SBA's Funding Priorities for Fiscal Year 2002, 107th Cong., 1st sess., May 1, 2002, S.Hrg. 107-237 (Washington: GPO, 2002), p. 45.

[64] Timothy Bates, "Government as Venture Capital Catalyst: Pitfalls and Promising Approaches," Economic Development Quarterly, vol. 16, no. 49 (2002): 58, at http://www. uk.sagepub.com/chaston/ Chaston%20Web%20readings%20chapters%201-12/Chapter% 204%20-%2045%20Bates.pdf.

[65] U.S. Congress, Senate Committee on Small Business, The President's Fiscal Year 2000 Budget Request for the Small Business Administration, 106th Cong., 1st sess., March 16, 1999, S.Hrg. 106-118 (Washington: GPO, 1999), pp. 125, 126; U.S. Congress, Senate Committee on Small Business and Entrepreneurship, SBA's Funding Priorities for Fiscal Year 2002, 107th Cong., 1st sess., May 1, 2001, S.Hrg. 107-237 (Washington: GPO, 2002), pp. 14, 15, 20, 26, 91-93; U.S. Congress, House Committee on Small Business, Small Business Investment Expansion Act of 2007 , report to accompany H.R. 3567, 110th Cong., 1st sess., September 25, 2007, H.Rept. 110-110 (Washington: GPO, 2007), pp. 5, 6; and U.S. Congress, Senate Committee on Small Business and Entrepreneurship, Small Business Venture Capital Act of 2007' , 110th Cong., 1st sess., October 16, 2007, S.Rept. 110-199 (Washington: GPO, 2007), pp. 5, 6, 9-11.

[66] P.L. 108-7, the Consolidated Appropriations Resolution, 2003; and U.S. Congress, Committee of Conference, Making Further Continuing Appropriations for the Fiscal Year 2003, and for Other Purposes, report to accompany H.J.Res. 2, 108th Cong., 1st sess., February 13, 2003, H.Rept. 108-10 (Washington: GPO, 2003), p. 787.

[67] During the 111th Congress, P.L. 111-240, the Small Business Jobs Act of 2010, Sec. 1115. New Markets Venture Capital Company Investment Limitations, included the following language: "Except to the extent approved by the Administrator, a covered New Markets Venture Capital company may not acquire or issue commitments for securities under this title for any single enterprise in an aggregate amount equal to more than 10 percent of the sum of—"(A) the regulatory capital of the covered New Markets Venture Capital company; and "(B) the total amount of leverage projected in the participation agreement of the covered New Markets Venture Capital."

[68] H.R. 2802, the Small Business Reauthorization and Manufacturing Revitalization Act of 2003, was introduced by Representative Donald Manzullo on July 21, 2003. It would have provided the NMVC program the additional funding over FY2004 and FY2005. S. 1886, the MADE in America Act, was introduced by Senator Tom Daschle on behalf of Senator John Kerry on November 18, 2003. It would have provided the NMVC program the additional funding over FY2005 and FY2006.

[69] H.R. 2802, the Small Business Reauthorization and Manufacturing Revitalization Act of 2003, was reported by the House Committee on Small Business on October 21, 2003; and placed on the Union Calendar on March 8, 2004. The House took no further action on the bill. S. 1886, the MADE in America Act, was referred to the Senate Committee on Small Business and Entrepreneurship. No further action took place on the bill.

[70] Representative Gwen Moore, "Consideration of H.R. 2862, the Science, State, Justice, Commerce, and Related Agencies Appropriations Act, 2006," House debate, Congressional Record, vol. 151, part 79 (June 15, 2005), p. H4511.

[71] Ibid., p. H4512.

[72] H.R. 4234, the Small Business Gulf Coast Revitalization Act of 2005, Sec. 104. Gulf Region New Markets Venture Capital Company. The bill was introduced by Representative Nydia Velázquez on November 5, 2005.

[73] H.R. 4303, the Securing Equity for the Economic Development of Low Income Areas Act of 2005, was introduced by Representative Gwen Moore on November 10, 2005.

[74] H.R. 4303, the Securing Equity for the Economic Development of Low Income Areas Act of 2005, was referred to the House Committee on Small Business. The House took no further action on the bill. H.R. 4234, the Small Business Gulf Coast Revitalization Act of 2005, was referred to the House Committee on Small Business. The House took no further action on the bill.

[75] H.R. 1719, the Securing Equity for the Economic Development of Low Income Areas Act of 2007, was introduced by Representative Gwen Moore on March 27, 2007. The bill was referred to the House Committee on Small Business. The House took no further action on the bill.

[76] H.R. 3567, the Small Business Investment Expansion Act of 2007, was introduced by Representative Jason Altmire on September 18, 2007. The bill was referred to the House Committee on Small Business and reported on September 25, 2007. The House passed it on September 27, 2007, by a vote of 325-72. The bill was received in the Senate on September 28, 2007, and referred to the Senate Committee on Small Business and Entrepreneurship. The Senate took no further action on the bill.

[77] S. 1663, the Securing Equity for the Economic Development of Low Income Areas Act of 2007, was introduced by Senator John Kerry on June 19, 2007 and referred to the Senate Committee on Small Business and Entrepreneurship. The additional funding for operational assistance training grants would have been available over FY2007 through FY2010. The bill was incorporated into S. 1662, the Small Business Venture Capital Act of 2007, which addressed the Small Business Administration's SBIC program. That bill, as amended, was reported by the Senate Committee on Small Business and Entrepreneurship on October 16, 2007. The Senate took no further action on the bill. S. 2920, the SBA Reauthorization and Improvement Act of 2008, was introduced by Senator John Kerry on April 24, 2008. The additional funding for operational assistance training grants would have been available over FY2008 through FY2010. The bill was placed on the Senate Legislative Calendar under General Orders under Read the First Time on September 24, 2008 and was placed on the Senate Legislative Calendar under General Orders under Read the Second Time on September 28, 2008. The Senate took no further action on the bill.

[78] H.R. 1491, the Securing Equity for the Economic Development of Low Income Areas Act of 2009, was introduced by Representative Gwen Moore on March 12, 2009, and referred to the House Committee on Small Business. The House took no further action on the bill.

[79] H.R. 3722, the Enhanced New Markets and Expanded Investment in Renewable Energy for Small Manufacturers Act of 2009, was introduced by Representative Ann Kirkpatrick on October 6, 2009, and referred to the House Committee on Small Business. The bill's provisions were incorporated into H.R. 3854, the Small Business Financing and Investment Act of 2009, which was introduced by Representative Kurt Schrader on October 20, 2009. That bill was reported by the House Committee on Small Business on October 26, 2009, and passed by the House, by a vote of 389- 32, on October 29, 2009. The bill was received in the Senate and referred to the Senate Committee on Small Business and Entrepreneurship on November 2, 2009. The Senate took no further action on the bill.

[80] 13 CFR §107.1150.

[81] U.S. Small Business Administration, "Impact Investment Initiative," Washington, DC, at http://www.sba.gov/content/small-business-investment-company-sbic-impact-investment-initiative-2. For further analysis and information concerning the SBA's impact investment initiative see CRS Report R41456, SBA Small Business Investment Company Program, by Robert Jay Dilger.

[82] A low or moderate income area (LMI Zone) means any area located within a HUBZone (as defined in 13 CFR 126.103), an Urban Empowerment Zone or Urban Enterprise Community (as designated by the Secretary of the Department of Housing and Urban Development), a Rural Empowerment Zone or Rural Enterprise Community (as designated by the Secretary of the Department of Agriculture), an area of Low Income or

Moderate Income (as recognized by the Federal Financial Institutions Examination Council), or a county with Persistent Poverty (as classified by the Economic Research Service of the Department of Agriculture). See 13 CFR §107.50.

[83] U.S. Small Business Administration, "All SBIC Program Licensees: Financing to Small Businesses Reported Between October 2008 and September 2009," Washington, DC; U.S. Small Business Administration, "All SBIC Program Licensees: Financing to Small Businesses Reported Between October 2009 and September 2010," Washington, DC; and U.S. Small Business Administration, "All SBIC Program Licensees: Financing to Small Businesses Reported Between October 2010 and September 2011," Washington, DC.

[84] U.S. Small Business Administration, "All SBIC Program Licensees: Financing to Small Businesses Reported Between October 2010 and September 2011," Washington, DC.

[85] U.S. Congress, Senate Committee on Small Business, Community Development and Venture Capital Act of 1999, report to accompany S. 1594, 106th Cong., 2nd sess., August 25, 2000, S.Rept. 106-383 (Washington: GPO, 2000), p. 3.

In: Small Business Administration ...
Editor: Alan R. Connoly

ISBN: 978-1-62417-674-6

Chapter 3

SMALL BUSINESS ADMINISTRATION 7(A) LOAN GUARANTY PROGRAM*

Robert Jay Dilger

SUMMARY

The Small Business Administration (SBA) administers several programs to support small businesses, including loan guaranty programs designed to encourage lenders to provide loans to small businesses "that might not otherwise obtain financing on reasonable terms and conditions." The SBA's 7(a) loan guaranty program is considered the agency's flagship loan guaranty program. It is named from Section 7(a) of the Small Business Act of 1953 (P.L. 83-163, as amended), which authorized the SBA to provide business loans and loan guaranties to American small businesses.

In FY2012, the SBA approved 44,377 7(a) loans amounting to more than $15.1 billion. Proceeds from 7(a) loans may be used to establish a new business or to assist in the operation, acquisition, or expansion of an existing business.

Congressional interest in the 7(a) loan guaranty program has increased in recent years because of concerns that small businesses might be prevented from accessing sufficient capital to enable them to assist in the economic recovery. Some, including President Obama, argue that the SBA should be provided additional resources to assist small businesses in acquiring capital necessary to start, continue, or expand operations with the expectation that in so doing small businesses will create jobs. Others worry about the long-term adverse economic effects of spending programs that increase the federal deficit. They advocate business tax reduction, reform of financial credit market regulation, and federal fiscal restraint as the best means to assist small business economic growth and job creation.

This report discusses the rationale provided for the 7(a) program; the program's borrower and lender eligibility standards and program requirements; and program statistics, including loan volume, loss rates, use of the proceeds, borrower satisfaction, and borrower demographics. It examines issues raised concerning the SBA's

* This is an edited, reformatted and augmented version of a Congressional Research Service publication, CRS Report for Congress R41146, prepared for Members and Committees of Congress, from www.crs.gov, dated October 11, 2012.

administration of the 7(a) program, including the oversight of 7(a) lenders and the program's lack of outcome-based performance measures.

It also examines congressional action taken during the 111th Congress to help small businesses gain greater access to capital. For example, P.L. 111-5, the American Recovery and Reinvestment Act of 2009 (ARRA), provided $375 million to temporarily subsidize the 7(a) and 504/CDC loan guaranty programs' fees and to temporarily increase the 7(a) program's maximum loan guaranty percentage to 90%. P.L. 111-240, the Small Business Jobs Act of 2010, provided $505 million to extend the fee subsidies and 90% loan guaranty percentage through December 31, 2010; increased the 7(a) program's gross loan limit from $2 million to $5 million; and established an alternative size standard for the 7(a) and 504/CDC loan programs. P.L. 111-322, the Continuing Appropriations and Surface Transportation Extensions Act, 2011, authorized the SBA to continue the fee subsidies and 90% loan guaranty percentage through March 4, 2011, or until available funding was exhausted (which occurred on January 3, 2011).

This report also examines three bills introduced during the 112th Congress that would affect the 7(a) program. S. 1828, a bill to increase small business lending, and for other purposes, would reinstate for a year following the date of its enactment ARRA's fee subsidies and 90% loan guaranty percentage for the 7(a) program. H.R. 2936, the Small Business Administration Express Loan Extension Act of 2011, would extend a one-year increase in the maximum loan amount for the SBAExpress program from $350,000 to $1 million for an additional year. That temporary increase expired on September 26, 2011. S. 532, the Patriot Express Authorization Act of 2011, would provide statutory authorization for the Patriot Express Pilot Program and increase its loan guaranty percentages and its maximum loan amount from $500,000 to $1 million.

Information concerning the 7(a) program's SBAExpress, Patriot Express, Small Loan Advantage, and Community Advantage programs is also provided.

Small Business Administration Loan Guaranty Programs

The Small Business Administration (SBA) administers programs to support small businesses, including loan guaranty programs to encourage lenders to provide loans to small businesses "that might not otherwise obtain financing on reasonable terms and conditions."[1] The SBA's 7(a) loan guaranty program is considered the agency's flagship loan program.[2] It is named from Section 7(a) of the Small Business Act of 1953 (P.L. 83-163, as amended), which authorizes the SBA to provide business loans to American small businesses.

The SBA also administers several 7(a) subprograms that offer streamlined and expedited loan procedures for particular groups of borrowers, including the SBAExpress, Patriot Express, Small Loan Advantage, and Community Advantage Pilot programs (see the Appendix for additional details). Although these subprograms have their own distinguishing eligibility requirements, terms, and benefits, they operate under the 7(a) program's authorization.[3]

Proceeds from 7(a) loans may be used to establish a new business or to assist in the operation, acquisition, or expansion of an existing business. Specific uses include to acquire land (by purchase or lease); improve a site (e.g., grading, streets, parking lots, and landscaping); purchase, convert, expand, or renovate one or more existing buildings; construct one or more new buildings; acquire (by purchase or lease) and install fixed assets;

purchase inventory, supplies, and raw materials; finance working capital; and refinance certain outstanding debts.[4]

In FY2012, the SBA approved 44,377 7(a) loans amounting to more than $15.1 billion.5 As will be discussed, the total number and amount of SBA 7(a) loans approved declined in FY2008 and FY2009, increased during FY2010 and FY2011, and then declined somewhat in FY2012.

The SBA attributed the decreased number and amount of 7(a) loans approved in FY2008 and FY2009 to a reduction in the demand for small business loans resulting from the economic uncertainty of the recession (December 2007 - June 2009) and to tightened loan standards imposed by lenders concerned about the possibility of higher loan default rates resulting from the economic slowdown. The SBA attributed the increased number and amount of 7(a) loans approved in FY2010 and FY2011 to legislation that provided funding to temporarily reduce the 7(a) program's loan fees and temporarily increase the 7(a) program's loan guaranty percentage to 90% for all standard 7(a) loans from up to 85% of loans of $150,000 or less and up to 75% of loans exceeding $150,000.[6] The fee subsidies and 90% loan guaranty percentage were in place during most of FY2010 and the first quarter of FY2011.[7]

Historically, one of the justifications presented for funding the SBA's loan guaranty programs has been that small businesses can be at a disadvantage, compared with other businesses, when trying to obtain access to sufficient capital and credit.[8] Congressional interest in the 7(a) loan program has increased in recent years because of concerns that small businesses might be prevented from accessing sufficient capital to enable them to assist in the economic recovery.

Some, including President Obama, argue that the SBA should be provided additional resources to assist small businesses in acquiring capital necessary to start, continue, or expand operations with the expectation that in so doing small businesses will create jobs.

Others worry about the longterm adverse economic effects of spending programs that increase the federal deficit. They advocate business tax reduction, reform of financial credit market regulation, and federal fiscal restraint as the best means to assist small business economic growth and job creation.

This report discusses the rationale provided for the 7(a) program; the program's borrower and lender eligibility standards and program requirements; and program statistics, including loan volume, loss rates, use of the proceeds, borrower satisfaction, and borrower demographics. It also examines issues raised concerning the SBA's administration of the 7(a) program, including the oversight of 7(a) lenders and the program's lack of outcome-based performance measures.

It then examines congressional action taken during the 111th Congress to help small businesses gain greater access to capital. For example, P.L. 111-5, the American Recovery and Reinvestment Act of 2009 (ARRA), provided $375 million to temporarily subsidize the 7(a) and 504/CDC loan guaranty programs' fees and to temporarily increase the 7(a) program's maximum loan guaranty percentage to 90%. P.L. 111-240, the Small Business Jobs Act of 2010, provided $505 million to extend the fee subsidies and 90% loan guaranty percentage through December 31, 2010; increased the 7(a) program's gross loan limit from $2 million to $5 million; and established an alternative size standard for the 7(a) and 504/CDC loan programs to enable more small businesses to qualify for assistance.

Also, P.L. 111-322, the Continuing Appropriations and Surface Transportation Extensions Act, 2011, authorized the SBA to continue the fee subsidies and the 7(a) program's 90% maximum loan guaranty percentage through March 4, 2011, or until available funding was exhausted (which occurred on January 3, 2011).

This report also examines three bills introduced during the 112th Congress that would affect the 7(a) program. S. 1828, a bill to increase small business lending, and for other purposes, would reinstate for a year following the date of its enactment the fee subsidies and 90% loan guaranty percentage for the 7(a) program, which were originally authorized by ARRA. H.R. 2936, the Small Business Administration Express Loan Extension Act of 2011, would extend a one-year increase in the maximum loan amount for the SBAExpress program from $350,000 to $1 million for an additional year. That temporary increase was authorized by P.L. 111-240 and expired on September 26, 2011. S. 532, the Patriot Express Authorization Act of 2011, would provide statutory authorization for the Patriot Express Pilot Program and increase its loan guaranty percentages and its maximum loan amount from $500,000 to $1 million.

Information concerning the SBAExpress, Patriot Express, Small Loan Advantage, and Community Advantage programs is also provided.

Borrower Eligibility Standards and Program Requirements

Borrower Eligibility Standards

To be eligible for an SBA business loan, a small business applicant must

- be located in the United States;
- be a for-profit operating business (except for loans to eligible passive companies);
- qualify as small under the SBA's size requirements;[9]
- demonstrate a need for the desired credit; and
- be certified by a lender that the desired credit is unavailable to the applicant on reasonable terms and conditions from non-Federal sources without SBA assistance.[10]

To qualify for an SBA 7(a) loan, applicants must be creditworthy and able to reasonably assure repayment. SBA requires lenders to consider the applicant's

- character, reputation, and credit history;
- experience and depth of management;
- strength of the business;
- past earnings, projected cash flow, and future prospects;
- ability to repay the loan with earnings from the business;
- sufficient invested equity to operate on a sound financial basis;
- potential for long-term success;

- nature and value of collateral (although inadequate collateral will not be the sole reason for denial of a loan request); and
- affiliates' effect on the applicant's repayment ability.[11]

Borrower Program Requirements

Use of Proceeds

Borrowers may use 7(a) loan proceeds to establish a new business or to assist in the operation, acquisition, or expansion of an existing business. 7(a) loan proceeds may be used to

- acquire land (by purchase or lease);
- improve a site (e.g., grading, streets, parking lots, landscaping), including up to 5% for community improvements such as curbs and sidewalks;
- purchase one or more existing buildings;
- convert, expand, or renovate one or more existing buildings;
- construct one or more new buildings;
- acquire (by purchase or lease) and install fixed assets;
- purchase inventory, supplies, and raw materials;
- finance working capital; and
- refinance certain outstanding debts.[12]

Borrowers are prohibited from using 7(a) loan proceeds to

- refinance existing debt where the lender is in a position to sustain a loss and the SBA would take over that loss through refinancing;
- effect a partial change of business ownership or a change that will not benefit the business;
- permit the reimbursement of funds owed to any owner, including any equity injection or injection of capital for the business's continuance until the loan supported by the SBA is disbursed;
- repay delinquent state or federal withholding taxes or other funds that should be held in trust or escrow; or
- pay for a non-sound business purpose.[13]

Loan Amounts

As mentioned previously, P.L. 111-240 increased the 7(a) program's maximum gross loan amount for any one 7(a) loan from $2 million to $5 million (up to $3.75 million maximum guaranty). In FY2012, the average loan amount was about $340,000.[14]

Loan Terms, Interest Rate, and Collateral

Loan Terms

7(a) loans are required to have the shortest appropriate term, depending upon the borrower's ability to repay. The maximum term is 10 years, unless the loan finances or refinances real estate or equipment with a useful life exceeding 10 years. In that case, the loan term can be up to 25 years, including extensions.[15]

Interest Rate

Lenders are allowed to charge borrowers "a reasonable fixed interest rate" or, with the SBA's approval, a variable interest rate.[16] The SBA uses a multi-step formula to determine the maximum allowable fixed interest rate and periodically publishes that rate and the maximum allowable variable interest rate in the *Federal Register*.[17]

The maximum allowable fixed interest rates in October 2012 for 7(a) loans with maturities less than seven years are 6.7% for loans greater than $50,000, 7.7% for loans over $25,000 but not exceeding $50,000, and 8.7% for loans of $25,000 or less. The maximum allowable fixed interest rates in October 2012 for 7(a) loans with maturities of seven years or more are 7.2% for loans greater than $50,000, 8.2% for loans over $25,000 but not exceeding $50,000, and 9.2% for loans of $25,000 or less.[18]

The 7(a) program's maximum allowable variable interest rate may be pegged to the lowest prime rate (3.25% in October 2012), the 30 day LIBOR rate plus 300 basis points (3.21% in October 2012), or the SBA optional peg rate (2.125% in the first quarter of FY2013).[19] The optional peg rate is a weighted average of rates the federal government pays for loans with maturities similar to the average SBA loan.[20]

Collateral

The SBA requires lenders to collateralize the loan to the maximum extent possible up to the loan amount. If business assets do not fully secure the loan, the lender must take available personal assets of the principals as collateral. Loans are considered "fully secured" if the lender has taken security interests in all available assets with a combined "liquidation value" up to the loan amount.[21]

LENDER ELIGIBILITY STANDARDS AND PROGRAM REQUIREMENTS

Lender Eligibility Standards

Lenders must have a continuing ability to evaluate, process, close, disburse, service, and liquidate small business loans; be open to the public for the making of such loans (and not be a financing subsidiary, engaged primarily in financing the operations of an affiliate); have continuing good character and reputation; and be supervised and examined by a state or federal regulatory authority, satisfactory to SBA. They must also maintain satisfactory performance, as determined by SBA through on-site review/examination assessments, historical performance measures (such as default rate, purchase rate, and loss rate), and loan volume to the extent that it affects performance measures.[22] There are currently about 3,500 active lenders providing SBA loans.[23]

Lender Program Requirements

The Application Process

Borrowers submit applications for a 7(a) business loan to private lenders. The lender reviews the application and decides if it merits a loan on its own or if it has some weaknesses which, in the lender's opinion, do not meet standard, conventional underwriting guidelines and requires additional support in the form of an SBA guaranty. The SBA guaranty assures the lender that if the borrower does not repay the loan and the lender has adhered to all applicable regulations concerning the loan, the SBA will reimburse the lender for its loss, up to the percentage of the SBA's guaranty. The small business borrowing the money remains obligated for the full amount due.[24]

If the lender determines that it is willing to provide the loan, but only with an SBA guaranty, it submits the application for approval through the mail, website, or e-mail to the Standard 7(a) Loan Guaranty Processing Center operating out of two locations: Citrus Heights, CA, and Hazard, KY.[25] This center has responsibility for processing 7(a) loan guaranty applications for lenders who do not have delegated authority to make 7(a) loans without the SBA's final approval.[26] The application must include the following documentation and forms:

- SBA Form 4, Application for Loan, which includes specific requirements for providing financial assistance to a small business located in a floodplain or a wetland, the use of lead-based paint, seismic safety of federal and federally assisted or regulated new building construction, coastal barrier protections, laws prohibiting discrimination on the grounds of race, color, national origin, religion, sex, marital status, disability or age, and rights under the Financial Privacy Act of 1978 (P.L. 95-630);
- SBA Form 4, Schedule A—Schedule of Collateral, or the lender may use their own form to list collateral and label it "Exhibit A";
- SBA Form 912, Statement of Personal History—required of all principals, officers, directors and owners of 20% or more of the small business applicant;
- 7(a) Eligibility Questionnaire;
- Personal Financial Statement, dated within 90 days of submission to the SBA, on all owners of 20% or more (including the assets of the owner's spouse and any minor children), and proposed guarantors. SBA Form 413 is available. However, lenders may use their own form;
- Business Financial Statements dated within 90 days of submission to the SBA, consisting of (1) year end balance sheets for the last three years, (2) year-end profit and loss statements for the last three years, (3) reconciliation of net worth, (4) interim balance sheet, (5) interim profit and loss statements, (6) affiliate and subsidiary financial statement requirements, and (7) cash flow projection— month-by-month for one year if less than three fiscal years provided and for all loans with a term of 18 months or less;

- history of the business, résumés of principals, and copy of lease, if applicable;
- detailed listing of machinery and equipment to be purchased with loan proceeds and cost quotes;
- if real estate is to be purchased with loan proceeds an appraisal, lender's environmental questionnaire, cost breakdown, and copy of purchase agreement;
- if purchasing an existing business with loan proceeds a (1) copy of buy-sell agreement, (2) copy of business valuation, (3) pro forma balance sheet for the business being purchased as of the date of transfer, (4) copy of seller's financial statements for the last three complete fiscal years or for the number of years in business if less than three years; (5) interim statements no older than 90 days from date of submission to SBA, and (6) if seller's financial statements are not available the seller must provide an alternate source of verifying revenues;
- Equity Injection Form—explanation of type and source of applicant's equity injection;
- Franchise Form—if listed on www.franchiseregistry.com a certification of material change or certification of no change or non-material change is required. If not listed on the registry, a copy of the Franchise Agreement and Federal Trade Commission Disclosure Report of Franchisor must be submitted;
- SBA Form 159 (7a), Fee Disclosure and Compensation Agreement, must be completed for each agent compensated by the applicant or lender and retained in lender's loan file;
- a copy of Internal Revenue Service (IRS) Form 4506-T, Request for Copy of Tax Return—lender must identify the date IRS Form 4506-T was sent to IRS;
- for non-citizens, a copy of the U.S. Citizenship and Immigration Services (USCIS) Form G-845, Document Verification Request—prior to disbursement, lenders must verify the USCIS status of each alien who is required to submit USCIS documents to determine eligibility. The lender must document the findings in the loan file;
- SBA Form 4-I, Lender's Application for Guaranty—must be completed in its entirety, including pro forma balance sheet and submitted with (1) explanation of use of proceeds and benefits of the loan, (2) lender's internal credit
- memorandum, (3) justification for new business, including change of ownership. For new businesses and change of ownership where historical repayment ability is not demonstrated, lender must provide a narrative addressing the business plan and cite any areas of concern and justification to overcome them, and (4) business valuation must be supplied by lender for change of ownerships;
- SBA Form 1846, Statement Regarding Lobbying, must be signed and dated by lender; and
- SBA National 7(a) Authorization Boilerplate language on-line "wizard" must be completed.[27]

The SBA established the Certified Lenders Program (CLP) on February 26, 1979, initially on a six-month pilot basis.[28] It is designed to provide expeditious service on 7(a) loan applications received from lenders who have a successful SBA lending track record and a thorough understanding of SBA policies and procedures. In recent years, CLP lenders have approved about 4.8% of the number of 7(a) loans approved each year and 7.4% of the amount of 7(a) loans approved each year.[29] For loan applications of $350,000 or less, CLP lenders must submit all forms and exhibits listed above for a standard 7(a) loan application and a draft authorization. For loan applications greater than $350,000, in addition to all of the standard 7(a) forms and exhibits, CLP lenders must submit a copy of its written credit analysis and must discuss SBA eligibility issues.[30]

The SBA started the Preferred Lenders Program (PLP) on March 1, 1983, initially on a pilot basis.[31] It is designed to streamline the procedures necessary to provide financial assistance to small businesses by delegating the final credit decision and most servicing and liquidation authority and responsibility to carefully selected PLP lenders.[32] In recent years, PLP lenders have approved about 22.5% of the number of 7(a) loans approved each year and about 55% of the amount of 7(a) loans approved each year.[33] PLP lenders must complete and retain in the lender's file all forms and exhibits listed above for the Standard 7(a) application. They must submit the following forms to the SBA for review: (1) a copy of page 1 of SBA Form 4, Application for Business Loan, (2) a copy of page 1 of SBA Form 4-I, Lender's Application for Guaranty or Participation (signed by two authorized officials of the lender), (3) a copy of Form 1920SX (Part B) "Supplemental Information for PLP/SBA Express Processing," and (4) a copy of Form 7, "Eligibility Information for Preferred Lender Participation (PLP) Loans." If the PLP loan is to refinance debt (not same institution debt), a fully completed business indebtedness schedule must be attached. If the PLP loan is to finance change of ownership and a business valuation is performed by the lender, a synopsis of the analysis must be submitted.[34]

SBA Guaranty and Servicing Fees

To offset its costs, the SBA charges lenders an upfront, one-time guaranty fee and an annual, ongoing servicing fee for each loan approved and disbursed. The maximum guaranty fee for 7(a) loans with maturities exceeding 12 months is set by statute. Also, the servicing fee cannot exceed 0.55% per year of the outstanding balance of the SBA's share of the loan.

The 7(a) program's guaranty fee is based on loan maturity and the amount of the guaranty portion of the loan. For loans with a maturity of 12 months or less, the SBA charges the lender a 0.25% guaranty fee, which the lender is required to submit with the application. The lender may charge the borrower for the fee when the loan is approved by the SBA.[35]

For loans with a maturity exceeding 12 months, the SBA charges the lender a 2% guaranty fee for the SBA guaranteed portion of loans of $150,000 or less, a 3% guaranty fee for the SBA guaranteed portion of loans exceeding $150,000 but not more than $700,000, and a 3.5% guaranty fee for the SBA guaranteed portion of loans exceeding $700,000. Loans with an SBA guaranteed portion in excess of $1 million are charged an additional 0.25% guaranty fee on the guaranteed amount in excess of $1 million.[36] These fees are the maximum allowed by law.[37] The lender must pay the SBA guaranty fee within 90 days of the date of loan's approval and may charge the borrower for the fee after the lender has made the first disbursement of the loan. Lenders are permitted to retain 25% of the up-front guaranty fee on loans with a gross amount of $150,000 or less.[38]

The annual ongoing servicing fee for all 7(a) loans is required to be no more than the "rate necessary to reduce to zero the cost to the Administration" of making guaranties and, as mentioned previously, cannot exceed 0.55% of the outstanding balance of the guaranteed portion of the loan.[39] The current rate is the maximum allowed by law—0.55% of the outstanding balance of the guaranteed portion of the loan.[40] The lender's annual service fee to the SBA cannot be charged to the borrower.[41]

Lender Packaging, Servicing and Other Fees

The lender may charge an applicant "reasonable fees" customary for similar lenders in the geographic area where the loan is being made for packaging and other services. The lender must advise the applicant in writing that the applicant is not required to obtain or pay for unwanted services. These fees are subject to SBA review at any time, and the lender must refund any such fee considered unreasonable by the SBA.[42]

The lender may also charge an applicant an additional fee if, subject to prior written SBA approval, all or part of a loan will have extraordinary servicing needs. The additional fee can not exceed 2% per year on the outstanding balance of the part requiring special servicing (e.g., field inspections for construction projects). The lender may also collect from the applicant necessary out-of-pocket expenses, including filing or recording fees, photocopying, delivery charges, collateral appraisals, environmental impact reports that are obtained in compliance with SBA policy, and other direct charges related to loan closing.[43] The lender is prohibited from requiring the borrower to pay any fees for goods and services, including insurance, as a condition for obtaining an SBA guaranteed loan, and from imposing on SBA loan applicants processing fees, origination fees, application fees, points, brokerage fees, bonus points, and referral or similar fees.[44]

The lender is also allowed to charge the borrower a late payment fee not to exceed 5% of the regular loan payment when the borrower is more than 10 days delinquent on its regularly scheduled payment. The lender may not charge a fee for full or partial prepayment of a loan.[45]

For loans with a maturity of 15 years or longer, the borrower must pay to the SBA a subsidy recoupment fee when the borrower voluntarily prepays 25% or more of its loan in any one year during the first three years after first disbursement. The fee is 5% of the prepayment amount during the first year, 3% the second year, and 1% in the third year.[46]

PROGRAM STATISTICS

Loan Volume

The SBA generally uses the number and amount of loans approved each fiscal year, as opposed to the number and amount of loans disbursed, for making comparisons of lending volume among its loan guaranty programs. Although loan disbursement data can be useful, loan disbursements in one fiscal year typically include significant amounts approved in previous fiscal years. For example, in FY2012, 38% of 7(a) loan disbursements were from loans approved prior to FY2012.[47]

The number of 7(a) loans approved annually is typically about 10% to 20% higher than the number of loans disbursed (e.g., some borrowers decide not to accept the loan or there is a change in business ownership.). The amount of 7(a) loans approved annually is typically about 10% to 15% higher than the amount disbursed.[48]

Table 1. 7(a) Loan Guaranty Program, Loan Volume, FY2007-FY2012

FY	Number of Loans Approved	Amount Approved	Total Unpaid Principal Balance
2007	99,606	$14. 3 billion	$46.1 billion
2008	69,434	$12.7 billion	$47.7 billion
2009	41,289	$9.2 billion	$48.6 billion
2010	47,002	$12.4 billion	$50.8 billion
2011	53,706	$19.6 billion	$56.4 billion
2012	44,377	$15.2 billion	$59.4 billion

Sources: U.S. Small Business Administration, Agency Financial Report Fiscal Year 2010, Washington, DC, November 15, 2010, p. 7; U.S. Small Business Administration, Fiscal Year 2011 Congressional Budget Justification and FY 2009 Annual Performance Report, Washington, DC, pp. 36, 125; U.S. Small Business Administration, "SBA Lending Statistics for Major Programs (as of 9/30/2012)," at http://www.sba.gov/about-sba-info/317721; and U.S. Small Business Administration, "Table 1 — Unpaid Principal Balance By Program," Washington, DC, http://www.sba.gov/sites/default/files/files/WDS_UPB_Report_2011Q3.pdf.

Notes: The number of 7(a) loans approved annually is typically about 10% to 20% higher than the number of loans disbursed (e.g., some borrowers decide not to accept the loan, there is a change in business ownership, etc.). The amount of 7(a) loans approved annually is typically about 10% to 15% higher than the amount disbursed. U.S. Small Business Administration, Office of Congressional and Legislative Affairs, correspondence with the author, September 17, 2012.

As shown in *Table 1*, the total number and amount of SBA 7(a) loans approved declined in FY2008 and FY2009, increased during FY2010 and FY2011, and then declined somewhat in FY2012.

As mentioned previously, the SBA attributed the decreased number and amount of 7(a) loans approved in FY2008 and FY2009 to a reduction in the demand for small business loans resulting from the economic uncertainty of the recession (December 2007 - June 2009) and to tightened loan standards imposed by lenders concerned about the possibility of higher loan default rates resulting from the economic slowdown. The SBA attributed the increased number of loans approved in FY2010 and FY2011 to legislation that provided funding to temporarily reduce the 7(a) program's loan fees and temporarily increase the 7(a) program's loan guaranty percentage to 90% for all standard 7(a) loans from up to 85% of loans of $150,000 or less and up to 75% of loans exceeding $150,000.[49] The fee subsidies and 90% loan guaranty percentage were in place during most of FY2010 and the first quarter of FY2011.[50]

Table 1 also provides, for comparison purposes, the total amount of the 7(a) program's unpaid principal balance. Precise measurements of the total credit market for small businesses is not available. However, the SBA has estimated that the credit market for small businesses (outstanding bank loans of $1 million or less, plus credit extended by finance companies) is roughly $1.0 trillion.[51] The SBA's 7(a) program's unpaid principal balance of $59.4 billion is about 5.9% of that amount.

Loss Rate and Appropriations for Subsidy Costs

Since its inception in 1953 through 2008, the 7(a) program (including subprograms) experienced a 5.83% loss rate (ratio of actual losses to disbursements).[52] In recent years, the loss rate for both 7(a) and 504/CDC programs has exceeded historical averages. As of June 30, 2012, the 7(a) program's loss rate since the program's inception in 1953 was 6.36%.[53]

One of the SBA's goals is to achieve a zero subsidy rate for its loan guaranty programs. A zero subsidy rate means that the SBA's loan guaranty programs do not require annual appropriations of budget authority for the issuance of new loan guarantees. From 2005 to 2009, the SBA did not request appropriations to subsidize the cost of any of its loan guaranty programs, including the 7(a) program. However, in recent years, SBA loan guaranty fees and loan liquidation recoveries, especially in the 7(a) loan guaranty program, have not generated enough revenue to cover loan losses, resulting in the need for additional appropriations to account for the shortfall. In FY2010 and in FY2011, the SBA was provided $80.0 million to subsidize the cost of SBA guaranteed loans. In FY2012, the SBA was provided $207.1 million for that purpose, and P.L. 112-175, the Continuing Appropriations Resolution, 2013 (which provides appropriations through March 27, 2013), provided a projected $333.6 billion for the cost of SBA loan guaranty program subsidies for FY2013.

The SBA reports that most of the agency's loan losses have occurred in the SBA's 7(a) loan guaranty program. For example, the SBA applied all of the FY2010 and FY2011 subsidy amounts ($80.0 million each year) to the 7(a) program, anticipates applying 67.3% ($139.4 million) of the FY2012 subsidy amount ($207.1 million) to the 7(a) program, and 67.6% ($224.5 million) of the FY2013 subsidy ($333.6 million) to the 7(a) program.[54]

Administrative Expenses

In FY2011, the SBA's spent $88.0 million on the 7(a) program for administrative expenses, including $44.2 million for loan making, $4.0 million for loan servicing, $26.8 million for loan liquidation, and $13.0 million for lender oversight. The SBA anticipates that the administrative costs for the 7(a) loan will be $89.5 million in FY2012 and $93.8 million in FY2013.[55]

Use of Proceeds and Borrower Satisfaction

In 2008, the Urban Institute released the results of an SBA-commissioned study of the SBA's loan guaranty programs. As part of its analysis, the Urban Institute surveyed a random sample of SBA loan guaranty borrowers. The survey indicated that borrowers used 7(a) loan proceeds to

- purchase or install new equipment (34%);
- finance working capital (23%);
- acquire original business (21%);
- other (19%);

- expand or renovate current building (14%);
- purchase new building (10%);
- refinance existing debt (8%);
- hire additional staff (6%);
- build new building (4%);
- purchase new land (3%); and
- improve land (2%).[56]

The Urban Institute also reported that most of the 7(a) borrowers responding to their survey rated their overall satisfaction with their 7(a) loan and loan terms as either excellent (18%) or good (50%). One out of every five 7(a) borrowers (20%) rated their overall satisfaction with their 7(a) loan and loan terms as fair, and 6% rated their overall satisfaction with their 7(a) loan and loan terms as poor (7% reported don't know or did not respond).[57] In addition, 90% of the survey's respondents reported that the 7(a) loan was either very important (62%) or somewhat important (28%) to their business success (2% reported somewhat unimportant, 3% reported very unimportant, and 4% reported don't know or did not respond).[58]

Borrower Demographics

The Urban Institute found that about 9.9% of conventional small business loans are issued to minority-owned small businesses and about 16% of conventional small business loans are issued to women-owned businesses.[59] In FY2012, 22.5% of 7(a) loan recipients were minority-owned businesses (12.1% Asian, 7.1% Hispanic, 2.4% African-American, and 0.9% other minority) and 16.6% were women-owned businesses.[60] Based on its comparative analysis of conventional small business loans and the SBA's loan guaranty programs, the Urban Institute concluded:

> SBA's loan programs are designed to enable private lenders to make loans to creditworthy borrowers who would otherwise not be able to qualify for a loan. As a result, there should be differences in the types of borrowers and loan terms associated with SBA-guaranteed and conventional small business loans.
>
> Our comparative analysis shows such differences. Overall, loans under the 7(a) and 504 programs were more likely to be made to minority-owned, women-owned, and start-up businesses (firms that have historically faced capital gaps) as compared to conventional small business loans. Moreover, the average amounts for loans made under the 7(a) and 504 programs to these types of firms were substantially greater than conventional small business loans to such firms. These findings suggest that the 7(a) and 504 programs are being used by lenders in a manner that is consistent with SBA's objective of making credit available to firms that face a capital opportunity gap.[61]

Congressional Issues

Access to Capital

Congressional interest in the 7(a) loan program has increased in recent years largely because of concerns that small businesses might be prevented from accessing sufficient capital to enable them to assist in the economic recovery. During the 111th Congress, several laws were enacted to increase the supply and demand for capital for both large and small businesses.[62] For example, in 2008, Congress adopted P.L. 110-343, the Emergency Economic Stabilization Act of 2008, which authorized the Troubled Asset Relief Program (TARP). Under TARP, the U.S. Department of the Treasury was authorized to purchase or insure up to $700 billion in troubled assets, including small business loans, from banks and other financial institutions. The law's intent was "to restore liquidity and stability to the financial system of the United States."[63] P.L. 111-203, the Dodd-Frank Wall Street Reform and Consumer Protection Act, reduced total TARP purchase authority from $700 billion to $475 billion. The Treasury Department's authority to make new financial commitments under TARP ended on October 3, 2010. The Department of the Treasury has disbursed approximately $389 billion in TARP funds, including $337 million to purchase SBA 7(a) loan guaranty program securities.[64]

In addition, as mentioned previously, in 2009, ARRA provided an additional $730 million for SBA programs, including $375 million to temporarily reduce fees in the SBA's 7(a) and 504/CDC loan guaranty programs and increase the 7(a) program's maximum loan guaranty percentage from up to 85% of loans of $150,000 or less and up to 75% of loans exceeding $150,000 to 90% for all standard 7(a) loans. Congress subsequently provided another $265 million, and authorized the SBA to reprogram another $40 million, to extend the fee reductions and loan modification through May 31, 2010, and the Small Business Jobs Act of 2010 provided another $510 million to extend the fee reductions and loan modification from September 27, 2010, through December 31, 2010. Also, P.L. 111-322, the Continuing Appropriations and Surface Transportation Extensions Act, 2011, authorized the use of any funding remaining from the Small Business Jobs Act of 2010 to extend the fee subsidies and 90% maximum loan guaranty percentage through March 4, 2011, or until the available funding was exhausted.[65] Funding for these purposes were exhausted on January 3, 2011.

The Obama Administration argued that TARP and the additional funding for the SBA's loan guaranty programs helped to improve the small business lending environment and supported "the retention and creation of hundreds of thousands of jobs."[66] Critics argued that small business tax reduction, reform of financial credit market regulation, and federal fiscal restraint are the best means to assist small business economic growth and job creation.[67]

Program Administration

The SBA's Office of Inspector General (OIG) and the U.S. Government Accountability Office (GAO) have independently reviewed the SBA's administration of the agency's loan guaranty programs. Both agencies have reported deficiencies in the SBA's administration of its loan guaranty programs that they argue need to be addressed, including issues involving the oversight of 7(a) lenders and the lack of outcome-based performance measures.

Oversight of 7(a) Lenders

The SBA's OIG has argued that the 7(a) loan guaranty program "is vulnerable to fraud and unnecessary losses because it relies on numerous third parties (e.g., borrowers, loan agents, and lenders)" to complete loan transactions for about 80% of the loans guaranteed annually by the SBA.[68] It has argued that the SBA needs to strengthen oversight of 7(a) lenders to "establish more robust controls to prevent waste, fraud, abuse, and inefficiencies."[69]

The SBA OIG has argued that the results of its review of the 7(a) program's FY2008 lending indicate the need for strengthened lender oversight. The SBA OIG found that the SBA's estimate of improper payments for FY2008 significantly understated the level of erroneous payments in the program. The SBA reported that improper payments were 0.53% of FY2008 program outlays, whereas the SBA's OIG estimated the improper payment rate to be 29% (approximately $248 million) of the $869 million in loan guaranties purchased between April 1, 2007, and March 31, 2008.[70] In addition, the SBA OIG's review of a sample of 30 7(a) loans issued in FY2008 found that 14 of the loans lacked evidence to support lender compliance with SBA origination, servicing, or liquidation requirements, resulting in improper payments totaling $723,293. In contrast, the SBA reported improper payments of $4,468 on two of the sampled loans.[71]

In 2009, GAO also recommended that the SBA strengthen its oversight of 7(a) program lenders. GAO argued that although the SBA's "lender risk rating system has enabled the agency to conduct some off-site monitoring of lenders, the agency does not use the system to target lenders for on-site reviews or to inform the scope of the reviews."[72] It also noted that

> the SBA targets for review those lenders with the largest SBA-guaranteed loan portfolios. As a result of this approach, 97 percent of the lenders that SBA's risk rating system identified as high risk in 2008 were not reviewed. Further, GAO found that the scope of the on-site reviews that SBA performs is not informed by the lenders' risk ratings, and the reviews do not include an assessment of lenders' credit decisions.[73]

GAO argued that although the SBA "has made improvements to its off-site monitoring of lenders, the agency will not be able to substantially improve its lender oversight efforts unless it improves its on-site review process."[74]

In a separate report concerning the SBA's administration of the 7(a) program, GAO also argued in 2009 that the SBA needs to "improve its oversight of lenders' compliance with the credit elsewhere requirement."[75] The Small Business Act specifies that "no financial assistance shall be extended pursuant to this subsection if the applicant can obtain credit elsewhere."[76] The SBA provides lenders the following six reasons for certifying in its application that the borrower meets the credit elsewhere requirement:

- the business needs a longer maturity than the lender's policy permits (for example, the business needs a loan that is not on a demand basis);
- the requested loan exceeds either the lender's legal lending limit or policy limit regarding the amount that it can lend to one customer;

- the lender's liquidity depends upon selling the guaranteed portion of the loan on the secondary market;
- the collateral does not meet the lender's policy requirements;
- the lender's policy normally does not allow loans to new businesses or businesses in the applicant's industry; or
- any other factors relating to the credit that, in the lender's opinion, cannot be overcome except for the guaranty. These other factors must be specifically documented in the loan file.[77]

GAO argued that "SBA's guidance to lenders on documenting compliance with the credit elsewhere requirement is limited" because it "does not specify the amount of detail lenders should include in their explanations."[78] GAO noted that "even with the lack of detail required," the SBA's own on-site reviews of 7(a) lenders over a recent six-quarter period indicated that nearly a third of the lenders reviewed had not consistently documented that borrowers met the credit elsewhere requirement.[79]

The SBA has argued that it currently "conducts a continuous risk-based, off-site analysis of lending partners through the Loan/Lender Monitoring System (L/LMS), a state-of-the-art portfolio monitoring system that incorporates credit scoring metrics for portfolio management purposes."[80] According to the SBA:

> The Loan/Lender Monitoring System focuses on 7(a) lenders, certified development companies and microloan intermediaries that pose the most risk to the SBA. In addition to overseeing lenders, the L/LMS provides policy, portfolio and program analysis. The Office of Credit Risk Management (OCRM) is divided into four teams: large lender oversight, small lender oversight, lender transaction, and program and policy analysis. The differentiation of lender oversight by lender size reflects the different forms of oversight needed for large lenders versus small lenders.[81]

The SBA asserts that

> The OCRM is continually enhancing and updating oversight programs and practices to provide a more robust and responsive system. Enhancements include: (1) better integration of delegated lending decisions into oversight practices; (2) addition of different types of lender reviews (targeted, desk, agreed upon procedures, etc.) to provide more options to obtain information in the most timely and efficient manner possible; (3) assessment of current on-site review practices to customize them based on risk factors and consider credit decisions made by lenders; (4) development of a lender certification program (particularly for community lenders); (5) quarterly reporting for non-bank lenders; (6) identification/ monitoring of risk related red flags and triggers; and (7) training for OCA staff, district office staff and lenders in the new process.[82]

In addition, in its FY2012 congressional budget request, the SBA reported that it had "created a more robust risk rating system, with more transparency in portfolios, and "best practices" for lender oversight (including more on-site and off-site lender monitoring)."[83]

Outcome-Oriented Performance Measures

GAO has argued that the 7(a) program's performance measures (e.g., number of loans approved, loans funded, and firms assisted across the subgroups of small businesses) provide limited information about the impact of the loans on participating small businesses:

> The program's performance measures focus on indicators that are primarily output measures–for instance, they report on the number of loans approved and funded. But none of the measures looks at how well firms do after receiving 7(a) loans, so no information is available on outcomes. As a result, the current measures do not indicate how well the agency is meeting its strategic goal of helping small businesses succeed.[84]

The SBA OIG has made a similar argument concerning the SBA's Microloan program's performance measures. Because the SBA uses similar program performance measures for its Microloan and 7(a) programs, the SBA OIG's recommendations could also be applied to the SBA's 7(a) program.

Specifically, as part of its audit of the SBA Microloan program's use of ARRA funds, the SBA OIG found that the SBA's performance measures for the Microloan program are based on the number of microloans funded, the number of small businesses assisted, and program's loan loss rate. It argued that these "performance metrics ... do not ensure the ultimate program beneficiaries, the microloan borrowers, are truly assisted by the program" and "without appropriate metrics, SBA cannot ensure the Microloan program is meeting policy goals."[85] It noted that the SBA does not track the number of microloan borrowers who remain in business after receiving a microloan to measure the extent to which the loans contributed to the success of borrowers and does not determine the effect that technical training assistance may have on the success of microloan borrowers and their ability to repay loans.[86] It recommended that the SBA "develop additional performance metrics to measure the program's achievement in assisting microloan borrowers in establishing and maintaining successful small businesses."[87]

In its response to GAO's recommendation to develop additional performance measures for the 7(a) program, the SBA indicated that there are legal constraints and cost considerations associated with tracking the success or failure of SBA borrowers and that it had, at that time, "a new administrator who may make changes to the agency's performance measures and goals."[88] In response to the SBA OIG's recommendation to develop additional performance metrics for the Microloan program, the SBA reported that it has "contracted with the Aspen Institute to advise on appropriate program and performance metrics for both microloans and technical assistance grants."[89] It also indicated that the program metrics developed will be used to assist the agency in measuring the Microloan program's effectiveness. Given that the Microloan program and 7(a) program use similar performance measures, it could be argued that the program metrics developed for the Microloan program may be applied to the 7(a) program as well.

LEGISLATIVE ACTIVITY DURING THE 111TH CONGRESS

Congress authorized several changes to the 7(a) program during the 111th Congress in an effort to increase the number, and amount, of 7(a) loans, including provisions contained in ARRA and the Small Business Jobs Act of 2010. Congress has not approved any changes to the 7(a) program during the 112th Congress.

The Obama Administration's Proposals

During the 111th Congress, the Obama Administration supported congressional efforts to temporarily subsidize fees for the 7(a) and 504/CDC loan guaranty programs and to increase the 7(a) program's loan guaranty percentage from up to 85% of loans of $150,000 or less and up to 75% of loans exceeding $150,000 to 90%. As mentioned previously, Congress subsequently provided more than $1.1 billion to subsidize fees for the 7(a) and 504/CDC loan guaranty programs and to increase the 7(a) program's maximum loan guaranty percentage to 90% for all standard 7(a) loans.

The Obama Administration also proposed the following modifications to several SBA programs, including the 7(a) program:

- increase the maximum loan size for 7(a) loans from $2 million to $5 million;
- increase the maximum loan size for the 504/CDC program from $2 million to $5 million for regular projects and from $4 million to $5.5 million for manufacturing projects;
- increase the maximum loan size for microloans to small business concerns from $35,000 to $50,000;
- increase the maximum loan limits for lenders in their first year of participation in the Microloan program, from $750,000 to $1 million, and from $3.5 million to $5 million in the subsequent years;
- temporarily increase the cap on SBAExpress loans from $350,000 to $1 million; and
- temporarily allow in FY2010 and FY2011, with an option to extend into FY2012, the refinancing of owner-occupied commercial real estate loans within one year of maturity under the SBA's 504/CDC program.[90]

Arguments for Increasing the SBA's Maximum Loan Limits

The Obama Administration argued that increasing the maximum loan limits for the 7(a), 504/CDC, Microloan, and SBAExpress programs would allow the SBA to "support larger projects," which will "allow the SBA to help America's small businesses drive long-term economic growth and the creation of jobs in communities across the country."[91] The Administration also argued that increasing the maximum loan limits for these programs will be "budget neutral" over the long run and "help improve the availability of smaller loans."[92]

Arguments Against Increasing the SBA's Maximum Loan Limits

Critics of the Obama Administration's proposals to increase the SBA's maximum loan limits argued that it might increase the risk of defaults, resulting in higher guaranty fees or the need to provide the SBA additional funding, especially for the SBAExpress program, which has experienced somewhat higher default rates than other SBA loan guaranty programs.[93] Others advocated a more modest increase in the maximum loan limits to ensure that the 7(a) program "remains focused on startup and early-stage small firms, businesses that have historically encountered the greatest difficulties in accessing credit" and "avoids making small borrowers carry a disproportionate share of the risk associated with larger loans."[94]

Others argued that creating a small business direct lending program within the SBA would reduce paperwork requirements and be more efficient in providing small businesses access to capital than modifying existing SBA programs that rely on private lenders to determine if they will issue the loans.[95] Also, as mentioned previously, others argued that providing additional resources to the SBA or modifying the SBA's loan programs as a means to augment small business access to capital is ill-advised. In their view, the SBA has limited impact on small access to capital. They argued that the best means to assist small business economic growth and job creation is to focus on small business tax reduction, reform of financial credit market regulation, and federal fiscal restraint.[96]

H.R. 3854, the Small Business Financing and Investment Act of 2009

H.R. 3854 would have authorized several new SBA programs and change several existing SBA programs, including the 7(a) program, in an effort to enhance job creation by increasing the availability of credit to small businesses. The bill was passed by the House, 389-32, on October 29, 2009. The Senate did not act on the bill.[97]

It would have

- increased the maximum loan size for 7(a) loans from $2 million to $3 million;
- increased the maximum loan size for 504/CDC loans from $1.5 million to $3 million for regular projects, from $2 million to $4 million for projects located in a low-income community, from $4 million to $8 million for manufacturers, and for up to $10 million for projects that constitute "a major source of employment" as determined by the Administration;
- extended ARRA's fee reductions and the 7(a) program's 90% loan guaranty limit through September 30, 2011;
- authorized the SBA to establish an alternative size standard for the 7(a) program that uses maximum tangible net worth and average net income as an alternative to the use of industry standards and established an interim size standard of a maximum tangible net worth of not more than $15 million and an average net income after federal taxes (excluding any carryover losses) for the preceding two fiscal years of not more than $5 million;
- extended, with modifications, ARRA's America's Recovery Capital Loan Program (ARC) which temporarily provides small businesses loan assistance for debt relief, through the end of FY2011;[98] and
- provided a 100% loan guaranty for small business concerns owned and controlled by veterans, and expanded and made permanent the SBA's secondary market lending authority.[99]

The bill would have also created a temporary SBA direct lending program following enactment that would be available to creditworthy small business borrowers that are unable to find credit elsewhere.[100]

S. 2869, the Small Business Job Creation and Access to Capital Act of 2009

S. 2869 was ordered to be reported by the Senate Committee on Small Business and Entrepreneurship on December 10, 2009. The Senate did not take further action on the bill, but many of its provisions were later included in P.L. 111-240. It would have authorized changes to several SBA programs, including the 7(a) program, and was designed to enhance job creation by increasing the availability of credit to small businesses.

It would have

- increased the maximum loan size for 7(a) loans from $2 million to $5 million;
- increased the maximum loan size for the 504/CDC loans from $1.5 million to $5 million for regular projects, from $2 million to $5 million for projects meeting one of the program's specified public policy goals, and from $4 million to $5.5 million for manufacturers;
- increased the maximum loan size for the Microloan program from $35,000 to $50,000;
- extended ARRA's fee reductions and the 7(a) program's 90% loan guaranty limit through December 31, 2010;
- authorized the SBA to establish an alternative size standard for the 7(a) and 504/CDC programs that uses maximum tangible net worth and average net income as an alternative to the use of industry standards and established an interim size standard of a maximum tangible net worth of not more than $15 million and an average net income after federal taxes (excluding any carryover losses) for the preceding two fiscal years of not more than $5 million; and
- allowed 504/CDC loans to be used to refinance up to $4 billion in short-term commercial real estate debt each fiscal year for two years after enactment into long-term fixed rate loans.[101]

P.L. 111-240, the Small Business Jobs Act of 2010

P.L. 111-240 was signed into law by President Obama on September 27, 2010. It increased the 7(a) program's loan guaranty limit from $2 million to $5 million, provided $510 million to extend the 7(a) program's 90% maximum loan guaranty percentage and 7(a) and 504/CDC loan guaranty programs' fee subsidies through December 31, 2010 (later extended to March 4, 2011), or until available funding was exhausted (which occurred on January 3, 2011). The act also includes all of the provisions listed above in S. 2869, the Small Business Job Creation and Access to Capital Act of 2009, except that it would allow 504/CDC loans to be used to refinance up to $7.5 billion in short-term commercial real estate debt each fiscal year for two years after enactment into longterm fixed rate loans instead of up to $4 billion each fiscal year.[102]

The act also authorizes the Secretary of the Treasury to establish a $30 billion Small Business Lending Fund (SBLF) to encourage community banks to provide small business loans ($4 billion was issued), a $1.5 billion State Small Business Credit Initiative to provide funding to participating states with small business capital access programs, and about $12 billion in tax relief for small businesses.[103] It also contains revenue raising provisions to offset the act's cost and authorizes a number of changes to other SBA loan and contracting programs.

LEGISLATIVE ACTIVITY DURING THE 112TH CONGRESS

As mentioned previously, Congress has not approved any changes to the 7(a) program during the 112th Congress. However, several bills have been introduced during the 112th Congress that would affect the 7(a) program.

S. 1828, a bill to increase small business lending, and for other purposes, was introduced on November 8, 2011 and referred to the Senate Committee on Small Business and Entrepreneurship. The bill would reinstate for a year following the date of its enactment the temporary fee subsidies for the 7(a) and 504/CDC loan guaranty programs and the 90% loan guaranty for standard 7(a) loans, which were originally authorized by ARRA and later extended by several laws, including the Small Business Jobs Act of 2010.

H.R. 2936, the Small Business Administration Express Loan Extension Act of 2011, introduced on September 15, 2011, and referred to the House Committee on Small Business, would extend a one-year increase in the maximum loan amount for the SBAExpress program from $350,000 to $1 million for an additional year. The temporary increase in that program's maximum loan amount was authorized by P.L. 111-240, the Small Business Jobs Act of 2010, and expired on September 26, 2011 (see *Appendix*).

S. 532, the Patriot Express Authorization Act of 2011, introduced on March 9, 2011, and referred to the Senate Committee on Small Business and Entrepreneurship, would provide statutory authorization for the Patriot Express Pilot Program (see *Appendix*). The bill would also increase the program's maximum loan amount from $500,000 to $1 million, and it would increase the guaranty percentage from up to 85% of loans of $150,000 or less and up to 75% of loans exceeding $150,000 to up to 85% of loans of $500,000 or less and up to 80% of loans exceeding $500,000.

CONCLUDING OBSERVATIONS

The congressional debate concerning the SBA's 7(a) program during the 111th Congress was not whether the federal government should act, but which federal policies would most likely enhance small business access to capital and result in job retention and creation. As a general proposition, some, including President Obama, argued that the SBA should be provided additional resources to assist small businesses in acquiring capital necessary to start, continue, or expand operations with the expectation that in so doing small businesses will create jobs.[104] Others worried about the long-term adverse economic effects of spending programs that increase the federal deficit. They advocated business tax reduction, reform of financial credit market regulation, and federal fiscal restraint as the best means to assist small business economic growth and job creation.[105]

In terms of specific program changes, increasing the 7(a) program's loan limit, extending the 7(a) program's temporary fee subsidies and 90% maximum loan guaranty percentage, and establishing an alternative size standard for the 7(a) program were all designed to achieve the same goal: to enhance job creation by increasing the ability of 7(a) borrowers to access credit at affordable rates. However, determining how specific changes in federal policy are most likely to enhance job creation is a challenging question. For example, a 2008 Urban Institute study concluded that differences in the term, interest rate, and amount of SBA financing "was not significantly associated with increasing sales or employment among firms receiving SBA financing."[106] However, they also reported that their analysis accounted for less than 10% of the variation in firm performance. The Urban Institute suggested that local economic conditions, local zoning regulations, state and local tax rates, state and local business assistance programs, and the business owner's charisma or business acumen also "may play a role in determining how well a business performs after receipt of SBA financing."[107]

As the Urban Institute study suggests, given the many factors that influence business success, measuring the SBA's 7(a) program's effect on job retention and creation is complicated. That task is made even more challenging by the absence of performance-oriented measures that could serve as a guide. Both GAO and the SBA's OIG have recommended that the SBA adopt outcome performance oriented measures for its loan guaranty programs, such as tracking the number of borrowers who remain in business after receiving a loan to measure the extent to which the program contributed to their ability to stay in business.[108] Other performance-oriented measures that Congress might also consider include requiring the SBA to survey 7(a) borrowers to measure the difficulty they experienced in obtaining a loan from the private sector and the extent to which the 7(a) loan or technical assistance received contributed to their ability to create jobs or expand their scope of operations.

Appendix. 7(a) Specialized Programs

The 7(a) program has four specialized programs that offer streamlined and expedited loan procedures for particular groups of borrowers, the SBAExpress, Patriot Express, Small Loan Advantage, and Community Advantage programs. Lenders must be approved by the SBA for participation in these programs.

SBAExpress Program

The SBAExpress program was established as a pilot program by the SBA on February 27, 1995, and made permanent through legislation, subject to reauthorization, in 2004 (P.L. 108-447, the Consolidated Appropriations Act, 2005). The program was designed to increase the availability of credit to small businesses by permitting lenders to use their existing documentation and procedures in return for receiving a reduced SBA guaranty on loans.[109] It provides a 50% loan guaranty on loan amounts up to $350,000.

In FY2012, the SBA approved 23,146 SBAExpress loans (52.2% of total 7(a) program loan approvals) amounting to $1.78 billion (11.8% of total 7(a) program amount approvals).[110] The SBA approved 26,838 SBAExpress loans amounting to $2.87 billion in FY2011 and 20,452 SBAExpress loans amounting to $1.55 billion in FY2010.[111] The program's higher loan volume in FY2011 was due, at least in part, to a provision in P.L. 111-240, the Small Business Jobs Act of 2010, which temporarily increased the SBAExpress program's loan limit to $1 million for one year following enactment (through September 26, 2011). H.R. 2936, the Small Business Administration Express Loan Extension Act of 2011, was introduced on September 9, 2011, and referred to House Committee on Small Business. As mentioned previously, the bill would have extended the higher loan limit for an additional year (through September 26, 2012). SBAExpress loan proceeds can be used for the same purposes as the 7(a) program (expansion, renovation, new construction, the purchase of land or buildings, the purchase of equipment, fixtures, and lease-hold improvements, working capital, to refinance debt for compelling reasons, seasonal line of credit, and inventory) except participant debt restructure cannot exceed 50% of the project and may be used for revolving credit. The program's loan terms are the same as the 7(a) program (the loan maturity for working capital, machinery, and equipment (not to exceed the life of the equipment) is typically 5 to 10 years and the loan maturity for real estate is up to 25 years), except that the term for a revolving line of credit cannot exceed 7 years. The SBAExpress loan's interest rates are negotiable with the lender, subject to maximums. Rates can be fixed or variable. Fixed rates may not exceed prime plus 6.5% on loans of $50,000 or less and prime plus 4.5% on loans over $50,000. Variable interest rates are based on either the prime rate (as published in The Wall Street Journal), the 30-day LIBOR plus 3.0%, or the SBA's optional peg rate (published quarterly in the Federal Register) plus 6.5% on loans of $50,000 or less and plus 4.5% on loans over $50,000.[112] The program's fees are the same as the 7(a) program. To account for the program's lower guaranty rate of 50%, lenders are allowed to perform their own loan analysis and procedures and receive SBA approval with a targeted 36-hour maximum turnaround time.[113] Also, collateral is not required for loans of $25,000 or less. Lenders are allowed to use their own established collateral policy for loans over $25,000.

Patriot Express Pilot Program

In 2007, the SBA created the Patriot Express Pilot Program "to support the entrepreneur segment of the Nation's military community (including spouses)."[114] Eligible businesses must be owned and controlled (51% or more) by one or more of the following groups: veteran, active duty military participating in the military's Transition Assistance Program, reservist or national guard member or a spouse of any of these groups, a widowed spouse of a service member who died while in service, or a widowed spouse of a veteran who died of a service-connected disability.[115] The SBA announced on December 10, 2010, that it will continue to operate the program for at least three more years.[116]

S. 532, the Patriot Express Authorization Act of 2011, was introduced on March 9, 2011, and referred to the Senate Committee on Small Business and Entrepreneurship. The bill would provide the Patriot Express program statutory authorization. Also, S.Amdt. 229, to establish the Patriot Express Loan Program, was introduced as an amendment to S. 493, the SBIR/STTR Reauthorization Act of 2011, on March 16, 2011. The Senate did not vote on the amendment as cloture on the base bill (S. 493) was not invoked.

The Patriot Express Pilot Program provides the same loan guaranty as the 7(a) program on loan amounts up to $500,000 (up to 85% of loans of $150,000 or less and up to 75% of loans exceeding $150,000). The loan proceeds can be used for the same purposes as the 7(a) program (expansion, renovation, new construction, the purchase of land or buildings, the purchase of equipment, fixtures, and lease-hold improvements, working capital, to refinance debt for compelling reasons, seasonal line of credit, and inventory) except participant debt restructure cannot exceed 15-25% of the project and may be used for revolving lines of credit. The loan terms are the same as the 7(a) program (the loan maturity for working capital, machinery, and equipment (not to exceed the life of the equipment) is typically 5 to 10 years and the loan maturity for real estate is up to 25 years), except that the term for a revolving line of credit cannot exceed 7 years. Also, collateral is not required for loans of $25,000 or less. Lenders are allowed to use their own established collateral policy for loans over $25,000 and up to $350,000. For loans exceeding $350,000, lenders must follow the SBA's regulations on collateral for standard 7(a) loans.[117]

The Patriot Express Pilot Program features streamlined documentation and processing features similar to the SBAExpress program, with a targeted SBA processing time of one business day. The program's interest rates are negotiable with the lender, subject to the same maximum rate limitations as the 7(a) program. It also has the same fees as the 7(a) program.[118]

The SBA has indicated in both testimony at congressional hearings and in press releases that it views the Patriot Express Program as a success. For example, in 2007, William Elmore, Associate Director of the SBA's Office of Veterans Business Development, testified at a congressional hearing shortly after the Patriot Express program's rollout that

> so far, the results have been good. The number of loans made to veterans increased from 4,800 in fiscal year 2000 to approximately 8,000 loans in fiscal year 2006.[119]

In 2010, Joseph Jordan, SBA's Associate Administrator for Contracting and Business Development, testified at a congressional hearing that

> SBA is committed to assisting veteran-owned small businesses access the capital they need. All of SBA's loan programs are available to veterans. In FY2009, veteran-owned small businesses received 8.00% of all 7(a) loans, totaling approximately $523 million, and 4.56% of all 504 development company loans, or $176 million. Additionally, veteran-owned small businesses received 4.33% of all microloans, totaling approximately $1.9 million. In total, SBA has supported more than $2 billion in recovery lending to veteran-owned small businesses. SBA also has a loan program dedicated to the military community—Patriot Express.... It features our lowest interest rates and fastest turnaround times, often within days.... In FY2009, we approved more than 2,300 Patriot Express loans and are on track to increase those numbers in FY2010.[120]

More recently, when the SBA announced in a December 10, 2010, press release that it was extending the Patriot Express Loan Program for another three years, the SBA characterized the program as "a very popular initiative that in just three-and-a-half years has provided more than $560 million in loan guarantees to nearly 7,000 veterans to start or expand their small businesses."[121]

Congressional testimony provided by various veteran service organizations provides a different perspective. For example, a representative of the American Legion testified at a congressional hearing in 2010 that being turned down for a SBA Patriot Express loan "is probably the largest, most frequent complaint that we receive from our business owners."[122] At that same congressional hearing, a representative of the Vietnam Veterans of America testified in response to that statement that

> I would have to concur ... in talking with some of the veterans with regard to the Patriot Express Loan, they are having difficulties also to acquire that capital. The rationale seems to be ... the banks in general seem to be tightening the credit, their lending practices, so that is ... what we are hearing.[123]

There are no empirical assessments of veterans' experiences with the SBA Patriot Express Loan program that would be useful for determining the relative ease or difficulty of veteran-owned small business owners accessing capital through the program.[124] The SBA does not conduct annual surveys of veteran-owned small businesses applying for SBA Patriot Express Loans similar to the annual survey the SBA currently sponsors for small businesses receiving services from the SBA's management and training programs.[125]

Small Loan Advantage and Community Advantage Programs

The Small Loan Advantage and Community Advantage programs became operational on February 15, 2011.[126] They are designed to increase lending to underserved low- and moderate-income communities. Both programs offer a streamlined application process for loans up to $250,000. The two programs replaced the Community Express Pilot Program, which was also designed to increase lending to underserved communities. It was created by the SBA in May 1999, and ended on April 30, 2011.[127]

The Small Loan Advantage program "is structured to encourage larger, existing SBA lenders to make lower-dollar loans, which often benefit businesses in underserved markets."[128] It provides the same loan guaranty as the 7(a) program on loan amounts up to $250,000 (85% for loans up to $150,000 and 75% for those greater than $150,000). The loan proceeds can be used for the same purposes as the 7(a) program (expansion, renovation, new construction, the purchase of land or buildings, the purchase of equipment, fixtures, and lease-hold improvements, working capital, to refinance debt for compelling reasons, seasonal line of credit, and inventory). The loan terms and guaranty fees are also the same as the 7(a) program.[129] The program's interest rates are negotiable with the lender, subject to the same maximum rate limitations as the 7(a) program.[130]

The program is available to lenders participating in the SBA's Preferred Lender Program (about 545 lenders, including most of the SBA's highest volume lenders). These lenders are authorized to use expedited loan processing procedures, which include a two-page application for borrowers and allow lenders to use their own note and guaranty agreements. Most Small Loan Advantage loans are expected "to be approved in a matter of minutes through electronic submission" or "within 5 to 10 days" otherwise.[131]

The Community Advantage pilot program is designed to increase lending in underserved communities by increasing "the number of SBA 7(a) lenders who reach underserved communities, targeting community-based, mission-focused financial institutions which were previously not able to offer SBA loan."[132] These mission-focused financial institutions include "Community Development Financial Institutions, SBA's Certified Development

Companies and SBA's nonprofit microlending intermediaries."[133] They are expected "to maintain at least 60% of their SBA loan portfolio in underserved markets, including loans to small businesses in, or that have more than 50% of their workforce residing in, low-to-moderate income (LMI) communities; in Empowerment Zones and Enterprise Communities; in HUBZones; start-ups (firms in business less than 2 years); and veteran-owned businesses and those that would be eligible for Patriot Express."[134]

The Community Advantage program is a three-year pilot program that provides the same loan guaranty as the 7(a) program on loan amounts up to $250,000 (85% for loans up to $150,000 and 75% for those greater than $150,000). The loan proceeds can be used for the same purposes as the 7(a) program (expansion, renovation, new construction, the purchase of land or buildings, the purchase of equipment, fixtures, and lease-hold improvements, working capital, to refinance debt for compelling reasons, seasonal line of credit, and inventory). The loan terms and guaranty fees are also the same as the 7(a) program.[135] The loan's maximum interest rate is prime, plus 6%.[136] The program has an expedited approval process which includes a two-page application for borrowers and a goal of completing the loan approval process within 5 to 10 days.[137]

The SBA has indicated that the Community Advantage program's goal is to "leverage the experience these institutions already have in lending to minority, women-owned and start-up companies in economically challenged markets, along with their management and technical assistance expertise, to help make their borrowers successful."[138]

End Notes

[1] U.S. Small Business Administration, Fiscal Year 2010 Congressional Budget Justification, p. 30.

[2] U.S. Congress, House Committee on Small Business, Subcommittee on Finance and Tax, Subcommittee Hearing on Improving the SBA's Access to Capital Programs for Our Nation's Small Business, 110th Cong., 2nd sess., March 5, 2008, H.Hrg. 110-76 (Washington: GPO, 2008), p. 2.

[3] U.S. Small Business Administration, "Express and Pilot Programs," at http://www.sba. gov/content/express-programs. The SBA also administers four special purpose loan guaranty programs that address particular business needs: the Community Adjustment and Investment Program (CAIP), CAPLines Program, Employee Trusts Program, and Pollution Control Program (currently not funded). See U.S. Small Business Administration, "Special Purpose Loans Program," at http://www.sba.gov/category/navigation-structure/loans-grants/small-business-loans/sba-loan-programs/ 7a-loan-program/special-purpose-loans-program.

[4] 13 C.F.R. §120.120.

[5] U.S. Small Business Administration, "SBA Lending Statistics for Major Programs (as of 9/30/2012)," at http://www.sba.gov/about-sba-info/317721. The number of 7(a) loans approved annually is typically about 10% to 20% higher than the number of loans disbursed (e.g., some borrowers decide not to accept the loan or there is a change in business ownership). The amount of 7(a) loans approved annually is typically about 10% to 15% higher than the amount disbursed.

[6] U.S. Small Business Administration, Press Office, "Recovery Loan Incentives Spurred Continued Rebound in SBA Lending in FY2010," October 4, 2010, at http://www.sba. gov/about-sba-services/7367/5527; and U.S. Small Business Administration, "Jobs Act Supported More Than $12 Billion in SBA Lending to Small Businesses in Just Three Months," January 3, 2011, at http://www.sba.gov/content/jobs-act-supported-more-12-billion-sba-lending-smallbusinesses-just-three-months.

[7] P.L. 111-5, the American Recovery and Reinvestment Act of 2009 (ARRA), enacted on February 17, 2009, provided the SBA $375 million to temporarily reduce fees in the 7(a) and 504/CDC loan guaranty programs, and increase the 7(a) program's maximum loan guaranty percentage to 90% for all standard 7(a) loans through September 30, 2010, or until available funds were exhausted. Due to the increased demand for 7(a) loans, available funding was anticipated to be exhausted in early January 2010. P.L. 111-118, the Department of Defense Appropriations Act, 2010, provided the SBA $125 million to continue the fee subsidies and 90%

maximum loan guaranty percentage through February 28, 2010. P.L. 111-144, the Temporary Extension Act of 2010, provided the SBA $60 million to continue the fee subsidies and 90% maximum loan guaranty percentage through March 28, 2010. P.L. 111-150, an act to extend the Small Business Loan Guarantee Program, and for other purposes, provided the SBA authority to reprogram $40 million in previously appropriated funds to continue the fee subsidies and 90% maximum loan guaranty percentage through April 30, 2010. P.L. 111-157, the Continuing Extension Act of 2010, provided the SBA $80 million to continue the SBA's fee subsidies and 90% maximum loan guaranty percentage through May 31, 2010. The fee subsidies and 90% loan guaranty percentage expired on May 31, 2010. P.L. 111-240, the Small Business Jobs Act of 2010, enacted on September 27, 2010, provided the SBA $505 million (plus an additional $5 million for related administrative expenses) to reinstate the fee subsidies and 90% maximum loan guaranty percentage through December 31, 2010, or until available funds were exhausted. P.L. 111-322, the Continuing Appropriations and Surface Transportation Extensions Act, 2011, authorized the SBA to use any funds remaining from the Small Business Jobs Act of 2010 to continue the fee subsidies and the 7(a) program's 90% maximum loan guaranty percentage through March 4, 2011, or until the available funding was exhausted. The funds were exhausted on January 3, 2011.

[8] U.S. Government Accountability Office, Small Business Administration: 7(a) Loan Program Needs Additional Performance Measures, GAO-08-226T, November 1, 2007, pp. 3, 9-11, at http://www.gao.gov/new.items/d08226t.pdf; and Veronique de Rugy, Why the Small Business Administration's Loan Programs Should Be Abolished, American Enterprise Institute for Public Policy Research, AEI Working Paper #126, April 13, 2006. Proponents of federal funding for the SBA's loan guarantee programs also argue that small business can promote competitive markets. See, P.L. 83-163, §2(a), as amended; and 15 U.S.C. §631a.

[9] For further analysis, see CRS Report R40860, Small Business Size Standards: A Historical Analysis of Contemporary Issues, by Robert Jay Dilger.

[10] 13 C.F.R. §120.100; and 13 C.F.R. §120.101. A list of ineligible businesses, such as non-profit businesses, insurance companies, and businesses deriving more than one-third of gross annual revenue from legal gambling activities, are contained in 13 C.F.R. §120.110.

[11] 13 C.F.R. §120.150.

[12] 13 C.F.R. §120.120.

[13] 13 C.F.R. §120.130; and U.S. Small Business Administration, "Use of 7(a) Loan Proceeds," at http://www.sba.gov/ content/use-7a-loan-proceeds.

[14] U.S. Small Business Administration, "SBA Lending Statistics for Major Programs (as of 9/30/2012)," at http://www.sba.gov/about-sba-info/317721.

[15] 13 C.F.R. §120.212. A portion of a 7(a) loan used to acquire or improve real property may have a term of 25 years plus an additional period needed to complete the construction or improvements.

[16] 13 C.F.R. §120.213.

[17] For fixed interest rates, the SBA first calculates a fixed base rate using the 30 day London Interbank Offered Rate (LIBOR) in effect on the first business day of the month as published in a national financial newspaper published each business day, adds to that 300 basis points (3%) and the average of the 5-year and 10-year LIBOR swap rates in effect on the first business day of the month as published in a national financial newspaper published each business day. For 7(a) fixed loans with maturities of less than seven years, the SBA adds 2.25% to the fixed base rate to arrive at the maximum allowable fixed rate. For 7(a) fixed loans with maturities of seven years or longer, the SBA adds 2.75% to the fixed base rate to arrive at the maximum allowable fixed rate. Lenders may increase the maximum fixed interest rate allowed by an additional 1% if the fixed rate loan is over $25,000 but not exceeding $50,000, and by an additional 2% if the fixed rate loan is $25,000 or less. See, U.S. Small Business Administration, "Business Loan Program Maximum Allowable Fixed Rate," 74 Federal Register 50263, 50264, September 30, 2009.

[18] Colson Services Corp., "SBA Base Rates," New York, at http://www.colsonservices. com/ main/news.shtml.

[19] Ibid.

[20] U.S. Small Business Administration, "7(a) Loan Program: Terms and Conditions," at http://www.sba.gov/content/7aterms-conditions.

[21] U.S. Small Business Administration, "SOP 50 10 5(E): Lender and Development Company Loan Programs," (effective June 1, 2012), pp. 188-189, at http://www.sba.gov/sites/ default/files/SOP%2050%2010%205(E)%20(5-16- 2012)%20clean.pdf. Liquidation value is the amount expected to be realized if the lender took possession after a loan default and sold the asset after conducting a reasonable search for a buyer and after deducting the costs of taking possession, preserving and marketing the asset, less the value of any existing liens.

[22] 13 C.F.R. §120.410.

[23] U.S. Small Business Administration, Fiscal Year 2013 Congressional Budget Justification and FY 2011 Annual Performance Report, p. 31.

[24] U.S. Small Business Administration, "7(a) Loan Program: How the Program Works," at http://archive.sba.gov/financialassistance/borrowers/guaranteed/7alp/FINANCIAL_GLP_7A_WORK.html.

[25] U.S. Small Business Administration, "SOP 50 10 5(E): Lender and Development Company Loan Programs," (effective June 1, 2012), p. 225, at http://www.sba.gov/sites/default/files/ SOP%2050%2010%205(E)%20(5-16- 2012)%20clean.pdf.

[26] U.S. Government Accountability Office, Small Business Administration: Opportunities Exist to Build on Leadership's Efforts to Improve Agency Performance and Employee Morale, GAO-08-995, September 24, 2008, p. 3, at http://www.gao.gov/new.items/d08995.pdf.

[27] U.S. Small Business Administration, "SOP 50 10 5(E): Lender and Development Company Loan Programs," (effective June 1, 2012), pp. 217-220, at http://www.sba.gov/sites/default/ files/SOP%2050%2010%205(E)%20(5-16- 2012)%20clean.pdf.

[28] U.S. Congress, Senate Select Committee on Small Business, SBA Loan Oversight, hearing on SBA loan oversight, 96th Cong., 1st sess., September 18, 1997 (Washington: GPO, 1997), p. 31; and U.S. General Accounting Office, SBA's Pilot Programs to Improve Guaranty Loan Procedures Need Further Development, CED-81-25, February 2, 1981, p. 7, at http://www.gao.gov/assets/140/131789.pdf; and U.S. General Accounting Office, SBA's Certified Lenders Program Falls Short of Expectations, RCED-83-99, June 7, 1983, p. 1, at http://www.gao.gov/assets/150/140126.pdf.

[29] U.S. Small Business Administration, Office of Congressional and Legislative Affairs, correspondence with the author, September 17, 2012.

[30] U.S. Small Business Administration, "SOP 50 10 5(E): Lender and Development Company Loan Programs," (effective June 1, 2012), p. 221, at http://www.sba.gov/sites/default/files/ SOP%2050%2010%205(E)%20(5-16- 2012)%20clean.pdf. CLP lenders are expected to perform a complete analysis of the application and, in return, the SBA promises a faster loan decision. The SBA still makes the final credit and eligibility decision, but by completing a credit review instead of an independently conducted analysis, the SBA attempts to arrive at its decision in three working days. See, U.S. Small Business Administration, "The Certified Lenders Program (CLP)," at http://www.sba.gov/content/ steps-participating-clp.

[31] U.S. General Accounting Office, SBA's Certified Lenders Program Falls Short of Expectations, RCED-83-99, June 7, 1983, p. 3, at http://www.gao.gov/ assets/150/ 140126.pdf.

[32] U.S. General Accounting Office, Small Business: Analysis of SBA's Preferred Lenders Program, GAO/RCED-92- 124, May 15, 1992, pp. 1-4, http://www.gao.gov/ assets/220/ 216229.pdf.

[33] PLP lenders approved 12,496 7(a) loans amounting to $8.4 billion in FY2012, 15,167 7(a) loans amounting to $10.7 billion in FY2011, and 13,168 7(a) loans amounting to $6.9 billion in FY2010. See U.S. Small Business Administration, "SBA Lending Statistics for Major Programs (as of 9/30/2012)," at http://www.sba.gov/about-sba-info/ 317721.

[34] U.S. Small Business Administration, "SOP 50 10 5(E): Lender and Development Company Loan Programs," (effective June 1, 2012), p. 221, at http://www.sba.gov/ sites/default/files/SOP%2050%2010%205(E)%20(5-16- 2012)%20clean.pdf. Lenders are considered for PLP status based on their record with SBA, and must have demonstrated a proficiency in processing and servicing SBA-guaranteed loans. The SBA continues to review the submitted materials to check loan eligibility criteria. See U.S. Small Business Administration, "The Preferred Lenders Program (PLP)," at http://www.sba.gov /content/preferred-lenders-program-plp. Of the 3,537 active lenders in the 7(a) program in FY2011, 545 participated in the Preferred Lenders Program.

[35] U.S. Small Business Administration, "SOP 50 10 5(E): Lender and Development Company Loan Programs," (effective June 1, 2012), pp. 83, 163, at http://www.sba.gov/sites/ default/files/SOP%2050%2010%205(E)%20(5-16- 2012)%20clean.pdf. The fee is refundable if the loan application is withdrawn prior to SBA approval, the SBA declines to guarantee the loan, or the SBA substantially changes the loan terms and those terms are unacceptable to the lender. Also, because the SBA does not approve or decline the credit for PLP loans, PLP lenders are required to send the guaranty fee directly to the SBA Denver Finance Center within 10 business days from the date the loan number is assigned and before the lender signs the Authorization for SBA.

[36] 15 U.S.C. 636(a)(18)(a).

[37] U.S. Small Business Administration, "Small Business Jobs Act: Implementation of Conforming and Technical Amendments," 76 Federal Register 63544, 63545, October 13, 2011.

[38] U.S. Small Business Administration, "SOP 50 10 5(E): Lender and Development Company Loan Programs," (effective June 1, 2012), p. 163, at http://www.sba.gov/sites/default/files/ SOP%2050%2010%205(E)%20(5-16- 2012)%20clean.pdf.

[39] 15 U.S.C. 636(a)(23)(a).

[40] U.S. Small Business Administration, "SBA Information Notice: 7(a) and 504 Fees Effective On October 1, 2012," at http://www.colsonservices.com/main/news/5000-1253%20-%207(a)%20and%20504%20Fees%20Effective%20On%20October%201%202012.pdf.

[41] 15 U.S.C. 636(a)(23)(b).

[42] 13 C.F.R. §120.221.

[43] Ibid.; and U.S. Small Business Administration, "SOP 50 10 5(E): Lender and Development Company Loan Programs," (effective June 1, 2012), p. 171, at http://www. sba.gov/sites/default/files/ SOP%2050%2010%205(E)%20(5-16-2012)%20clean.pdf.

[44] 13 C.F.R. §120.222. A commitment fee may be charged for a loan made under the Export Working Capital Loan Program.

[45] 13 C.F.R. §120.221; and U.S. Small Business Administration, "SOP 50 10 5(E): Lender and Development Company Loan Programs," (effective June 1, 2012), p. 172, at http://www.sba.gov/sites/default/files/SOP%2050%2010%205(E)%20(5-16-2012)% 20 clean.pdf.

[46] 13 C.F.R. §120.223; and U.S. Small Business Administration, "SOP 50 10 5(E): Lender and Development Company Loan Programs," (effective June 1, 2012), p. 172, at http://www.sba.gov/ sites/default/files/SOP%2050%2010%205(E)%20(5-16-2012)% 20clean.pdf.

[47] U.S. Small Business Administration, Office of Congressional and Legislative Affairs, correspondence with the author, September 17, 2012. The SBA maintains selected disbursement data and will provide that data to congressional offices by request.

[48] U.S. Small Business Administration, "SBA Lending Report for Major Programs, Fiscal Year 2010," October 4, 2010, at http://archive.sba.gov/idc/groups/public/documents/ sba_homepage/serv_fa_lending_ major_progs.pdf; and U.S. Small Business Administration, Office of Congressional and Legislative Affairs, correspondence with the author, September 17, 2012.

[49] U.S. Small Business Administration, Press Office, "Recovery Loan Incentives Spurred Continued Rebound in SBA Lending in FY2010," October 4, 2010, at http://www.sba. gov/about-sba-services/7367/5527; and U.S. Small Business Administration, "Jobs Act Supported More Than $12 Billion in SBA Lending to Small Businesses in Just Three Months," January 3, 2011, at http://www.sba.gov/content/jobs-act-supported-more-12-billion-sba-lending-smallbusinesses-just-three-months.

[50] P.L. 111-5, the American Recovery and Reinvestment Act of 2009 (ARRA), enacted on February 17, 2009, provided the SBA $375 million to temporarily reduce fees in the 7(a) and 504/CDC loan guaranty programs, and increase the 7(a) program's maximum loan guaranty percentage to 90% for all standard 7(a) loans through September 30, 2010, or until available funds were exhausted. Due to the increased demand for 7(a) loans, available funding was anticipated to be exhausted in early January 2010. P.L. 111-118, the Department of Defense Appropriations Act, 2010, provided the SBA $125 million to continue the fee subsidies and 90% maximum loan guaranty percentage through February 28, 2010. P.L. 111-144, the Temporary Extension Act of 2010, provided the SBA $60 million to continue the fee subsidies and 90% maximum loan guaranty percentage through March 28, 2010. P.L. 111-150, an act to extend the Small Business Loan Guarantee Program, and for other purposes, provided the SBA authority to reprogram $40 million in previously appropriated funds to continue the fee subsidies and 90% maximum loan guaranty percentage through April 30, 2010. P.L. 111-157, the Continuing Extension Act of 2010, provided the SBA $80 million to continue the SBA's fee subsidies and 90% maximum loan guaranty percentage through May 31, 2010. The fee subsidies and 90% loan guaranty percentage expired on May 31, 2010. P.L. 111-240, the Small Business Jobs Act of 2010, enacted on September 27, 2010, provided the SBA $505 million (plus an additional $5 million for related administrative expenses) to reinstate the fee subsidies and 90% maximum loan guaranty percentage through December 31, 2010, or until available funds were exhausted. P.L. 111-322, the Continuing Appropriations and Surface Transportation Extensions Act, 2011, authorized the SBA to use any funds remaining from the Small Business Jobs Act of 2010 to continue the fee subsidies and the 7(a) program's 90% maximum loan guaranty percentage through March 4, 2011, or until the available funding was exhausted. The funds were exhausted on January 3, 2011.

[51] U.S. Small Business Administration, Office of Advocacy, "Frequently Asked Questions About Small Business Finance," September 2011, at http://www.sba.gov/sites/default/ files/Finance%20FAQ%208-25-11%20FINAL%20for%20web.pdf.

[52] U.S. Small Business Administration, FY 2008 Small Business Administration (SBA) Loss Report, p. 7, at http://archive.sba.gov/idc/groups/public/documents/ sba_program_office/ cfo_2008_loss_report.pdf. Loans include those made through the SBA's 7(a), 8(A), FIS 8a, Economic Opportunity, Small Business Energy, Handicap Assistance, Veterans, Pollution Control, Import Export, Foreign Trade, USCAIP (NAFTA) and Reconstruction Finance Corporation Business programs.

[53] U.S. Small Business Administration, Office of Congressional and Legislative Affairs, correspondence with the author, September 17, 2012. 7(a) program loan loss was calculated by subtracting total 7(a) loan purchases from total 7(a) program disbursements, and then adding total 7(a) loan recoveries.

[54] U.S. Small Business Administration, FY 2013 Congressional Budget Justification and FY 2011 Annual Performance Report, p. 19, at http://www.sba.gov/sites/default/files/files/ FY%202013%20CBJ%20FY%202011%20APR.pdf.

[55] U.S. Small Business Administration, Fiscal Year 2013 Congressional Budget Justification and FY 2011 Annual Performance Report, p. 21.

[56] Christopher Hayes, An Assessment of Small Business Administration Loan and Investment Performance: Survey of Assisted Businesses (Washington, DC: The Urban Institute, 2008), p. 3, at http://www.urban.org/ UploadedPDF/ 411599_assisted_business_survey.pdf. The percentage total exceeds 100 because recipients were allowed to name more than one use for the loan proceeds.

[57] Ibid., p. 5.

[58] Ibid.

[59] Kenneth Temkin, Brett Theodos, with Kerstin Gentsch, Competitive and Special Competitive Opportunity Gap Analysis of the 7(A) and 504 Programs (Washington, DC: The Urban Institute, 2008), p. 13, at http:// www.urban.org/ UploadedPDF/411596_504_gap_ analysis.pdf.

[60] U.S. Small Business Administration, "SBA Lending Statistics for Major Programs (as of 9/30/2012)," at http://www.sba.gov/about-sba-info/317721.

[61] Kenneth Temkin, Brett Theodos, with Kerstin Gentsch, Competitive and Special Competitive Opportunity Gap Analysis of the 7(A) and 504 Programs (Washington, DC: The Urban Institute, 2008), p. 21, at http://www.urban.org/UploadedPDF/411596_504_gap_ analy sis.pdf.

[62] For further analysis, see CRS Report R40985, Small Business: Access to Capital and Job Creation, by Robert Jay Dilger.

[63] P.L. 110-343, the Emergency Economic Stabilization Act of 2008.

[64] U.S. Department of the Treasury, Troubled Assets Relief Program Monthly 105(a) Report – November 2010, December 10, 2010, pp. 2-4, at http://www.financialstability.gov/docs/ November%20105(a)%20FINAL.pdf. On March 16, 2009, President Obama announced that the Department of the Treasury would use TARP funds to purchase up to $15 billion of SBA-guaranteed loans to "immediately unfreeze the secondary market for SBA loans and increase the liquidity of community banks." The plan was deferred after it met resistance from lenders. Some lenders objected to TARP's requirement that participating lenders comply with executive compensation limits and issue warrants to the federal government. Smaller, community banks objected to the program's paperwork requirements, such as the provision of a small-business lending plan and quarterly reports. See The White House, "Remarks by the President to Small Business Owners, Community Leaders, and Members of Congress," March 16, 2009, at http://www.whitehouse.gov/the_press_office/Remarks-by-the-President-to-small-business-owners/.

[65] P.L. 111-240, the Small Business Jobs Act of 2010, §1111. Section 7(A) Business Loans. The Senate had adopted H.R. 4213, the American Workers, State, and Business Relief Act of 2010, on March 10, 2010, by a 62-36 vote. It would have provided $560 million to extend the fee reductions and 90% loan guarantee limit through December 31, 2010. The House approved an amended version of the bill, renamed the American Jobs and Closing Tax Loopholes Act of 2010, on May 28, 2010, by a 245-171 vote. It would have provided $505 million to extend the fee reductions and 90% loan guarantee limit through December 31, 2010. The extension provision was subsequently removed from the bill, which became P.L. 111-205, the Unemployment Compensation Extension Act of 2010.

[66] U.S. Small Business Administration, "Administration Announces New Small Business Commercial Real Estate and Working Capital Programs," February 5, 2010, at http://www.sba.gov/sites/default/files/ sba_rcvry_factsheet_cre_refi.pdf.

[67] Susan Eckerly, "NFIB Responds to President's Small Business Lending Initiatives," Washington, DC, October 21, 2009, at http://www.nfib.com/newsroom/newsroom-item/cmsid/50080/; and NFIB, "Government Spending," Washington, DC, at http://www.nfib.com/issues-elections/issues-elections-item/cmsid/49051/.

[68] U.S. Small Business Administration, Office of Inspector General, "Semiannual Report to Congress, Fall 2009," p. 5, at http://www.sba.gov/office-of-inspector-general/867/12348.

[69] Ibid., p. 3.

[70] Ibid., p. 5.

[71] Ibid.

[72] U.S. Government Accountability Office, Small Business Administration: Actions Needed to Improve the Usefulness of the Agency's Lender Risk Rating System, GAO-1—53, November 6, 2009, p. i, at http://www.gao.gov/new.items/ d1053.pdf.

[73] Ibid., pp. i, 27-30.

[74] Ibid., p. 35.

[75] U.S. Government Accountability Office, Small Business Administration: Additional Guidance on Documenting Credit Elsewhere Decisions Could Improve 7(a) Program Oversight, GAO-09-228, February 12, 2009, p. 3, at http://www.gao.gov/new.items/d09228.pdf.

[76] 15 U.S.C. 636(a)(1)(A). The act defines credit elsewhere as "the availability of credit from non-Federal sources on reasonable terms and conditions taking into consideration the prevailing rates and terms in the community in or near where the concern transacts business, or the homeowner resides, for similar purposes and periods of time." See 15 U.S.C. 632(h).

[77] U.S. Small Business Administration, "SOP 50 10 5(E): Lender and Development Company Loan Programs," (effective June 1, 2012), p. 102, at http://www.sba.gov/sites/ default/files/SOP%2050%2010%205(E)%20(5-16- 2012)%20clean.pdf.

[78] U.S. Government Accountability Office, Small Business Administration: Additional Guidance on Documenting Credit Elsewhere Decisions Could Improve 7(a) Program Oversight, GAO-09-228, February 12, 2009, pp. 25-26, at http://www.gao.gov/new.items/d09228.pdf.

[79] Ibid., p. 26.

[80] U.S. Small Business Administration, Fiscal Year 2011 Congressional Budget Justification and FY 2009 Annual Performance Report, p. 6.

[81] Ibid., p. 43.

[82] Ibid.

[83] U.S. Small Business Administration, Fiscal Year 2012 Congressional Budget Justification and FY 2010 Annual Performance Report, p. 7.

[84] U.S. Government Accountability Office, Small Business Administration: 7(a) Loan Program Needs Additional Performance Measures, GAO-08-226T, November 1, 2007, p. 2, at http://www.gao.gov/ new.items/d08226t.pdf.

[85] U.S. Small Business Administration, Office of the Inspector General, SBA's Administration of the Microloan Program under the Recovery Act, December 28, 2009, p. 6, at http://www.sba.gov/sites/default/files/om10-10.pdf.

[86] Ibid.

[87] Ibid., p. 7.

88 U.S. Government Accountability Office, Small Business Administration: 7(a) Loan Program Needs Additional Performance Measures, GAO-08-226T, November 1, 2007, p. 8, at http://www.gao.gov/ new.items/d08226t.pdf.

[89] U.S. Small Business Administration, Office of the Inspector General, SBA's Administration of the Microloan Program under the Recovery Act, December 28, 2009, p. 9, at http://www.sba.gov/sites/default/files/om10-10.pdf.

[90] U.S. Small Business Administration, "Administration Announces New Small Business Commercial Real Estate and Working Capital Programs," February 5, 2010, at http://www. sba.gov/sites/default/files/ sba_rcvry_factsheet_cre_refi.pdf.

[91] Ibid.

[92] Ibid.

[93] Robb Mandelbaum, "Small Business Incentives Face a Hard Road in Congress," New York Times, February 12, 2010, at http://boss.blogs.nytimes.com/2010/02/12/small-business-incentives-face-a-hard-road-in-congress/; and U.S. Congress, House Committee on Small Business, House Committee on Small Business Views With Regard to the Fiscal Year (FY) 2010 Budget, Letter from Nydia Velázquez, Chair, House Committee on Small Business, to John M. Spratt, Jr., Chair, House Committee on the Budget, 111th Cong., 2nd sess., March 11, 2009, p. 3, at http://www.house.gov/ smbiz/democrats/Reports/FY%202010% 20Views %20and%20Estimates%20v2.pdf.

[94] U.S. Congress, House Committee on Small Business, Small Business Financing and Investment Act Of 2009, report to accompany H.R. 3854, 111th Cong., 2nd sess., October 26, 2009, H.Rept. 111-315 (Washington: GPO, 2009), p. 1.

[95] Robb Mandelbaum, "Why Won't the S.B.A. Lend Directly to Small Businesses?" New York Times, March 10, 2010, at http://boss.blogs.nytimes.com/2010/03/10/why-wont-the-s-b-a-loan-directly-to-small-businesses/.

[96] Susan Eckerly, "NFIB Responds to President's Small Business Lending Initiatives," Washington, DC, October 21, 2009, at http://www.nfib.com/newsroom/newsroom-item/ cmsid/50080/; and NFIB, "Government Spending," Washington, DC, at http://www. nfib.com/issues-elections/issues-elections-item/cmsid/49051/.

[97] For further analysis, see CRS Report R40985, Small Business: Access to Capital and Job Creation, by Robert Jay Dilger.

[98] ARC's loan limit would be increased from $35,000 to $50,000, and to $75,000 in areas of high unemployment, and borrowers would be allowed to use ARC loans to refinance existing SBA loan debt. The ARC program ended on September 30, 2010.

[99] H.R. 3854, the Small Business Financing and Investment Act of 2009.

[100] Ibid. For further analysis, see CRS Report R40985, Small Business: Access to Capital and Job Creation, by Robert Jay Dilger.

[101] S. 2869, the Small Business Job Creation and Access to Capital Act of 2009; and H.R. 4213, the American Workers, State and Business Relief Act.

[102] P.L. 111-240, the Small Business Jobs Act of 2010, §1122. Low-Interest Refinancing Under the Local Development Business Loan Program.

[103] For further analysis of P.L. 111-240, the Small Business Jobs Act of 2010, see CRS Report R41385, Small Business Legislation During the 111th Congress, by Robert Jay Dilger and Gary Guenther. For further analysis of the Small Business Lending Fund, see CRS Report R42045, The Small Business Lending Fund, by Robert Jay Dilger. For further analysis of the State Small Business Credit Initiative, see CRS Report R42581, State Small Business Credit Initiative: Implementation and Funding Issues, by Robert Jay Dilger.

[104] Representative Nydia Velázquez, "Small Business Financing and Investment Act of 2009," House debate, Congressional Record, daily edition, vol. 155, no. 159 (October 29, 2009), pp. H12074, H12075; Senator Mary Landrieu, "Statements on Introduced Bills and Joint Resolutions," remarks in the Senate, Congressional Record, daily edition, vol. 155, no. 185 (December 10, 2009), p. S12910; and The White House, "Remarks by the President on Job Creation and Economic Growth," December 8, 2009, at http://www.whitehouse.gov/the-press-office/remarkspresident-job-creation-and-economic-growth.

[105] Susan Eckerly, "NFIB Responds to President's Small Business Lending Initiatives," Washington, DC, October 21, 2009, at http://www.nfib.com/newsroom/newsroom-item/cmsid/50080/; and NFIB, "Government Spending," Washington, DC, at http://www. nfib.com/issues-elections/issues-elections-item/cmsid/49051/.

[106] Shelli B. Rossman and Brett Theodos, with Rachel Brash, Megan Gallagher, Christopher Hayes, and Kenneth Temkin, Key Findings from the Evaluation of the Small Business Administration's Loan and Investment Programs: Executive Summary (Washington, DC: The Urban Institute, January 2008), p. 58, at http://www.urban.org/ Uploaded PDF/ 411602_executive_summary.pdf.

[107] Ibid.

[108] U.S. Government Accountability Office, Small Business Administration: 7(a) Loan Program Needs Additional Performance Measures, GAO-08-226T, November 1, 2007, p. 2, at http://www.gao.gov/ new.items/d08226t.pdf; and U.S. Small Business Administration, Office of the Inspector General, SBA's Administration of the Microloan Program under the Recovery Act, December 28, 2009, pp. 6-7, at http://www.sba.gov/sites/default/files/om10-10.pdf.

[109] U.S. Small Business Administration, "The SBA Express Pilot Program: Inspection Report," June 1998, p. 3, at http://archive.sba.gov/idc/groups/public/ documents/sba/ oig_ loarchive_980601.pdf.

[110] U.S. Small Business Administration, "SBA Lending Statistics for Major Programs (as of 9/30/2012)," at http://www.sba.gov/about-sba-info/317721.

[111] Ibid.

[112] U.S. Small Business Administration, "SBAExpress," at http://www.sba.gov/content/sba-express.

[113] Ibid.

[114] U.S. Small Business Administration, "SOP 50 10 5(E): Lender and Development Company Loan Programs," (effective June 1, 2012), p. 42, at http://www.sba.gov/sites/ default/files/SOP%2050%2010%205(E)%20(5-16-2012)%20clean.pdf.

[115] Ibid., pp. 83, 127.

[116] U.S. Small Business Administration, "Popular SBA Patriot Express Loan Initiative Renewed for Three More Years," December 10, 2010, at http://www.sba.gov/content/popular-sba-patriot-express-loan-initiative-renewed-threemore-years.

[117] U.S. Small Business Administration, "SOP 50 10 5(E): Lender and Development Company Loan Programs," (effective June 1, 2012), pp. 83, 146, 148-153, at http://www.sba. gov/sites/default/files/SOP% 2050%2010%205(E)%20(5-16-2012)%20 clean.pdf.

[118] Ibid., pp. 84, 172-173.

[119] U.S. Congress, Senate Committee on Small Business and Entrepreneurship, Assessing Federal Small Business Assistance Programs for Veterans and Reservists, hearing, 110th Cong., 1st sess., January 31, 2007, S.Hrg. 110-209 (Washington: GPO, 2007), p. 32.

[120] U.S. Congress, House Committee on Veterans' Affairs, Subcommittee on Economic Opportunity, Status of Veterans Small Business, hearing, 111th Cong., 2nd sess., April 29, 2010, House Committee on Veterans' Affairs Serial No. 111- 74 (Washington: GPO, 2010), p. 75.

[121] U.S. Small Business Administration, "Popular SBA Patriot Express Loan Initiative Renewed for Three More Years," December 10, 2010, at http://www.sba.gov/content/popular-sba-patriot-express-loan-initiative-renewed-threemore-years.

[122] U.S. Congress, House Committee on Veterans' Affairs, Subcommittee on Economic Opportunity, Status of Veterans Small Business, hearing, 111th Cong., 2nd sess., April 29, 2010, House Committee on Veterans' Affairs Serial No. 111- 74 (Washington: GPO, 2010), p. 17.

[123] Ibid.

[124] In FY2010, the SBA's Veterans Business Outreach Centers Program, which provides management and technical assistance training for veteran-owned small businesses, conducted its sixth annual "Customer Satisfaction Survey." The centers surveyed 1% of their total veteran customer population (408 of the 485 clients surveyed responded). The FY2010 survey found that 85% of the clients using the centers were satisfied or highly satisfied with the quality, relevance and timeliness of the assistance provided. Clients evaluating the centers gave 85% ratings for the training programs provided and 85% ratings for program evaluation. See U.S. Small Business Administration, "FY2012 Congressional Budget Justification and FY2010 Annual Performance Report," p. 73. In FY2011, the Veterans Business Outreach Centers Program conducted its seventh annual "Customer Satisfaction Survey." The FY2011 survey found that 91% of the clients using the centers were satisfied or highly satisfied with the quality, relevance, and timeliness of the assistance provided. See U.S. Small Business Administration, "FY2013 Congressional Budget Justification and FY2011 Annual Performance Report," 2012, p. 62.

[125] For further information and analysis, see CRS Report R41352, Small Business Management and Technical Assistance Training Programs, by Robert Jay Dilger; U.S. Small Business Administration, Office of Entrepreneurial Development, "Impact Study of Entrepreneurial Development Resources: Face to Face Counseling," November 9, 2011, at http://www. sba.gov/sites/default/files/ SBA%20ED%20Resources% 20Impact%20Study%20Nov %20 2011%20Final%20Report.pdf; and P.L. 96-302, the Small Business Development Center Act of 1980.

[126] U.S. Small Business Administration, "Small Loan Advantage," at http://www.sba.gov/ content/small-loan-advantage; and U.S. Small Business Administration, "SBA Announces New Initiatives Aimed at Increasing Lending in Underserved Communities," December 15, 2010, at http://www.sba.gov/content/sba-announces-new-initiatives-aimedincreasing-lending-underserved-communities.

[127] U.S. Congress, House Committee on Small Business, Small Business Financing and Investment Act Of 2009, report to accompany H.R. 3854, 111th Cong., 2nd sess., October 26, 2009, H.Rept. 111-315 (Washington: GPO, 2009), p. 7. The SBA indicated that the Community Express Pilot Program "has had mixed outcomes," providing loans "to new businesses, minority businesses and other underserved sectors" but with "significantly higher default rates (almost 40% of loans defaulted in certain cohorts) compared with other similarly sized 7(a) loans." See U.S. Small Business Administration, "Community Express Pilot Program," 75 Federal Register 80562, December 22, 2010.

[128] U.S. Small Business Administration, "Advantage Loan Initiatives," at http://www.sba. gov/advantage.

[129] U.S. Small Business Administration, "Small Loan Advantage," at http://www.sba.gov /content/small-loan-advantage.

[130] Ibid.

[131] Ibid.

[132] U.S. Small Business Administration, "Advantage Loan Initiatives," at http://www. sba. gov/advantage.

[133] Ibid.

[134] Ibid.

[135] Ibid.

[136] U.S. Small Business Administration, "Community Advantage Participant Guide," p. 18, at http://www.sba.gov/sites/ default/files/files/CA%20-%20Participants%20Guide.pdf; and U.S. Small Business Administration, "Community Advantage Pilot Program," 77 Federal Register 6619, February 8, 2012.

[137] U.S. Small Business Administration, "Community Advantage," at http://www.sba.gov/ content/community-advantage.

[138] U.S. Small Business Administration, "SBA Announces New Initiatives Aimed at Increasing Lending in Underserved Communities," December 15, 2010, at http://www.sba.gov/ content/sba-announces-new-initiatives-aimedincreasing-lending-underserved-communities. The SBA maintains a list of approved Community Advantage pilot program lenders on its website at http://www.sba.gov/content/community-advantage-approved-lenders.

In: Small Business Administration ...
Editor: Alan R. Connoly
ISBN: 978-1-62417-674-6

Chapter 4

SMALL BUSINESS ADMINISTRATION 504/CDC LOAN GUARANTY PROGRAM*

Robert Jay Dilger

SUMMARY

The Small Business Administration (SBA) administers programs to support small businesses, including several loan guaranty programs designed to encourage lenders to provide loans to small businesses "that might not otherwise obtain financing on reasonable terms and conditions."

The SBA's 504 Certified Development Company (504/CDC) loan guaranty program is administered through non-profit Certified Development Companies (CDC). It provides long-term fixed rate financing for major fixed assets, such as land, buildings, equipment, and machinery. Of the total project costs, a third-party lender must provide at least 50% of the financing, the CDC provides up to 40% of the financing through a 100% SBA-guaranteed debenture, and the applicant provides at least 10% of the financing.

It is named from Section 504 of the Small Business Investment Act of 1958 (P.L. 85-699, as amended), which authorized the program. In FY2012, the SBA approved 9,471 504/CDC loans amounting to about $6.7 billion.

Congressional interest in the SBA's 504/CDC program has increased in recent years because of concern that small businesses might be prevented from accessing sufficient capital to assist in the economic recovery. During the 111th Congress, P.L. 111-240, the Small Business Jobs Act of 2010, increased the 504/CDC program's loan guaranty limits from $1.5 million to $5 million for "regular" borrowers, from $2 million to $5 million if the loan proceeds are directed toward one or more specified public policy goals, and from $4 million to $5.5 million for manufacturers. It also temporarily expanded, for two years, the types of projects eligible for 504/CDC program refinancing of existing debt, created an alternative 504/CDC size standard to increase the number of businesses eligible for assistance, and provided $510 million to extend temporary fee subsidies for the 504/CDC and 7(a) loan guaranty programs and a temporary increase in the 7(a) program's maximum loan guaranty percentage to 90%.

* This is an edited, reformatted and augmented version of a Congressional Research Service publication, CRS Report for Congress R41184, prepared for Members and Committees of Congress, from www.crs.gov, dated October 9, 2012.

The temporary fee subsidies and 90% loan guaranty percentage ended on January 3, 2011, and the temporary expansion of the projects eligible for 504/CDC program refinancing of existing debt expired on September 27, 2012.

This report opens with a discussion of the rationale provided for the 504/CDC program, the program's borrower and lender eligibility standards, program requirements, and program statistics, including loan volume, loss rates, use of the proceeds, borrower satisfaction, and borrower demographics.

It then examines congressional action taken during the 111th Congress to help small businesses gain greater access to capital, including the enactment of P.L. 111-5, the American Recovery and Reinvestment Act of 2009 (ARRA), and P.L. 111-240, the Small Business Jobs Act of 2010. It also discusses congressional efforts during the 112th Congress to extend the temporary expansion of the projects eligible for 504/CDC program refinancing of existing debt, which expired on September 27, 2012.

For example, H.R. 2950, the Small Business Administration 504 Loan Refinancing Extension Act of 2011, would extend that expiration date another year and S. 3572, the Restoring Tax and Regulatory Certainty to Small Businesses Act of 2012, would extend that expiration date another year and a half. S. 1828, a bill to increase small business lending, and for other purposes, is also discussed. It would reinstate for a year following the date of its enactment the temporary fee subsidies for the 504/CDC and 7(a) programs and the 90% loan guaranty percentage for the 7(a) program, which ended on January 3, 2011. Issues raised concerning the SBA's administration of the program, including the oversight of 504/CDC lenders, are also discussed.

Small Business Administration Loan Guaranty Programs

The Small Business Administration (SBA) administers programs to support small businesses, including several loan guaranty programs designed to encourage lenders to provide loans to small businesses "that might not otherwise obtain financing on reasonable terms and conditions."[1] The SBA's 504 Certified Development Company (504/CDC) loan guaranty program provides longterm fixed rate financing for major fixed assets, such as land, buildings, equipment, and machinery. It is named from Section 504 of the Small Business Investment Act of 1958 (P.L. 85- 699, as amended), which authorized the program.[2] It is administered through non-profit Certified Development Companies (CDCs). Of the total project costs, a third-party lender must provide at least 50% of the financing, the CDC provides up to 40% of the financing backed by a 100% SBA-guaranteed debenture, and the applicant provides at least 10% of the financing.

The SBA's debenture is backed with the full faith and credit of the United States and is sold to underwriters who form debenture pools. Investors purchase interests in the debenture pools and receive certificates representing ownership of all or part of the pool. The SBA and CDCs use various agents to facilitate the sale and service of the certificates and the orderly flow of funds among the parties.[3] After a 504/CDC loan is approved and disbursed, accounting for the loan is set up at the Central Servicing Agent (CSA, currently Colson Services Corporation), not the SBA. The SBA guarantees the timely payment of the debenture. If the small business is behind in its loan payments, the SBA pays the difference to the investor on every semi-annual due date.[4] In FY2012, the SBA approved 9,471 504/CDC loans amounting to about $6.7 billion.[5]

Historically, one of the justifications presented for funding the SBA's loan guaranty programs has been that small businesses can be at a disadvantage, compared with other businesses, when trying to obtain access to sufficient capital and credit.[6] Congressional interest in small business access to capital, in general, and the 504/CDC program, in particular, has increased in recent years because of concern that small businesses might be prevented from accessing sufficient capital to enable them to assist in the economic recovery. For example, senior loan officers at private lending institutions have indicated in Federal Reserve Board surveys that they have tightened small business lending standards, largely in reaction to relatively high loan default rates and increased numbers of noncurrent (past due) loans.[7]

Congress authorized several changes to the 504/CDC program during the 111th Congress in an effort to increase the number, and amount, of 504/CDC loans. For example, P.L. 111-5, the American Recovery and Reinvestment Act of 2009 (ARRA), provided $375 million to temporarily reduce fees in the SBA's 7(a) and 504/CDC loan guaranty programs and to temporarily increase the 7(a) program's maximum loan guaranty percentage to 90%. Congress subsequently appropriated another $265 million, and authorized the SBA to reprogram another $40 million, to extend those subsidies and loan modification through May 31, 2010. ARRA also authorized the SBA to allow, under specified circumstances, the use of 504/CDC program funds to refinance existing debt for business expansion.[8]

P.L. 111-240, the Small Business Jobs Act of 2010, increased the 504/CDC program's loan guaranty limits from $1.5 million to $5 million for "regular" borrowers, from $2 million to $5 million if the loan proceeds are directed toward one or more specified public policy goals, and from $4 million to $5.5 million for manufacturers. The act also temporarily expanded for two years after the date of enactment (until September 27, 2012) the types of projects eligible for refinancing of existing debt under the 504/CDC program; provided $510 million to continue the 504/CDC program's fee subsidies from its date of enactment through December 31, 2010; and established an alternative size standard that allows more companies to qualify for 504/CDC assistance. P.L. 111-322, the Continuing Appropriations and Surface Transportation Extensions Act, 2011, authorized the SBA to continue the fee subsidies and the 7(a) program's 90% maximum loan guaranty percentage through March 4, 2011, or until funding provided for these purposes in P.L. 111-240 was exhausted (which occurred on January 3, 2011).

This report examines the 504/CDC program's borrower and lender eligibility standards; program requirements; and program statistics, including loan volume, loss rates, use of the proceeds, borrower satisfaction, and borrower demographics. It then examines congressional action taken during the 111th Congress to help small businesses gain greater access to capital, including the enactment of ARRA and P.L. 111-240, the Small Business Jobs Act of 2010. It also discusses H.R. 2950, the Small Business Administration 504 Loan Refinancing Extension Act of 2011; S.Amdt. 1833, the INVEST in America Act of 2012 — an amendment in the nature of a substitute for H.R. 3606, the Jumpstart Our Business Startups Act; and S. 3572, the Restoring Tax and Regulatory Certainty to Small Businesses Act of 2012. They would extend the temporary expansion of the projects eligible for 504/CDC program refinancing of existing debt, which expired on September 27, 2012. S. 1828, a bill to increase small business lending, and for other purposes, is also discussed. It would reinstate for a year following the date of its enactment the temporary fee subsidies for the 504/CDC and 7(a) programs and the 90% loan guaranty percentage for the 7(a) program, which ended on January 3, 2011.

The report also examines issues raised concerning the SBA's administration of the program, including the oversight of 504/CDC lenders.

PROGRAM PARTICIPANTS AND FINANCING CONTRIBUTION

As shown in *Table 1,* 504/CDC projects generally have three main participants: a third-party lender provides 50% or more of the financing; a CDC provides up to 40% of the financing through a 504/CDC debenture, which is guaranteed 100% by the SBA; and the borrower contributes at least 10% of the financing. No more than 50% of eligible costs can be from federal sources.

Table 1. 504/CDC Loan Structures and Contribution Requirements

Participant	Standard Loan	New Business or Limited or Special Purpose Property Loan	Both New Business and Limited or Special Purpose Property Loan
Third Party Lender	at least 50%	at least 50%	at least 50%
CDC/SBA	maximum 40%	maximum 35%	maximum 30%
Borrower	at least 10%	at least 15%	at least 20%

Source: U.S. Small Business Administration, "U.S. Small Business Administration, "SOP 50 10 5(E): Lender and Development Company Loan Programs," (effective June 1, 2012), p. 266, at http://www.sba.gov/sites/default/files/SOP% 2050%2010%205(E)%20(5-16-2012)%20clean.pdf.

The CDC's contribution, and the amount of the SBA's 100% guaranteed debenture, cannot exceed 40% of the financing for standard 504/CDC loans and 35% of the financing for new businesses (defined as "a business that is two years old or less at the time the loan is approved") or if the loan is for a limited-market property (defined as "a property with a unique physical design, special construction materials, or a layout that restricts its utility to the use for which it is designed") or for a special purpose property. The SBA lists 27 limited or special purpose properties (e.g., dormitories, golf courses, hospitals, and bowling alleys).[9] The CDC's contribution cannot exceed 30% of the financing when the borrower is both a new businesses and the loan is for either a limited-market property or a special purpose property.

Borrowers must contribute at least 10% of the financing for standard 504/CDC loans and at least 15% of the financing if they are a new business or if the loan is for a limited-market property or for a special purpose property. They must contribute at least 20% of the financing if they are both a new businesses and the loan is for either a limited-market property or a special purpose property.

Borrower Eligibility Standards and Program Requirements

Borrower Eligibility Standards

To be eligible for an SBA business loan, a small business applicant must

- be located in the United States;
- be a for-profit operating business (except for loans to eligible passive companies);
- qualify as small;[10]
- demonstrate a need for the desired credit and that the funds are not available from alternative sources, including personal resources of the principals; and
- be certified by a lender that the desired credit is unavailable to the applicant on reasonable terms and conditions from non-federal sources without SBA assistance.[11]

Several types of businesses are prohibited from participating in the program. For example, financial businesses primarily engaged in the business of lending, such as banks and finance companies; life insurance companies; businesses located in a foreign country; businesses deriving more than one-third of gross annual revenue from legal gambling activities; businesses that present live performances of a prurient sexual nature; and businesses with an associate who is incarcerated, on probation, on parole, or has been indicted for a felony or a crime of moral turpitude are ineligible.[12]

To qualify for a SBA business loan, applicants must be creditworthy and able to reasonably assure repayment. The SBA requires lenders to consider the applicant's

- character, reputation, and credit history;
- experience and depth of management;
- strength of the business;
- past earnings, projected cash flow, and future prospects;
- ability to repay the loan with earnings from the business;
- sufficient invested equity to operate on a sound financial basis;
- potential for long-term success;
- nature and value of collateral (although inadequate collateral will not be the sole reason for denial of a loan request); and
- affiliates' effect on the applicant's repayment ability.[13]

Borrower Program Requirements

Use of Proceeds

A 504/CDC loan can be used to

- purchase land and make necessary improvements to the land, such as adding streets, curbs, gutters, parking lots, utilities, and landscaping;

- finance short-term debt ("bridge financing") on the land as long as there is no building currently on the land and the financing term is three years or less;
- purchase buildings and make improvements to the buildings, such as altering the building's facade and updating its heating and electrical systems, plumbing, and roofing;
- purchase, transport, dismantle, or install machinery and equipment, provided the machinery and equipment have a useful life of at least 10 years;
- purchase essential furniture and fixtures;
- pay professional fees that are directly attributable and essential to the project, such as title insurance, title searches and abstract costs, surveys and zoning matters;
- pay interim financing costs, including points, fees, and interest;
- create a contingency fund, provided that the fund does not exceed 10% of the project's construction costs; and
- finance permissible debt refinancing related to business expansion.[14] A 504/CDC loan cannot be used for working capital or inventory.

Job Creation and Retention Requirement

All 504/CDC borrowers must meet one of two specified economic development objectives.

First, borrowers, other than small manufacturers, must create or retain at least one job for every $65,000 of project debenture. Borrowers who are small manufacturers (defined as a small business with its primary North American Industry Classification System Code in Sectors 31, 32, and 33, and all of its production facilities are located in the United States) must create or retain one job per $100,000 of project debenture.

The jobs created do not have to be at the project facility, but 75% of the jobs must be created in the community where the project is located. Using job retention to satisfy this requirement is allowed only if the CDC "can reasonably show that jobs would be lost to the community if the project was not done."[15]

Second, if the borrower does not meet the job creation or retention requirement, the borrower can retain eligibility by meeting any one of five community development goals or ten public policy goals, provided the CDC meets its required job opportunity average of at least one job opportunity created or retained for every $65,000 in project debenture, or for every $75,000 in project debenture for projects located in special geographic areas (Alaska, Hawaii, state-designated enterprise zones, empowerment zones, enterprise communities, and labor surplus areas). Loans to small manufacturers are excluded from the calculation of this average.[16]

The five community development goals are

- improving, diversifying or stabilizing the economy of the locality;
- stimulating other business development;
- bringing new income into the community;
- assisting manufacturing firms; or
- assisting businesses in labor surplus areas as defined by the U.S. Department of Labor.

The ten public policy goals are

- revitalizing a business district of a community with a written revitalization or redevelopment plan;
- expansion of exports;
- expansion of small businesses owned and controlled by women;
- expansion of small businesses owned and controlled by veterans (especially service-disabled veterans);
- expansion of minority enterprise development;
- aiding rural development;
- increasing productivity and competitiveness (e.g., retooling, robotics, modernization, and competition with imports);
- modernizing or upgrading facilities to meet health, safety, and environmental requirements;
- assisting businesses in or moving to areas affected by federal budget reductions, including base closings, either because of the loss of federal contracts or the reduction in revenues in the area due to a decreased federal presence; or
- reducing unemployment rates in labor surplus areas, as determined by defined by the U.S. Department of Labor.[17]

Loan Amounts

The minimum 504/CDC debenture is $25,000. P.L. 111-240 increased the maximum gross debenture amount

- from $1.5 million for regular 504/CDC loans to $5 million,
- from $2 million if the loan proceeds are directed toward one or more of the public policy goals described above to $5 million,
- from $4 million for small manufacturers to $5.5 million,
- from $4 million for projects that reduce the borrower's energy consumption by at least 10% to $5.5 million, and
- from $4 million for projects for plant, equipment, and process upgrades of renewable energy sources, such as the small-scale production of energy for individual buildings or communities consumption (commonly known as micropower), or renewable fuel producers, including biodiesel and ethanol producers to $5.5 million.[18]

Loan Terms, Interest Rate, and Collateral

Loan Terms

The SBA determines the 504/CDC program's loan terms and publishes those terms in the *Federal Register*.[19] The current maturities for 504/CDC loans are

- 20 years for real estate,
- 10 years for machinery and equipment, and

- 10 or 20 years based upon a weighted average of the useful life of the assets being financed.[20]

The maturities for the first mortgage issued by the third-party lender must be at least seven years when the CDC/504 loan is for a term of 10 years, and 10 years when the loan is for 20 years.[21]

Interest Rate

The interest rate for 504/CDC debentures is set by the SBA and approved by the Secretary of the Treasury.[22] It is based on market conditions for long-term government debt at the time of sale, and pegged to an increment above the current market rate for 5-year and 10-year U.S. Treasury issues. The rate for October 2012 is 4.28%.[23] In addition, the SBA sets the maximum interest rate that can be charged by any third party lender for a commercial loan which funds any portion of the cost of a 504/CDC project. That rate "must be reasonable" and published in the *Federal Register*. The current maximum interest rate that a third-party lender is allowed to charge for a commercial loan that funds any portion of the cost of a 504/CDC project is 6% over the New York prime rate or the maximum interest rate permitted in that state, whichever is less.[24]

Collateral

The SBA usually takes a second lien position on the project property to secure the loan. The SBA's second lien position is considered adequate when the applicant meets all of the following criteria:

- strong, consistent cash flow that is sufficient to cover the debt;
- demonstrated, proven management;
- the applicant's business has been in operation for more than two years; and
- the proposed project is a logical extension of the applicant's current operations.[25]

If one or more of the above factors is not met, additional collateral or increased equity contributions may be required. All collateral must be insured against such hazards and risks as the SBA may require, with provisions for notice to the SBA and the CDC in the event of impending lapse of coverage.[26] However, for 504/CDC loans, the applicant's cash flow is the primary source of repayment, not the liquidation of collateral. Thus, "if the lender's financial analysis demonstrates that the applicant lacks reasonable assurance of repayment in a timely manner from the cash flow of the business, the loan request must be declined, regardless of the collateral available."[27]

LENDER ELIGIBILITY STANDARDS, OPERATING REQUIREMENTS, AND PROGRAM REQUIREMENTS

Lender Eligibility Standards

CDCs apply to the SBA for certification to participate in the 504/CDC program. A CDC must be a non-profit corporation and

- be in good standing in the state in which it is incorporated;
- be in compliance with all laws, including taxation requirements, in the state in which it is incorporated and any other state in which it conducts business;
- have satisfactory performance as determined by the SBA in its discretion. Examples of the factors that may be considered in determining satisfactory performance include the CDC's risk rating, on-site review and examination assessments, historical performance measures (like default rate, purchase rate and loss rate), loan volume to the extent that it impacts performance measures, and other performance related measurements and information (such as contribution toward SBA's mission); and
- provide the SBA a copy of its IRS tax exempt status.[28]

In addition, when applying for certification a CDC must

- indicate its area of operations, which is the state of the CDC's incorporation;[29]
- report its membership, which must include at least 25 members who actively support economic development in their area of operations and represent (1) government organizations, (2) financial institutions (lenders), (3) community organizations, such as chambers of commerce, trade associations, colleges, or small business development centers, and (4) businesses in the area of operations;
- meet other specified membership requirements, such as meeting at least annually, requiring a quorum to transact business, and prohibiting any person or entity from owning or controlling more than 10% of the CDC's voting membership; and
- have a board of directors which meet specified requirements, such as being chosen from the membership by the members and representing at least three of the four membership groups.[30]

If approved by the SBA, newly certified CDCs are on probation for two years. At the end of this time, the CDC must petition for either permanent CDC status or a single, one-year extension of probation. There are about 260 CDCs actively participating in the program.[31]

Lender Operating Requirements

The CDC's board of directors is allowed to establish a loan committee composed of members of the CDC who may or may not be on its board of directors. The loan committee reports to the board, and must meet specified requirements, such as having at least one member with commercial lending experience acceptable to the SBA, having all of its members live or work in the area of operations of the state where the 504/CDC project they are voting on is located, allowing CDC staff to serve on the committee, and requiring a quorum of at least five committee members authorized to vote in order to hold a meeting.[32] In addition, multi-state CDCs are required to have a separate loan committee "for each state into which the CDC expands."[33]

The SBA also has a number of requirements concerning CDC staff, such as requiring CDCs to "have qualified full-time professional staff to market, package, process, close and service loans" and "directly employ full-time professional management," typically including an executive director (or the equivalent) to manage daily operations.[34]

CDCs are also required to operate "in accordance with all SBA loan program requirements" and provide the SBA "current and accurate information about all certification and operational requirements."[35] CDCs with 504/CDC loan portfolio balances of $20 million or more are required to submit financial statements audited in accordance with Generally Accepted Accounting Principles (GAAP) by an independent Certified Public Accountant (CPA). CDCs with 504/CDC loan portfolio balances of less than $20 million must, at a minimum, submit a review of their loan portfolio balances by an independent CPA or independent accountant in accordance with GAAP. The auditor's opinion must state that the financial statements are in conformity with GAAP.[36]

Lender Program Requirements

The Application Process

CDCs must analyze each application in a commercially reasonable manner, consistent with prudent lending standards. The CDC's analysis must include

- a financial analysis of the applicant's pro forma balance sheet. The pro forma balance sheet must reflect the loan proceeds, use of the loan proceeds, and any other adjustments such as required equity injection or stand-by debt;
- a financial analysis of repayment ability based on historical income statements, tax returns (if an existing business) and projections, including the reasonableness of the supporting assumptions;
- a ratio analysis of the financial statements including comments on any trends and a comparison with industry averages;
- a discussion of the owners' and managers' relevant experience in the type of business, as well as their personal credit histories;
- an analysis of collateral adequacy, including an evaluation of the collateral and lien position offered as well as the liquidation value;
- a discussion of the applicant's credit experience, including a review of business credit reports and any experience the CDC may have with the applicant; and
- other relevant information (e.g., if the application involves a franchise and the success of the franchise).[37]

Lenders submit this information, using required SBA forms, to the Sacramento, CA, Loan Processing Center. The SBA's goal is to process all 504/CDC regular loans within six business days and all loans submitted by members of the Accredited Lender Program (ALP) within three business days.[38]

Accredited Lender Program Status

In 1991, the SBA established the Accredited Lenders Program (ALP) on a pilot basis to provide CDCs "which have developed a good partnership with their SBA field office in promoting local economic development and have demonstrated a good track record in the submission of documentation needed for making and servicing of sound loans" an expedited process for approving loan applications and servicing actions.[39] P.L. 103-403, the Small Business Administration Reauthorization and Amendments Act of 1994, authorized the SBA to establish the ALP on a permanent basis.

CDCs may apply to the SBA for ALP status. Selection is based on several factors, including the CDC's experience as a CDC, the number of 504/CDC loans approved, the size of their portfolio, their record of compliance with SBA loan program requirements, and their record of cooperation with all SBA offices.[40] The SBA is able to process loan requests from ALP-CDCs more quickly than from regular CDCs because it relies on their credit analysis when making the decision to guarantee the debenture. About one-third of CDCs have ALP status and ALP CDCs approve about two-thirds of total 504/CDC loan amounts each year.[41]

Premier Certified Lenders Program Status

P.L. 103-403, the Small Business Administration Reauthorization and Amendments Act of 1994, authorized the SBA's Premier Certified Lenders Program (PCLP) on a pilot basis through October 1, 1997. The program's authorization was later extended through October 1, 2002, and given permanent statutory authorization by P.L. 106-554, the Consolidated Appropriations Act, 2001 (§1: H.R. 5667, the Small Business Reauthorization Act of 2000).[42]

ALP-CDCs must apply to the SBA for PCLP status. CDCs provided PCLP status have increased authority to process, close, service and liquidate 504/CDC loans. The loans are subject to the same terms and conditions as other 504/CDC loans, but the SBA delegates to the PCLP-CDC all loan approval decisions, except eligibility. Selection is based on several factors, including all of the factors used to assess ALP status plus evidence that the CDC is "in compliance with its Loan Loss Reserve Fund (LLRF) requirements [described below], has established a PCLP processing goal of 50%, and has a demonstrated ability to process, close, service and liquidate 504 and/or PCLP loans."[43]

PCLP-CDCs are required to establish and maintain a LLRF for its financings under the program. The LLRF is used to reimburse the SBA for 10% of any loss sustained by the SBA resulting from a default in the payment of principal or interest on a PCLP debenture. Each LLRF must equal 1% of the original principal amount of each PCLP debenture.[44]

About one out of every 14 CDCs have PCLP status.[45] In recent years, the number and amount of 504/CDC loans made through the PCLP program has declined. In FY2009, PCLP CDCs approved 441 504/CDC loans amounting to $238.0 million. Those figures declined to 129 504/CDC loans amounting to $69.8 million in FY2010, 37 504/CDC loans amounting to $16.1 million in FY2011, and 23 504/CDC loans amounting to $8.6 million in FY2012.[46]

Real Estate Appraisals

As part of its analysis of each application, CDCs are required to have an independent appraisal conducted of the real estate if the estimated value of the project property is greater than $250,000, or $250,000 or less "if such appraisal is necessary for appropriate evaluation of creditworthiness."[47] The appraiser must have no appearance of a conflict of interest and be either state-licensed or state-certified. When the project property's estimated value is over $1 million, the appraiser must be state-certified.[48]

Closing

The CDC closes the loan in time to meet a specific debenture funding date. At the time of closing, the project must be complete (except funds put into a construction escrow account to complete a minor portion of the project). The SBA's district counsel reviews the closing package and notifies the CSA (currently Colson Services Corporation) and the CDC via e-mail if the loan is approved for debenture funding. If the loan is approved, the CDC forwards specified documents needed for the debenture funding directly to the CSA using a transmittal letter or spreadsheet. Because the 504/CDC program provides permanent or "take-out" financing, an interim lender (either the third party lender or another lender) typically provides financing to cover the period between SBA approval of the project and the debenture sale. Proceeds from the debenture sale are used to repay the interim lender for the amount of the project costs that it advanced on an interim basis.[49]

Loan Guaranty and Servicing Fees

Borrowers are currently charged fees amounting to about 3.5% of the net debenture proceeds plus annual servicing and guaranty fees of about 1.5% of the unpaid debenture balance. Some of these fees are charged by the SBA to the CDC and others are charged by the CDC directly to the borrower.

SBA Fees

The SBA is authorized to charge CDCs five fees: a guaranty fee, servicing fee, funding fee, development company fee, and participation fee.

Guaranty Fee

The SBA is authorized to charge CDCs a one time, up-front guaranty fee of 0.5% of the debenture.[50] The SBA elected not to charge this fee in FY2009, FY2010, and FY2011. The SBA is charging this fee in FY2012.[51]

Servicing Fee

The SBA is authorized to charge CDCs an ongoing, annual servicing fee that is adjusted annually based on the date the loan was approved. By statute, the fee is the lesser of the amount necessary to cover the estimated cost of purchasing and guaranteeing debentures under the 504/CDC program or 0.9375% of the unpaid principal balance of the loan.[52] The SBA's annual servicing fee for FY2012 is the maximum fee permitted under law – 0.9375% of the unpaid principal balance.[53]

Funding Fee

The SBA charges CDCs a funding fee, not to exceed 0.25% of the debenture, to cover costs incurred by the trustee, fiscal agent, and transfer agent.[54]

Development Company Fee

For SBA loans approved after September 30, 1996, the SBA charges CDCs an annual development company fee of 0.125% of the debenture's outstanding principal balance. The fee must be paid from the servicing fees collected by the CDC and cannot be paid from any additional fees imposed on the borrower.[55]

Participation Fee

The SBA charges third-party lenders a one time participation fee of 0.5% of the senior mortgage loan if in a senior lien position to the SBA and the loan was approved after September 30, 1996.[56] The fee may be paid by the third party lender, CDC, or borrower.

CDC Fees

CDCs are allowed to charge borrowers a processing (or packaging) fee, closing fee, servicing fee, late fee, assumption fee, Central Servicing Agent (CSA) fee, other agent fees, and an underwriters' fee.

Processing (or Packaging) Fee

The CDC is allowed to charge borrowers a processing (or packaging) fee of up to 1.5% of the net debenture proceeds. Two-thirds of this fee is considered earned and may be collected by the CDC when the SBA issues an "Authorization for the Debenture." The portion of the processing fee paid by the borrower may be reimbursed from the debenture proceeds.[57]

Closing Fee

The CDC is also allowed to charge "a reasonable closing fee sufficient to reimburse it for the expenses of its in-house or outside legal counsel, and other miscellaneous closing costs."[58] Up to $2,500 in closing costs may be financed out of the debenture proceeds.[59]

Servicing Fee

CDCs can also charge a monthly servicing fee of at least 0.625% per annum and no more than 2% per annum on the unpaid balance of the loan as determined at five-year anniversary intervals. A servicing fee greater than 1.5% for rural areas and 1% elsewhere requires the SBA's prior written approval, based on evidence of substantial need. The servicing fee may be paid only from loan payments received. The fees may be accrued without interest and collected from the CSA when the payments are made. CSAs are entities that receive and disburse funds among the various parties involved in 504/CDC financing under a master servicing agent agreement with the SBA.[60]

Late Fee and Assumption Fee

Loan payments received after the 15th of each month may be subject to a late payment fee of 5% of the late payment or $100, whichever is greater. Late fees will be collected by the CSA on behalf of the CDC. Also, with the SBA's written approval, CDCs may charge an assumption fee not to exceed 1% of the outstanding principal balance of the loan being assumed.[61]

Central Servicing Agent Fee

CSAs are allowed to charge an initiation fee on each loan and an ongoing monthly servicing fee of 0.1% under the terms of the master servicing agreement (with the CSA receiving three sixty-fourths of the servicing fee and the remainder going to the SBA). Also, "agent fees and charges necessary to market and service debentures and certificates may be assessed to the borrower or the investor."[62] CDCs must review the agent's services and related fees "to determine if the fees are necessary and reasonable when there is an indication from a third party that an agent's fees might be excessive, or when an applicant complains about the fees charged by an agent."[63] In cases where fees appear to be unreasonable, CDCs "should contact" the SBA which, after conducting an investigation, can "reduce the fee to an amount SBA deems reasonable, refund any sum in excess of that amount to the applicant, and refrain from charging or collecting from the applicant any funds in excess of the amount SBA deems reasonable."[64]

Underwriters' Fee

Borrowers are also charged an up front underwriters' fee of 0.4% for 20-year loans and 0.375% for 10-year loans. The underwriters' fee is paid by the borrower to the underwriter.[65] As mentioned previously, underwriters are approved by the SBA to form debenture pools and arrange for the sale of certificates.

Fee Subsidies

As mentioned previously, the SBA was provided more than $1.1 billion in additional funding in 2009 and 2010 to subsidize the 504/CDC program's third party participation fee and CDC processing fee, subsidize the SBA's 7(a) program's guaranty fee, and increase the 7(a) program's maximum loan guaranty percentage from up to 85% of loans of $150,000 or less and up to 75% of loans exceeding $150,000 to 90% for all standard 7(a) loans.[66] The last extension, P.L. 111-322, the Continuing Appropriations and Surface Transportation Extensions Act, 2011, authorized the SBA to continue the fee subsidies and the 7(a) program's 90% maximum loan guaranty percentage through March 4, 2011, or until funding provided by the Small Business Jobs Act of 2010 for this purpose was exhausted (which occurred on January 3, 2011).[67]

The Obama Administration argued that additional funding for the SBA's loan guaranty programs, including the 504/CDC program's fee subsidies, improved the small business lending environment, increased both the number and amount of SBA guaranteed loans, and supported "the retention and creation of hundreds of thousands of jobs."[68] Critics argued that small business tax reduction, reform of financial credit market regulation, and federal fiscal restraint are a better means to assist small business economic growth and job creation.[69]

PROGRAM STATISTICS

Loan Volume

The SBA generally uses the number and amount of loans approved each fiscal year, as opposed to the number and amount of loans disbursed, for making comparisons of lending volume among its loan guaranty programs. Although loan disbursement data can be useful, loan disbursements in one fiscal year typically include significant amounts approved in previous fiscal years.

For example, in FY2011, 67.0% of 504/CDC loan disbursements were from loans approved prior to FY2011.[70]

As shown in *Table 2,* the number and amount of 504/CDC loans approved by the SBA declined in FY2008 and FY2009. The most likely causes for the decline were decreased small business demand for capital during the recession; difficulties in secondary credit markets, especially from October 2008 to February 2009; and a tightening of small business credit lending standards. The number and amount of 504/CDC loans increased during FY2010 and FY2011, and reached pre-recession levels in FY2012.

The SBA attributed the increased number and amount of 504/CDC loans approved in FY2010 and FY2011 to the continuation of 504/CDC fee subsidies, which were in place through most of FY2010 and the first quarter of FY2011.[71]

Table 2. 504/CDC Loans and Amounts Approved, FY2006 - FY2012 ($ amounts in billions)

Fiscal Year	Number of Loans Approved	Amount of the Debentures Approved
2006	9,943	$5.7
2007	10,669	$6.3
2008	8,883	$5.3
2009	6,608	$3.8
2010	7,833	$4.4
2011	7,983	$4.8
2012	9,471	$6.7

Source: U.S. Small Business Administration, "SBA Lending Report for Major Programs, Fiscal Year 2010," October 4, 2010, at http://archive.sba.gov/idc/ groups/public/documents/sba_homepage/ serv_fa_lending_major_progs.pdf; and U.S. Small Business Administration, "SBA Lending Statistics for Major Programs (as of 9/30/2012)," at http://www.sba.gov/about-sba-info/317721.

Note: Based on previous experience, the number of loans approved is typically about 4% to 5% higher than the actual number of loans issued (e.g., some borrowers decide not to accept the loan or there is a change in ownership).

Loss Rate and Appropriations for Subsidy Costs

Since the program's inception in FY1958 through FY2008, the SBA experienced a 2.36% loss rate (ratio of actual losses to disbursements) on its 504/CDC business loans. The loss rate for 504/CDC guaranteed loans from FY1958 through FY2008 was 1.9%, and 26.9% for direct loans (last issued in FY1988).[72] In recent years, the loss rate for 504/CDC guaranteed loans has increased. In FY2010, the loss rate was 4.2%. In FY2011, the loss rate was 6.0%.[73]

One of the SBA's goals is to achieve a zero subsidy rate for its loan guaranty programs. A zero subsidy rate means that the SBA's loan guaranty programs do not require annual appropriations of budget authority for the issuance of new loan guarantees. From 2005 to 2009, the SBA did not request appropriations to subsidize the cost of any of its loan guaranty programs, including the 504/CDC program. However, in recent years, loan guaranty fees and loan liquidation recoveries, especially in the 7(a) loan guaranty program, have not generated enough revenue to cover loan losses, resulting in the need for additional appropriations to account for the shortfall. In FY2010 and FY2011, the SBA was provided $80.0 million to subsidize the cost of SBA guaranteed loans. In FY2012, the SBA was provided $207.1 million for that purpose, and P.L. 112-175, the Continuing Appropriations Resolution, 2013 (which provides appropriations through March 27, 2013), provided a projected $333.6 billion for the cost of SBA loan guaranty program subsidies for FY2013. The SBA reports that most of the agency's loan losses have occurred in the SBA's 7(a) loan guaranty program. For example, there were no subsidy costs for the 504/CDC program in FY2011. However, the SBA anticipates subsidy costs of about $67.7 million for the 504/CDC program in FY2012, and $113.0 million in FY2013.[74]

Use of Proceeds and Borrower Satisfaction

In 2008, the Urban Institute released the results of a SBA-commissioned study of the SBA's loan guaranty programs. As part of its analysis, the Urban Institute surveyed a random sample of SBA loan guaranty borrowers. The survey indicated that borrowers used 504/CDC loan proceeds to

- build a new building (36%),
- purchase a new building (33%),
- purchase new land (16%),
- purchase or install new equipment (15%),
- acquire original business (8%),
- expand or renovate current building (7%),
- other (7%),
- improve land (6%),
- finance working capital (4%),
- refinance existing debt (3%), or
- hire additional staff (2%).[75]

The Urban Institute also reported that two-thirds the 504/CDC borrowers responding to their survey rated their overall satisfaction with their loan and loan terms as either excellent (21%) or good (45%). About one out of every four borrowers (23%) rated their overall satisfaction with their loan and loan terms as fair, 8% rated their overall satisfaction as poor, and 4% reported that they don't know or did not respond.[76]

In addition, 87% of the survey's respondents reported that the 504/CDC loan was either very important (53%) or somewhat important (34%) to their business success (4% reported somewhat unimportant, 4% reported very unimportant, and 6% reported that they don't know or did not respond).[77]

Borrower Demographics

The Urban Institute found that about 9.9% of private sector small business loans are issued to minority-owned small businesses and about 16% of those loans are issued to women-owned businesses.[78] In FY2012, 19.4% of 504/CDC loan recipients were minority-owned businesses (11.9% Asian, 5.9% Hispanic, 1.4% African American, and 0.2% Native American) and 14.3% were women-owned businesses.[79] Based on its comparative analysis of private sector small business loans and the SBA's loan guaranty programs, the Urban Institute concluded

> Overall, loans under the 7(a) and 504 programs were more likely to be made to minority-owned, women-owned, and start-up businesses (firms that have historically faced capital gaps) as compared to conventional small business loans. Moreover, the average amounts for loans made under the 7(a) and 504 programs to these types of firms were substantially greater than conventional small business loans to such firms. These findings suggest that the 7(a) and 504 programs are being used by lenders in a manner that is consistent with SBA's objective of making credit available to firms that face a capital opportunity gap.[80]

CONGRESSIONAL ISSUES

Fee Subsidies and the 7(a) Program's 90% Maximum Loan Guaranty Percentage

Congress included provisions in ARRA to encourage both lenders and small businesses to use the SBA's loan guaranty programs. For example, ARRA provided an additional $730 million for SBA programs. As mentioned previously, included in that amount was $375 million to subsidize the 504/CDC program's third party participation fee and CDC processing fee, subsidize the SBA's 7(a) program's guaranty fee, and increase the 7(a) program's maximum loan guaranty percentage from up to 85% of loans of $150,000 or less and up to 75% of loans exceeding $150,000 to 90% for all standard 7(a) loans.[81]

ARRA's funding for the fee subsidies and 7(a) program's 90% loan guaranty percentage was exhausted on November 23, 2009. Congress subsequently approved an additional $305 million to extend the fee reductions and the 90% loan guaranty percentage through May 31, 2010.[82] P.L. 111-240, the Small Business Jobs Act of 2010, provided $505 million (plus an additional $5 million for related administrative expenses) to continue the fee subsidies and the 7(a) program's 90% loan guaranty percentage through December 31, 2010. P.L. 111-322, the Continuing Appropriations and Surface Transportation Extensions Act, 2011, authorized the SBA to continue the fee subsidies and the 90% loan guaranty percentage through March 4,

2011, or until the funding provided by the Small Business Jobs Act of 2010 for these purposes was exhausted (which occurred on January 3, 2011).[83]

The Obama Administration argued that additional funding for the SBA's loan guaranty programs, including the 504/CDC program, improved the small business lending environment, increased both the number and amount of SBA guaranteed loans, and supported "the retention and creation of hundreds of thousands of jobs."[84] Critics argued that small business tax reduction, reform of financial credit market regulation, and federal fiscal restraint are a better means to assist small business economic growth and job creation.[85]

Program Administration

The SBA's Office of Inspector General (OIG) and the U.S. Government Accountability Office (GAO) have independently reviewed the administration of SBA's loan guaranty programs. Both agencies have reported deficiencies which they argued needed to be addressed, including issues involving the oversight of 504/CDC lenders.

On March 23, 2010, the SBA's OIG released the results of an audit of "25 of 100 statistically selected CDC/504 loans approved under Premier Certified Lender (PCL) authority that were disbursed during fiscal year (FY) 2008."[86] The loans "had been approved by 3 of the most active of the 24 PCLs" operating in 2008.[87]

The audit was initiated "based on concerns that PCLs were engaging in risky underwriting practices and that five PCLs were paying their executives excessive compensation."[88]

The OIG determined that

> PCLs may not have used prudent practices in approving and disbursing 68% of the sampled loans, totaling nearly $8.9 million, due to poor loan underwriting, and eligibility or loan closing issues. Specifically, 40% of the loans had faulty underwriting repayment analyses, and 52% of the loans had eligibility and/or loan closing issues.... Projecting our sample results to the universe of CDC/504 loans disbursed in 2008 by these three PCLs, we estimate with 90% confidence that at least 572 loans, totaling nearly $254.9 million in CDC/504 loan proceeds, had weaknesses in the underwriting process, eligibility determinations or loan closing. Of this amount, we estimate that a minimum of 183 loans, totaling $56.4 million or more, were made to borrowers based on faulty repayment analyses. We also estimate that lenders disbursed $209 million or more to borrowers who had eligibility and/or loan closing issues.[89]

In terms of dollars paid for CDC executive compensation, the OIG found that

> 4 of the 5 CDCs reviewed were among the top 10 highest for executive compensation.... In terms of percentage of gross receipts spent on executive compensation, 3 of the 5 questioned CDCs ranked among the top 10 highest of the 56 CDCs that had gross receipts over $1 million.[90]

The OIG made several recommendations to address these issues, including changing the SBA's Standard Operating Procedures (SOP) to require lenders to use

> (1) the actual cash flow method to determine borrower repayment ability for businesses using accrual accounting, (2) historical salary levels to estimate salaries of the borrower's officers, and (3) historical sales data to make sales projections.[91]

It also recommended that the SBA develop a process "to ensure that corrective actions are taken in response to the Agency's onsite reviews to ensure these conditions do not continue, and/or guidance for these reviews should be modified, as appropriate, to ensure that reviewers properly assess lender determinateon of borrower repayment ability and eligibility."[92]

The OIG reported that the SBA

> disagreed that SOP 50 10 should be revised to strengthen lender repayment analyses by requiring the use of the actual cash flow method and historical salary and sales data. The Agency also did not believe an additional process was needed to ensure that corrective actions are taken to improve lender performance, but acknowledged that better use of onsite review results are needed to make more informed lender decisions and programmatic determinations.[93]

In 2009, GAO released an analysis of the SBA's oversight of the lending and risk management activities of lenders that extend 7(a) and 504/CDC loans to small businesses. GAO recommended that the SBA strengthen its oversight of these lenders. GAO argued that although the SBA's "lender risk rating system has enabled the agency to conduct some off-site monitoring of lenders, the agency does not use the system to target lenders for on-site reviews or to inform the scope of the reviews."[94] It also noted that

> the SBA targets for review those lenders with the largest SBA-guaranteed loan portfolios. As a result of this approach, 97% of the lenders that SBA's risk rating system identified as high risk in 2008 were not reviewed. Further, GAO found that the scope of the on-site reviews that SBA performs is not informed by the lenders' risk ratings, and the reviews do not include an assessment of lenders' credit decisions.[95]

GAO argued that although the SBA "has made improvements to its off-site monitoring of lenders, the agency will not be able to substantially improve its lender oversight efforts unless it improves its on-site review process."[96]

As mentioned previously, in recent years, both the number and amount of 504/CDC loans made through the PCL program has declined. In FY2009, PCLP CDCs approved 441 504/CDC loans amounting to $238.0 million. Those figures declined to 129 504/CDC loans amounting to $69.8 million in FY2010, 37 504/CDC loans amounting to $16.1 million in FY2011, and 23 504/CDC loans amounting to $8.6 million in FY2012.[97]

Legislative Activity During the 111th Congress

Congress authorized several changes to the 504/CDC program during the 111th Congress in an effort to increase the number, and amount, of 504/CDC loans, including provisions contained in ARRA and the Small Business Jobs Act of 2010. Congress has not approved any changes to the program during the 112th Congress.

The Obama Administration's Proposals

The Obama Administration supported congressional efforts to temporarily subsidize fees for the 7(a) and 504/CDC loan guaranty programs and to increase the 7(a) program's loan guaranty percentage from up to 85% of loans of $150,000 or less and up to 75% of loans exceeding $150,000 to 90%. As mentioned previously, the latest extension of the fee subsidies and 7(a) program's 90% maximum loan guaranty percentage was authorized by the Continuing Appropriations and Surface Transportation Extensions Act, 2011. The act authorized the SBA to continue the fee subsidies and the 7(a) program's 90% maximum loan guaranty percentage through March 4, 2011, or until the funding provided by the Small Business Jobs Act of 2010 for these purposes was exhausted (which occurred on January 3, 2011).[98]

In an effort to make the SBA's loan guaranty programs more attractive to small businesses, the Obama Administration also proposed the following modifications to several SBA programs, including the 504/CDC program:

- increase the maximum loan size for the 504/CDC program from $2 million to $5 million for regular projects and from $4 million to $5.5 million for manufacturing projects;
- temporarily allow in FY2010 and FY2011, with an option to extend into FY2012, the refinancing of owner-occupied commercial real estate loans within one year of maturity under the 504/CDC program;
- increase the maximum loan size for standard 7(a) loans from $2 million to $5 million;
- increase the maximum loan size for microloans to small business concerns from $35,000 to $50,000;
- increase the maximum loan limits for lenders in their first year of participation in the Microloan program, from $750,000 to $1 million, and from $3.5 million to $5 million in the subsequent years; and
- temporarily increase the cap on SBAExpress loans from $350,000 to $1 million.[99]

H.R. 3854, the Small Business Financing and Investment Act of 2009

H.R. 3854 would have authorized several new SBA programs and change several existing SBA programs, including the 504/CDC program, in an effort to enhance job creation by increasing the availability of credit to small businesses. The bill was passed by the House, 389-32, on October 29, 2009. The Senate did not take action on the bill.[100]

It would have

- increased the maximum loan size for 504/CDC loans from $1.5 million to $3 million for regular projects, from $2 million to $4 million for projects located in a low-income community, from $4 million to $8 million for manufacturers, and for up to $10 million for projects that constitute "a major source of employment" as determined by the Administration;
- extended ARRA's fee reductions and loan modifications through September 30, 2011;
- increased the maximum loan size for 7(a) loans from $2 million to $3 million;
- extended, with modifications, ARRA's America's Recovery Capital Loan Program (ARC), which temporarily provided small businesses loan assistance for debt relief, through the end of FY2011;[101] and
- provided a 100% loan guaranty for small business concerns owned and controlled by veterans, and expanded and made permanent the SBA's secondary market lending authority.[102]

The bill would have also created a temporary SBA direct lending program following enactment that would have been available to creditworthy small business borrowers that were unable to find credit elsewhere.[103]

S. 2869, the Small Business Job Creation and Access to Capital Act of 2009

S. 2869 was ordered to be reported by the Senate Committee on Small Business and Entrepreneurship on December 10, 2009. The Senate did not take further action on the bill, but several of its provisions were later included in the Small Business Jobs Act of 2010. It would have

- increased the maximum loan size for the 504/CDC loans from $1.5 million to $5 million for regular projects, from $2 million to $5 million for projects meeting one of the program's specified public policy goals, and from $4 million to $5.5 million for manufacturers;
- allowed 504/CDC loans to be used to refinance up to $4 billion in short-term commercial real estate debt each fiscal year for two years after enactment into long-term fixed rate loans;
- authorized the SBA to establish an alternative size standard for the 7(a) and 504/CDC programs that uses maximum tangible net worth and average net income as an alternative to the use of industry standards;
- extended ARRA's fee reductions and loan modifications through December 31, 2010;
- increased the maximum loan size for 7(a) loans from $2 million to $5 million; and
- increased the maximum loan size for the Microloan program from $35,000 to $50,000.[104]

P.L. 111-240, the Small Business Jobs Act of 2010

P.L. 111-240 was signed into law by President Obama on September 27, 2010. The act authorizes the Secretary of the Treasury to establish a $30 billion Small Business Lending Fund (SBLF) to encourage community banks to provide small business loans ($4 billion was issued), a $1.5 billion State Small Business Credit Initiative to provide funding to participating states with small business capital access programs, and about $12 billion in tax relief for small businesses.[105] It also contains revenue raising provisions to offset the act's cost, a number of changes to the SBA's loan and contracting programs, and establishes an alternative SBA small business eligibility size standard.[106]

As mentioned previously, the act also increased the 504/CDC program's loan limits from $1.5 million to $5 million for regular 504/CDC loans; from $2 million to $5 million if the loan proceeds are directed toward one or more of the program's specified public policy goals; from $4 million to $5.5 million for small manufacturers; from $4 million to $5.5 million for projects that reduce the borrower's energy consumption by at least 10%; and from $4 million to $5.5 million for projects for plant, equipment, and process upgrades of renewable energy sources, such as the small-scale production of energy for individual buildings or communities consumption (commonly known as micropower), or renewable fuel producers, including biodiesel and ethanol producers.[107]

P.L. 111-240 also provided $505 million (plus an additional $5 million for related administrative expenses) to continue the fee subsidies for the 7(a) and 504/CDC loan guaranty programs and the temporary increase in the 7(a) program's loan guaranty percentage from up to 85% of loans of $150,000 or less and up to 75% of loans exceeding $150,000 to 90% for all standard 7(a) loans from September 27, 2010, through December 31, 2010. The fee subsidies and 90% loan guaranty percentage had expired on May 31, 2010.

In addition, the act temporarily allowed, for two years from the date of enactment, 504/CDC loans to be used to refinance projects not involving expansions as long as the financing did not exceed 90% of the value of the collateral for the financing, "except that, if the appraised value of the eligible fixed assets serving as collateral for the financing is less than the amount equal to 125% of the amount of the financing, the borrower may provide additional cash or other collateral to eliminate any deficiency."[108] The refinancing could be used only for commercial indebtedness incurred not less than two years before the date of the application for assistance and only for eligible fixed assets (to acquire land, buildings, or equipment, or to construct a building). The refinancing could not be used for indebtedness subject to a federal guarantee, and it had to be collateralized by eligible fixed assets. The borrower also had to be current on all payments due on the existing debt for not less than one year before the date of the application. The act authorized the SBA to issue up to $7.5 billion in refinancing annually, for two fiscal years.[109] This temporary refinancing provision expired on September 27, 2012.

Finally, the act required the SBA to establish an alternative size standard for the 504/CDC and 7(a) loan programs that uses maximum tangible net worth and average net income as an alternative to the use of industry size standards.[110] At the time of passage, the 7(a) program used industry specific size standards and the 504/CDC program used maximum net worth of $8.5 million and maximum average net income of $3 million to determine program eligibility. The act establishes on an interim basis "until the date on which the alternative size standard [is] established" the following alternative size standard for both the

504/CDC and 7(a) programs: the business qualifies as small if it does not have a tangible net worth in excess of $15 million and does not have an average net income after federal taxes (excluding any carry-over losses) in excess of $5 million for two full fiscal years before the date of application.[111]

LEGISLATIVE ACTIVITY DURING THE 112TH CONGRESS

As mentioned previously, Congress has not approved any changes to the 504/CDC program during the 112th Congress. However, legislation has been introduced during the 112th Congress that would affect the 504/CDC program.

H.R. 2950, the Small Business Administration 504 Loan Refinancing Extension Act of 2011, was introduced on September 15, 2011, and referred to the House Committee on Small Business. The bill would allow 504/CDC loans to be used to refinance projects not involving expansions as long as the financing does not exceed 90% of the value of the collateral for the financing for an additional year beyond the two years from the date of enactment which was authorized by the Small Business Jobs Act of 2010.

S.Amdt. 1833, the INVEST in America Act of 2012—an amendment in the nature of a substitute for H.R. 3606, the Jumpstart Our Business Startups Act—was introduced on March 15, 2012. It would have allowed 504/CDC loans to be used to refinance projects not involving expansions for an additional year beyond the two years from the date of enactment authorized by the Small Business Jobs Act of 2010.[112] The amendment was ruled non-germane by the chair on March 21, 2012, and was not included in the final version of the bill which was approved by the Senate the following day.[113]

S. 3572, the Restoring Tax and Regulatory Certainty to Small Businesses Act of 2012, was introduced on September 19, 2012, and referred to the Senate Committee on Small Business and Entrepreneurship and the Senate Committee on Finance. It would, among other provisions, allow 504/CDC loans to be used to refinance projects not involving expansions for an additional year and a half beyond the two years from the date of enactment authorized by the Small Business Jobs Act of 2010.

S. 1828, a bill to increase small business lending, and for other purposes, was introduced on November 8, 2011, and referred to the Senate Committee on Small Business and Entrepreneurship. The bill would reinstate for a year following the date of its enactment the fee subsidies for the 504/CDC and 7(a) loan guaranty programs and the 90% loan guaranty percentage for the 7(a) program which were originally funded by ARRA.

CONCLUSION

During the 111th Congress, congressional debate concerning proposed changes to the SBA's loan guaranty programs, including the 504/CDC program, centered on the likely impact the changes would have on small business access to capital, job retention, and job creation. As a general proposition, some, including the chairs of the House and Senate Committees on Small Business and President Obama, argued that economic conditions made it imperative that the SBA be provided additional resources to assist small businesses in acquiring capital necessary to start, continue, or expand operations and create jobs.[114] Others worried about the long-term adverse economic effects of spending programs that increase the federal deficit. They advocated business tax reduction, reform of financial credit market regulation, and federal fiscal restraint as the best means to assist small business economic growth and job creation.[115]

In terms of specific program changes, continuing the 504/CDC program's temporary fee subsidies, increasing its loan limits, temporarily expanding its refinancing options, and requiring the SBA to establish an alterative size standard were designed to achieve the same goal: to enhance job creation and retention by increasing the ability of 504/CDC borrowers to obtain credit at affordable rates. For example, the Obama Administration argued that increasing the maximum loan limits for the 504/CDC, 7(a), Microloan, and SBAExpress programs will allow the SBA to "support larger projects" which will "allow the SBA to help America's small businesses drive long-term economic growth and the creation of jobs in communities across the country."[116] The Administration also argued that increasing the maximum loan limits for these programs will be "budget neutral" over the long run and "help improve the availability of smaller loans."[117]

Critics argued that increasing these loan limits might increase the risk of defaults and result in higher guaranty fees or the need to provide the SBA additional funding, especially for the SBAExpress program, which had experienced somewhat higher losses than other SBA loan guaranty programs.[118] Others advocated a more modest increase in the maximum loan limits to ensure that the programs focus on start-ups and early-stage small firms, "businesses that have historically encountered the greatest difficulties in accessing credit" and "avoids making small borrowers carry a disproportionate share of the risk associated with larger loans."[119]

During the 112th Congress, Congress focused on the SBA's administration of the program changes enacted during the 111th Congress, the impact of these changes on the SBA's lending, and ways to address and minimize increased costs associated with loan losses. Although there is widespread congressional support for providing assistance to small businesses, federal fiscal constraints may impede efforts to expand the 504/CDC program in the near future, especially given that the program is expected to continue to require federal assistance to cover the cost of loan losses. In addition, unless there is a change in law, the SBA faces a potential loss of about $75 million in federal funding in January 2013 (including $29 million of $359 million in the SBA's business loans program account) as part of the sequestration process under P.L. 112-25, the Budget Control Act of 2011.[120]

Given existing fiscal constraints, it is likely that Congress will, in the coming months, continue to focus on the SBA's administration of the 504/CDC program to ensure that the program is as efficient as possible, request information concerning the program's efficacy in job retention and creation, and explore ways to address and minimize costs associated with 504/CDC loan losses.

End Notes

[1] U.S. Small Business Administration, Fiscal Year 2010 Congressional Budget Justification, p. 30.

[2] The 504/CDC program was preceded by a 501 state development company program (1958-1982), a 502 local development company program (1958-1995), and a 503/CDC program (1980-1986). The 504/CDC program

started in 1986. There are a small number of for-profit CDCs that participated in these predecessor programs that have been grandfathered into the current 504/CDC program. See U.S. Small Business Administration, "SOP 50 10 5(E): Lender and Development Company Loan Programs," (effective June 1, 2012), p. 49, at http://www.sba.gov/sites/default/files/SOP%2050%2010%205(E)%20(5-16-2012)%20 clean.pdf.

3 13 C.F.R. §120.801. 504/CDC debentures are normally sold and proceeds disbursed on the Wednesday after the second Sunday of each month. See U.S. Small Business Administration, "SOP 50 10 5(E): Lender and Development Company Loan Programs," (effective June 1, 2012), p. 348, at http://www.sba.gov/sites/default/files/SOP%2050% 20 10%205(E)%20(5-16-2012)%20clean.pdf.

4 U.S. Small Business Administration, "Monthly Purchase of 504 Debentures for Accelerated Loans," at http://archive.sba.gov/aboutsba/sbaprograms/elending/notices/BANK_ 5000_ 602_MONTHLY_PURC_504.html.

5 U.S. Small Business Administration, "SBA Lending Statistics for Major Programs (as of 9/30/2012)," at http://www.sba.gov/about-sba-info/317721.

6 U.S. Government Accountability Office, Small Business Administration: 7(a) Loan Program Needs Additional Performance Measures, GAO-08-226T, November 1, 2007, pp. 3, 9-11, at http://www.gao.gov/new.items/d08226t.pdf; and Veronique de Rugy, Why the Small Business Administration's Loan Programs Should Be Abolished, American Enterprise Institute for Public Policy Research, AEI Working Paper #126, April 13, 2006, at http://www.aei.org/ docLib/20060414_wp126.pdf. Proponents of federal funding for the SBA's loan guarantee programs also argue that small business can promote competitive markets. See P.L. 83-163, §2(a), as amended; and 15 U.S.C. §631a.

7 Federal Reserve Board, "Senior Loan Officer Opinion Survey on Bank Lending Practices," at http://www.federalreserve.gov/boarddocs/SnLoanSurvey/.

8 The specified circumstances include the following: the amount of existing indebtedness does not exceed 50% of the project cost of the expansion; the proceeds of the indebtedness were used to acquire land, including the building situated thereon, to construct a building thereon, or to purchase equipment; the existing indebtedness is collateralized by fixed assets; the existing indebtedness was incurred for the benefit of a small business; the financing is used only for refinancing existing indebtedness or costs related to the project being financed; the refinancing provides a substantial benefit to the borrower; the borrower has been current on all payments due on the existing debt for not less than one year preceding the date of refinancing; and the financing provided will have better terms or rate of interest than the existing indebtedness. See P.L. 111-5, the American Recovery and Reinvestment Act of 2009, Section 504. Stimulus for Community Development Lending.

9 The SBA considers the following as a limited or special purpose property: amusement parks; bowling alleys; car wash properties; cemeteries; clubhouses; cold storage facilities where more than 50% of total square footage is equipped for refrigeration; dormitories; farms, including dairy facilities; funeral homes with crematoriums; gas stations; golf courses; hospitals, surgery centers, urgent care centers and other health medical facilities; hotels and motels; marinas; mines; museums; nursing homes, including assisted living facilities; oil wells; quarries, including gravel pits; railroads; sanitary landfills; service centers (e.g., oil and lube, brake or transmission centers) with pits; sports arenas; swimming pools; tennis clubs; theaters; and wineries. See U.S. Small Business Administration, "SOP 50 10 5(E): Lender and Development Company Loan Programs" (effective June 1, 2012), p. 269, at http://www.sba.gov/sites/default/files/ SOP%2050%2010%205(E)%20(5-16-2012)% 20 clean.pdf.

10 P.L. 111-240, the Small Business Jobs Act of 2010, requires the SBA to establish an alternative size standard for the 504/CDC and 7(a) loan programs that uses maximum tangible net worth and average net income as an alternative to the use of industry standards. At the time of passage, the 7(a) program used industry specific size standards and the 504/CDC program used maximum net worth of $8.5 million and maximum average net income of $3 million to determine program eligibility. The act establishes the following alternative size standard for both the 504/CDC and 7(a) programs on an interim basis: the business qualifies as small if it does not have a tangible net worth in excess of $15 million and does not have an average net income after federal taxes (excluding any carry-over losses) in excess of $5 million for two full fiscal years before the date of application. For further analysis concerning SBA size standards see CRS Report R40860, Small Business Size Standards: A Historical Analysis of Contemporary Issues, by Robert Jay Dilger.

11 13 C.F.R. §120.100; and 13 C.F.R. §120.101.

12 13 C.F.R. §120.110. Nineteen types of businesses are ineligible for 504/CDC loans. Also, an associate is an officer, director, owner of more than 20% of the equity, or key employee of the small business; any entity in which one or more individuals referred to above owns or controls at least 20% of the equity; and any

individual or entity in control of or controlled by the small business, except a Small Business Investment Company licensed by the SBA. See 13 C.F.R. §120.10.

[13] 13 C.F.R. §120.150.

[14] U.S. Small Business Administration, "SOP 50 10 5(E): Lender and Development Company Loan Programs," (effective June 1, 2012), pp. 309-313, at http://www.sba.gov/sites/default/ files/SOP%2050%2010% 205(E)%20(5-16- 2012)%20clean.pdf. Expansion "includes any project that involves the acquisition, construction or improvement of land, building or equipment for use by the small business applicant." See Ibid., p. 309.

[15] Ibid., p. 305.

[16] A job opportunity is defined as a full time (or equivalent) permanent job created within two years of receipt of 504/CDC funds, or retained in the community because of a 504/CDC loan. See Ibid., pp. 56, 264, 305-307.

[17] 13 C.F.R. §120.862.

[18] P.L. 111-240, the Small Business Jobs Act of 2010, §1112. Maximum Loan Amounts Under 504 Program.

[19] 13 C.F.R. §120.933.

[20] U.S. Small Business Administration, "SOP 50 10 5(E): Lender and Development Company Loan Programs," (effective June 1, 2012), p. 332, at http://www.sba.gov/sites/default/files /SOP%2050%2010%205(E)%20(5-16- 2012)%20clean.pdf.

[21] 13 C.F.R. §120.921.

[22] 13 C.F.R. §120.932.

[23] Capital Certified Development Corporation, "504/CDC Program Interest Rates," Austin, TX, at https://www.capitalcdc.com/loan-programs/the-sba-504-program. The interest rate for March 2012 was 4.59%

[24] 13 C.F.R. §120.921; and U.S. Small Business Administration, "Reporting and Recordkeeping Requirements Under OMB Review," 77 Federal Register 59447, September 27, 2012.

[25] U.S. Small Business Administration, "SOP 50 10 5(E): Lender and Development Company Loan Programs," (effective June 1, 2012), p. 316, at http://www.sba.gov/sites/ default/files/SOP%2050%2010%205(E)%20(5-16- 2012)%20clean.pdf.

[26] 13 C.F.R. §120.934.

[27] U.S. Small Business Administration, "SOP 50 10 5(E): Lender and Development Company Loan Programs," (effective June 1, 2012), p. 180, at http://www.sba.gov/sites/ default/files/ SOP%2050%2010%205(E)%20(5-16- 2012)%20clean.pdf.

[28] Ibid., p. 49.

[29] A CDC can apply to be a multi-state CDC "provided the State the CDC seeks to expand into is contiguous to the State of the CDC's incorporation; the CDC demonstrates that its membership meets the requirements in 13 CFR §120.822 separately for its State of incorporation and for each additional State in which it seeks to operate as a Multi-State CDC; and the CDC has a loan committee meeting the requirements of 13 CFR §120.823." See ibid., p. 77.

[30] Ibid., pp. 49-51.

[31] U.S. Small Business Administration, "CDC/504 Loan Program," at http://www.sba.gov/ content/cdc504-loan-program; and National Association of Development Companies, "504 Loan Approval Statistics," at http://www.nadco.org/i4a/pages/index.cfm?pageid=3558.

32 U.S. Small Business Administration, "SOP 50 10 5(E): Lender and Development Company Loan Programs," (effective June 1, 2012), pp. 50, 51, at http://www.sba.gov/sites/ default/files/SOP%2050% 2010%205(E)%20(5-16- 2012)%20clean.pdf.

33 Ibid., p. 51.

[34] Ibid.

[35] Ibid., p. 53.

[36] Ibid.

[37] Ibid., pp. 180, 181.

[38] Ibid., pp. 328, 329.

[39] U.S. Small Business Administration, "Loans to State and Local Development Companies Accredited Lenders Program for Certified Development Companies," 60 Federal Register 20391, April 26, 1995.

[40] U.S. Small Business Administration, "SOP 50 10 5(E): Lender and Development Company Loan Programs," (effective June 1, 2012), pp. 68, 69, at http://www.sba.gov/sites/ default/files/SOP%2050%2010%205(E) %20(5-16- 2012)%20clean.pdf.

[41] U.S. Small Business Administration, Office of Congressional and Legislative Affairs, correspondence with the author, April 7, 2010; and U.S. Small Business Administration, Office of Congressional and Legislative Affairs, correspondence with the author, September 17, 2012.

[42] P.L. 105-135, the Small Business Reauthorization Act of 1997, extended the program's authorization to October 1, 2002.

[43] U.S. Small Business Administration, "SOP 50 10 5(E): Lender and Development Company Loan Programs," (effective June 1, 2012), p. 70, at http://www.sba.gov/sites/ default/files/SOP%2050%2010%205(E)%20(5-16-2012)%20clean.pdf.

[44] Ibid., p. 71.

[45] U.S. Small Business Administration, Office of Congressional and Legislative Affairs, correspondence with the author, April 7, 2010. All PCLP-CDCs have ALP status as that is a requirement for being provided PCLP authority.

[46] U.S. Small Business Administration, "SBA Lending Statistics for Major Programs (as of 9/30/2011)," at http://www.sba.gov/about-sba-info/26641; and U.S. Small Business Administration, "SBA Lending Statistics for Major Programs (as of 9/30/2012)," at http://www.sba.gov/about-sba-info/317721.

[47] U.S. Small Business Administration, "SOP 50 10 5(E): Lender and Development Company Loan Programs," (effective June 1, 2012), p. 318, at http://www.sba.gov/sites/ default/files/SOP%2050%2010%205(E)%20(5-16- 2012)%20clean.pdf.

[48] Ibid.

[49] Ibid., p. 267.

[50] 13 C.F.R. §120.971(d).

[51] U.S. Small Business Administration, "SBA Information Notice: 7(a) and 504 Fees Effective On October 1, 2011," Washington, DC, September 30, 2011, http://www.sba.gov/sites/ default/files/5000-1223.pdf.

[52] 15 U.S.C. §697(b)(7)(A)(i); and 13 C.F.R. §120.971(d). The SBA's annual servicing fee was 0.749% in FY2011 and 0.389% in FY2010.

[53] U.S. Small Business Administration, "SBA Information Notice: 7(a) and 504 Fees Effective On October 1, 2011," Washington, DC, September 30, 2011, at http://www.sba.gov/sites/ default/files/5000-1223.pdf.

[54] 13 C.F.R. §120.971(e).

[55] 13 C.F.R. §120.972.

[56] Ibid. When there are different liens on a property, the senior lien must be satisfied before junior liens in the event of a default.

[57] U.S. Small Business Administration, "SOP 50 10 5(E): Lender and Development Company Loan Programs," (effective June 1, 2012), p. 347, at http://www.sba.gov/sites/default/ files/SOP%2050%2010%205(E)%20(5-16- 2012)%20clean.pdf; and 13 C.F.R. §120.971(a)(1).

[58] 13 C.F.R. §120.971(a)(2).

[59] U.S. Small Business Administration, "SOP 50 10 5(E): Lender and Development Company Loan Programs," (effective June 1, 2012), p. 356, at http://www.sba.gov/sites/default/ files/SOP%2050%2010%205(E)%20(5-16- 2012)%20clean.pdf; and 13 C.F.R. §120.883(e).

[60] 13 C.F.R. §120.971(a)(3); and U.S. Small Business Administration, "SOP 50 10 5(E): Lender and Development Company Loan Programs," (effective June 1, 2012), pp. 264, 350, at http://www.sba.gov/sites/default/ files/SOP%2050%2010%205(E)%20(5-16-2012)%20clean.pdf.

[61] 13 C.F.R. §120.971(a)(4); 13 C.F.R. §120.971(a)(5); and U.S. Small Business Administration, "SOP 50 10 5(E): Lender and Development Company Loan Programs," (effective June 1, 2012), p. 350, at http://www.sba.gov/sites/ default/files/SOP%2050%2010%205(E)%20(5-16-2012)%20clean.pdf.

[62] 13 C.F.R. §120.971(c).

[63] U.S. Small Business Administration, "SOP 50 10 5(E): Lender and Development Company Loan Programs," (effective June 1, 2012), p. 355, at http://www.sba.gov/sites/default/files/ SOP%2050%2010%205(E)%20(5-16- 2012)%20clean.pdf.

[64] Ibid.

[65] Ibid., p. 351.

[66] P.L. 111-5, the American Recovery and Reinvestment Act of 2009, provided $375 million for fee subsidies and the 7(a) program's 90% guaranty for all standard 7(a) loans. ARRA's funding for these purposes was exhausted on November 23, 2009. P.L. 111-118, the Department of Defense Appropriations Act, 2010, enacted on December 19, 2009, provided $125 million to extend the fee subsidies and 90% guaranty through February 28, 2010. P.L. 111-144, the Temporary Extension Act of 2010, enacted on March 2, 2010, provided $60 million to extend the fee subsidies and 90% guaranty through March 28, 2010. P.L. 111-150, an act to

extend the Small Business Loan Guarantee Program, enacted on March 26, 2010, authorized the use of $40 million in SBA appropriated funds to extend the fee subsidies and 90% guaranty through April 30, 2010. P.L. 111-157, the Continuing Extension Act of 2010, enacted on April 15, 2010, provided $80 million to extend the fee subsides and 90% guaranty through May 31, 2010. P.L. 111-240, the Small Business Jobs Act of 2010, enacted on September 27, 2010, provided $505 million (plus $5 million for related administrative expenses) to extend the fee subsidies and 90% guaranty through December 31, 2010. P.L. 111-322, the Continuing Appropriations and Surface Transportation Extensions Act, 2011, authorized the SBA to continue the fee subsidies and 90% guaranty through March 4, 2011, or until the funding provided by the Small Business Jobs Act of 2010 for these purposes was exhausted (which occurred on January 3, 2011).

[67] On January 3, 2011, the SBA announced that it had formed a SBA Loan Queue for loan applicants should any funding with the enhancements should become available from loan cancellations. Typically, 7% to 10% of previously approved SBA loans are later cancelled by the borrower or lender and are not disbursed for a variety of reasons. See U.S. Small Business Administration, "Jobs Act Supported More Than $12 Billion in SBA Lending to Small Businesses in Just Three Months," Washington, DC, January 3, 2011, at http://www.sba.gov/content/jobs-act-supported-more-12- billion-sba-lending-small-businesses-just-three-months.

[68] U.S. Small Business Administration, "Administration Announces New Small Business Commercial Real Estate and Working Capital Programs," February 5, 2010, at http://www.sba.gov/sites/default/files/ sba_rcvry_factsheet_cre_refi.pdf; and U.S. Small Business Administration, "SBA Recovery Lending Extended Through April 30," March 29, 2010, at http://www.sba.gov/about-sba-services/7367/5883.

[69] Susan Eckerly, "NFIB Responds to President's Small Business Lending Initiatives," Washington, DC, October 21, 2009, at http://www.nfib.com/newsroom/newsroom-item/cmsid/50080/; and NFIB, "Government Spending," Washington, DC, at http://www.nfib.com/issues-elections/issues-elections-item/cmsid/49051/.

[70] U.S. Small Business Administration, Office of Congressional and Legislative Affairs, correspondence with the author, September 17, 2012. The SBA maintains selected disbursement data and will provide that data to congressional offices by request.

[71] U.S. Small Business Administration, Press Office, "Recovery Loan Incentives Spurred Continued Rebound in SBA Lending in FY2010," October 4, 2010, at http://www.sba.gov/about-sba-services/7367/5527; and U.S. Small Business Administration, "Jobs Act Supported More Than $12 Billion in SBA Lending to Small Businesses in Just Three Months," January 3, 2011, at http://www.sba.gov/content/jobs-act-supported-more-12-billion-sba-lending-smallbusinesses-just-three-months.

[72] U.S. Small Business Administration, "2008 Loss Report," Washington, DC, p. 8, http://archive.sba.gov/idc/groups/ public/documents/sba_program_office/cfo_2008_loss_report.pdf.

[73] U.S. Small Business Administration, "Agency Financial Report: Fiscal Year, 2010," p. 66, at http://www.sba.gov/ sites/default/files/afr_2010_final.pdf; and U.S. Small Business Administration, "Agency Financial Report: Fiscal Year, 2011," p. 71, at http://www. sba.gov/sites/default/files/Agency%20 Financial%20 Report%20FY%202011_0.pdf.

[74] U.S. Small Business Administration, FY 2013 Congressional Budget Justification and FY 2011 Annual Performance Report, p. 19, at http://www.sba.gov/sites/default/files/ files/FY%202013%2 0CBJ%20FY% 202011%20APR.pdf.

[75] Christopher Hayes, An Assessment of Small Business Administration Loan and Investment Performance: Survey of Assisted Businesses (Washington, DC: The Urban Institute, 2008), p. 3, at http://www.urban.org/UploadedPDF/ 411599_assisted_business_survey.pdf. The percentage total exceeds 100 because recipients were allowed to name more than one use for the loan proceeds.

[76] Ibid., p. 5.

[77] Ibid.

[78] Kenneth Temkin, Brett Theodos, with Kerstin Gentsch, Competitive and Special Competitive Opportunity Gap Analysis of the 7(A) and 504 Programs (Washington, DC: The Urban Institute, 2008), p. 13, at http://www.urban.org/ UploadedPDF/411596_504 _gap_ analysis.pdf.

[79] U.S. Small Business Administration, "SBA Lending Statistics for Major Programs (as of 9/30/2012)," at http://www.sba.gov/about-sba-info/317721.

[80] Kenneth Temkin, Brett Theodos, with Kerstin Gentsch, Competitive and Special Competitive Opportunity Gap Analysis of the 7(A) and 504 Programs (Washington, DC: The Urban Institute, 2008), p. 21, at http://www.urban.org/ UploadedPDF/411596_504_ gap_ analysis.pdf.

[81] P.L. 111-5, the American Recovery and Reinvestment Act of 2009, Section 501. Fee Reductions.

[82] P.L. 111-118, the Department of Defense Appropriations Act, 2010, enacted on December 19, 2009, provided $125 million to extend ARRA's "fee reductions and eliminations" for the SBA's 7(a) and 504/CDC programs and 90% maximum loan guarantee limit for the SBA's 7(a) program through February 28, 2010. P.L. 111-144, the Temporary Extension Act of 2010, enacted on March 2, 2010, provided $60 million to extend those fee reductions and loan modifications through March 28, 2010. P.L. 111-150, an act to extend the Small Business Loan Guarantee Program, enacted on March 26, 2010, authorized the use of $40 million in SBA appropriated funds to extend those fee reductions and loan modifications through April 30, 2010. P.L. 111-157, the Continuing Extension Act of 2010, enacted on April 15, 2010, provided $80 million to extend those fee reductions and loan modifications through May 31, 2010.

[83] On January 3, 2011, the SBA announced that it had formed a SBA Loan Queue for loan applicants should any funding with the enhancements should become available from loan cancellations. Typically, 7% to 10% of previously approved SBA loans are later cancelled by the borrower or lender and are not disbursed for a variety of reasons. See U.S. Small Business Administration, "Jobs Act Supported More Than $12 Billion in SBA Lending to Small Businesses in Just Three Months," January 3, 2011, at http://www.sba.gov/ content/jobs-act-supported-more-12-billion-sbalending-small-businesses-just-three-months.

[84] U.S. Small Business Administration, "Administration Announces New Small Business Commercial Real Estate and Working Capital Programs," February 5, 2010, at http://www.sba.gov/sites/default/files/ sba_rcvry_factsheet_cre_refi.pdf; and U.S. Small Business Administration, "SBA Recovery Lending Extended Through April 30," March 29, 2010, at http://www.sba.gov/about-sba-services/7367/5883.

[85] Susan Eckerly, "NFIB Responds to President's Small Business Lending Initiatives," Washington, DC, October 21, 2009, at http://www.nfib.com/newsroom/newsroom-item/cmsid/50080/; and NFIB, "Government Spending," Washington, DC, at http://www. nfib.com/issues-elections/issues-elections-item/cmsid/49051/.

[86] U.S. Small Business Administration, Office of the Inspector General, "Report on Audit of Premier Certified Lenders in the Section 504 Loan Program," March 23, 2010, at p. 20, http://www.sba.gov/office-of-inspector-general/868/5032.

[87] Ibid.

[88] Ibid., p. 1.

[89] Ibid., pp. 3, 4.

[90] Ibid., p. 4.

[91] Ibid., pp. 4, 5.

[92] Ibid., p. 5.

[93] Ibid.

[94] U.S. Government Accountability Office, Small Business Administration: Actions Needed to Improve the Usefulness of the Agency's Lender Risk Rating System, GAO-1-53, November 6, 2009, p. i, at http://www.gao.gov/new.items/ d1053.pdf.

[95] Ibid., pp. i, 27-30.

[96] Ibid., p. 35.

[97] U.S. Small Business Administration, "SBA Lending Statistics for Major Programs (as of 9/30/2011)," at http://www.sba.gov/about-sba-info/26641; and U.S. Small Business Administration, "SBA Lending Statistics for Major Programs (as of 9/30/2012)," at http://www.sba.gov/about-sba-info/317721.

[98] U.S. Small Business Administration, "Jobs Act Supported More Than $12 Billion in SBA Lending to Small Businesses in Just Three Months," January 3, 2011, at http://www.sba.gov/content/jobs-act-supported-more-12-billionsba-lending-small-businesses-just-three months

[99] U.S. Small Business Administration, "Administration Announces New Small Business Commercial Real Estate and Working Capital Programs," February 5, 2010, http://www.sba.gov/sites/default/files/sba_ rcvry_factsheet_cre_refi.pdf. For an analysis of the pros and cons associated with these actions see CRS Report R41146, Small Business Administration 7(a) Loan Guaranty Program, by Robert Jay Dilger.

[100] For further analysis see CRS Report R40985, Small Business: Access to Capital and Job Creation, by Robert Jay Dilger.

1[01] ARC's loan limit would have been increased from $35,000 to $50,000, and to $75,000 in areas of high unemployment, and borrowers would be allowed to use ARC loans to refinance existing SBA loan debt. The ARC program ended on September 30, 2010.

[102] H.R. 3854, the Small Business Financing and Investment Act of 2009.

[103] Ibid. For further analysis see CRS Report R40985, Small Business: Access to Capital and Job Creation, by Robert Jay Dilger.

[104] S. 2869, the Small Business Job Creation and Access to Capital Act of 2009.

[105] For further analysis of P.L. 111-240, the Small Business Jobs Act of 2010, see CRS Report R41385, Small Business Legislation During the 111th Congress, by Robert Jay Dilger and Gary Guenther. For further analysis of the Small Business Lending Fund see CRS Report R42045, The Small Business Lending Fund, by Robert Jay Dilger. For further analysis of the State Small Business Credit Initiative see CRS Report R42581, State Small Business Credit Initiative: Implementation and Funding Issues, by Robert Jay Dilger.

[106] For further analysis of the SBA's size standards see CRS Report R40860, Small Business Size Standards: A Historical Analysis of Contemporary Issues, by Robert Jay Dilger.

[107] P.L. 111-240, the Small Business Jobs Act of 2010, §1112. Maximum Loan Amounts Under 504 Program.

[108] P.L. 111-240, the Small Business Jobs Act of 2010, §1122. Low-Interest Refinancing Under the Local Development Business Loan Program.

[109] Ibid. The House Committee on Small Business has indicated that it will examine the refinancing program for termination because it does not believe that the program's fees "will cover the subsidy costs of the program." U.S. Congress, House Committee on Small Business, Budget Views and Estimates, 112th Cong., 1st sess., March 17, 2011, p. 3, http://smbiz.house.gov/UploadedFiles/March_17_Views_and_Estimates_Letter.pdf.

[110] P.L. 111-240, the Small Business Jobs Act of 2010, §1116. Alternative Size Standards.

[111] Ibid.

[112] Senator Harry Reid, "Consideration of H.R. 3606, the Jumpstart our Business Startups Act," Text of Amendments, Congressional Record, vol. 158, part 43 (March 15, 2012), p. S1754.

[113] H.R. 3606, the Jumpstart Our Business Startups Act, was passed by the House on March 8, 2012. The bill did not contain a provision concerning 504/CDC refinancing. President Obama signed the bill, as amended, into law on April 5, 2012 (P.L. 112-106, the Jumpstart Our Business Startups).

[114] Representative Nydia Velázquez, "Small Business Financing and Investment Act of 2009," House debate, Congressional Record, daily edition, vol. 155, no. 159 (October 29, 2009), pp. H12074, H12075; Senator Mary Landrieu, "Statements on Introduced Bills and Joint Resolutions," remarks in the Senate, Congressional Record, daily edition, vol. 155, no. 185 (December 10, 2009), p. S12910; and The White House, "Remarks by the President on Job Creation and Economic Growth," December 8, 2009, at http://www.whitehouse.gov/the-press-office/remarkspresident-job-creation-and-economic-growth.

115 Susan Eckerly, "NFIB Responds to President's Small Business Lending Initiatives," Washington, DC, October 21, 2009, at http://www.nfib.com/newsroom/newsroom-item/cmsid/50080/; and NFIB, "Government Spending," Washington, DC, at http://www. nfib.com/issues-elections/issues-elections-item/cmsid/49051/.

[116] U.S. Small Business Administration, "Administration Announces New Small Business Commercial Real Estate and Working Capital Programs," February 5, 2010, at http://www. sba.gov/sites/default/files/ sba_rcvry_ factsheet_cre_refi.pdf.

[117] Ibid.

[118] Robb Mandelbaum, "Small Business Incentives Face a Hard Road in Congress," New York Times, February 12, 2010, at http://boss.blogs.nytimes.com/2010/02/12/small-business-incentives-face-a-hard-road-in-congress/; and U.S. Congress, House Committee on Small Business, House Committee on Small Business Views With Regard to the Fiscal Year (FY) 2010 Budget, Letter from Nydia Velázquez, Chair, House Committee on Small Business, to John M. Spratt, Jr., Chair, House Committee on the Budget, 111th Cong., 2nd sess., March 11, 2009, p. 3, at http://www.house.gov/ smbiz/democrats/Reports/FY%202010% 20Views%20and%2 0Estimates%20v2.pdf.

[119] U.S. Congress, House Committee on Small Business, Small Business Financing and Investment Act of 2009, report to accompany H.R. 3854, 111th Cong., 2nd sess., October 26, 2009, H.Rept. 111-315 (Washington: GPO, 2009), p. 1.

[120] U.S. Office of Management and Budget, "OMB Report Pursuant to the Sequestration Transparency Act of 2012 (P.L. 112-112–155)," p. 193, at http://www.whitehouse.gov/sites/ default/files/omb/assets/legislative_reports/ stareport.pdf.

In: Small Business Administration ...
Editor: Alan R. Connoly

ISBN: 978-1-62417-674-6

Chapter 5

SMALL BUSINESS ADMINISTRATION MICROLOAN PROGRAM*

Robert Jay Dilger

SUMMARY

The Small Business Administration's (SBA's) Microloan program provides direct loans to qualified non-profit intermediary Microloan lenders who, in turn, provide "microloans" of up to $50,000 to small business owners, entrepreneurs, and non-profit child care centers. It also provides marketing, management, and technical assistance to Microloan borrowers and potential borrowers. The program was authorized in 1991 as a five-year demonstration project and became operational in 1992. It was made permanent, subject to reauthorization, in 1997. The SBA's Microloan program is designed to assist women, low-income, veteran, and minority entrepreneurs and small business owners and other individuals possessing the capability to operate successful business concerns by providing them small-scale loans for working capital or the acquisition of materials, supplies, or equipment. In FY2012, Microloan intermediaries provided 3,973 Microloans amounting to $44.7 million. The average Microloan was $11,254 and had a 8.18% interest rate. Critics of the SBA's Microloan program argue that it is expensive relative to alternative programs, duplicative of the SBA's 7(a) loan guaranty program, and subject to administrative shortfalls. The program's advocates argue that it provides assistance that reaches many who otherwise would not be served by the private sector and is an important source of capital and training assistance for low-income women and minority business owners. Congressional interest in the Microloan program has increased in recent years, primarily because microloans are viewed as a means to assist very small businesses, especially women- and minority-owned startups, to get loans that enable them to create and retain jobs. Job creation, always a congressional interest, has taken on increased importance given the nation's current economic difficulties.

This report opens with a discussion of the rationale provided for having a Microloan program, describes the program's eligibility standards and operating requirements for lenders and borrowers, and examines the arguments presented by the program's critics and by its advocates. It concludes with an examination of changes to the program

---

* This is an edited, reformatted and augmented version of Congressional Research Service, Publication No. R41057, dated October 16, 2012.

authorized by P.L. 111-240, the Small Business Jobs Act of 2010. The Small Business Jobs Act increased the Microloan program's loan limit for borrowers from $35,000 to $50,000, and for intermediaries after their first year of participation in the program from $3.5 million to $5 million. It also authorized the SBA to waive, in whole or in part through FY2012, the non-federal share requirement for loans to the Microloan program's intermediaries and for grants made to Microloan intermediaries for small business marketing, management, and technical assistance for up to a fiscal year.

SMALL BUSINESS MICROLOANS AND TRAINING ASSISTANCE

The Small Business Administration (SBA) administers programs that support small businesses, including loan guarantees to lenders to encourage them to provide loans to small businesses "that might not otherwise obtain financing on reasonable terms and conditions" and grants to nonprofit organizations to provide marketing, management, and technical training assistance to small business owners.[1] Historically, one of the justifications presented for funding the SBA's loan guarantee programs has been that small businesses can be at a disadvantage, compared with other businesses, when trying to obtain access to sufficient capital and credit.[2] It has been argued that this disadvantage is particularly acute for startups and microbusinesses (firms with fewer than five employees):

> Traditional lending institutions, such as banks and investors, are unlikely to offer loans and investment capital to microfirms due to a variety of reasons. One barrier to microlending is a concern that startups and smaller enterprises are risky investments since growing businesses typically exhibit erratic bursts of growth and downturn. The perceived risk of these types of companies reduces the chances of a microbusiness to obtain financing. Another issue is that microbusinesses by and large require smaller amounts of capital, and thus banks or investment companies often believe that it is not efficient use of their time or resources, nor will they receive a substantive return on investment from such a small loan amount.[3]

An Urban Institute survey of SBA 7(a), 504/Certified Development Company (504/CDC), Small Business Investment Company (SBIC), and Microloan borrowers conducted in 2007 found that Microloan borrowers reported having the most difficulty in finding acceptable financing elsewhere. Less than one-third (31%) of Microloan borrowers reported that they would have been able to find acceptable financing elsewhere, compared with 35% of SBIC borrowers, 40% of 7(a) borrowers, and 48% of 504/CDC borrowers.[4]

The SBA has provided loan guarantees to encourage lenders to issue small businesses loans since the agency's inception in 1953.[5] Interest in creating a separate loan program to address the specific needs of startups and microbusinesses increased during the 1980s, primarily due to the growth and experience of microlending institutions abroad and evidence concerning private lending practices that led Congress to the conclusion that a new loan program was necessary "to reach very small businesses that were not being served by traditional lenders of SBA's credit programs."[6] To address the perceived disadvantages faced by very small businesses in gaining access to capital, Congress authorized the SBA's Microloan lending program in 1991 (P.L. 102-140, the Departments of Commerce, Justice, and State, the Judiciary, and Related Agencies Appropriations Act, 1992). The program became operational in 1992. Its stated purpose is

> to assist women, low-income, veteran ... and minority entrepreneurs and business owners and other individuals possessing the capability to operate successful business concerns; to assist small business concerns in those areas suffering from a lack of credit due to economic downturns; ... to make loans to eligible intermediaries to enable such intermediaries to provide small-scale loans, particularly loans in amounts averaging not more than $10,000, to start-up, newly established, or growing small business concerns for working capital or the acquisition of materials, supplies, or equipment; [and] to make grants to eligible intermediaries that, together with non-Federal matching funds, will enable such intermediaries to provide intensive marketing, management, and technical assistance to microloan borrowers.[7]

The SBA's Microloan lending program was authorized initially as a five-year demonstration project. It was made permanent, subject to reauthorization, in 1997 (P.L. 105-135, the Small Business Reauthorization Act of 1997).

Congressional interest in the Microloan program has increased in recent years, primarily because microloans are viewed as a means to assist very small businesses, especially women- and minority-owned startups, obtain loans that enable them to create jobs. Job creation and preservation, always a congressional interest, has taken on increased importance given the nation's current economic difficulties.[8] This report describes the Microloan program's eligibility standards and operating requirements for lenders and borrowers, and examines the arguments presented by the program's critics and by its advocates. It concludes with an examination of changes to the program authorized by P.L. 111- 240, the Small Business Jobs Act of 2010. P.L. 111-240 authorizes the Secretary of the Treasury to establish a $30 billion Small Business Lending Fund (SBLF) to encourage community banks to provide small business loans ($4.0 billion was issued), a $1.5 billion State Small Business Credit Initiative to provide funding to participating states with small business capital access programs, and about $12 billion in tax relief for small businesses.[9] It also authorizes changes to the SBA's loan guaranty programs, including increasing the Microloan program's loan limit for borrowers from $35,000 to $50,000, and for intermediaries after their first year of participation in the program from $3.5 million to $5 million. It also authorized the SBA to waive, in whole or in part through FY2012, the non-federal share requirement for loans to the Microloan program's intermediaries and for grants made to Microloan intermediaries for small business marketing, management, and technical assistance for up to a fiscal year.

THE SBA MICROLOAN PROGRAM: FUNDING, ELIGIBILITY

Standards, Program Requirements, and Statistics

Unlike the SBA's 7(a) and 504/CDC loan guarantee programs, the SBA Microloan program does not guarantee loans.[10] Instead, it provides direct loans to qualified non-profit intermediary Microloan lenders who, in turn, provide "microloans" of up to $50,000 to small business owners, entrepreneurs, and non-profit child care centers.[11] There are 181 intermediaries participating in the program, located in 48 states, the District of Columbia, and Puerto Rico.[12]

Funding

The program received an appropriation of $3.678 million in FY2012, which was expected to support about $25.0 million in lending to intermediaries.[13] The Obama Administration recommended that the program receive an appropriation of $2.844 million for FY2013, which was expected to support about $18.0 million in lending to intermediaries.[14] P.L. 112-175, the Continuing Appropriations Resolution, 2013, which provides appropriations for FY2013 through March 27, 2013, provided the program a projected $3,700,509 for FY2013 (the FY2012 appropriation amount plus 0.612%).

Microloan intermediaries and qualified "non-lending technical assistance providers" selected by the SBA also received $20.0 million in FY2012 to provide Microloan borrowers and prospective borrowers marketing, management, and technical training assistance.[15] The Obama Administration recommended that the Microloan technical assistance program receive $19.76 million in FY2013.[16] P.L. 112-175, the Continuing Appropriations Resolution, 2013, which provides appropriations through March 27, 2013, provided the program a projected $20.124 million for FY2013 (the FY2012 appropriation amount plus 0.612%).

The Microloan technical assistance program provided counseling services to 15,892 small businesses in FY2012.[17]

Intermediary Microloan Lender Eligibility Standards

To become a qualified intermediary Microloan lender, an applicant must be organized as a nonprofit organization, quasi-governmental economic development corporation, or an agency established by a Native American Tribal Government. It must also have made and serviced short-term, fixed rate loans of not more than $50,000 to newly established or growing small businesses for at least one year and have at least one year of experience providing technical assistance to its borrowers.[18] If accepted into the program by the SBA, it can borrow no more than $750,000 from the SBA during its first year of participation, and no more than an aggregate of $5 million in later years.[19]

Intermediary Microloan Lender Program Requirements

After receiving an SBA microloan, intermediaries are not required to make any interest payments on the loan during the first year, but interest accrues from the date that the SBA disburses the loan proceeds to the intermediary. After that, the SBA determines the schedule for periodic payments. Loans must be repaid within 10 years.[20]

The interest rate charged to the intermediary is based on the five-year Treasury rate, adjusted to the nearest one-eighth percent, less 1.25%. The SBA's interest rate is updated on a monthly basis. In addition, intermediaries that maintain an average loan size of $10,000 or less are charged an interest rate based on the five-year Treasury rate, adjusted to the nearest one-eighth percent, less 2.0%. Portfolios are evaluated annually to determine the applicable rate.[21]

Intermediaries are required to contribute not less than 15% of the loan amount in cash from nonfederal sources and, as security for repayment of the loan, must provide the SBA first lien position on all notes receivable from any microloans issued under the program.[22] Unlike the SBA's 7(a) and 504/CDC loan guarantee programs, the SBA does not charge intermediaries upfront or on-going service fees under the Microloan program.[23]

As mentioned previously, P.L. 111-240, the Small Business Jobs Act of 2010, temporarily allowed the SBA to waive, in whole or in part through FY2012, the intermediary's 15% non-federal share requirement under specified circumstances (e.g., the economic conditions affecting the intermediary and the intermediary's performance) for up to a fiscal year.[24]

Intermediaries are required to deposit the proceeds from the SBA's loans, their 15% contribution, and payments from their microloan borrowers into an interest-bearing Microloan Revolving Fund. Intermediaries may only withdraw from this account funds necessary to make microloans to borrowers, repay the SBA, and establish and maintain an interest-bearing Loan Loss Reserve Fund to pay any shortage in the Microloan Revolving Fund caused by delinquencies or losses on its microloans.[25] They are required, until they have been in the program for at least five years, to maintain a balance in the Loan Loss Reserve Fund equal to 15% of the outstanding balance of the notes receivable from their microloan borrowers.[26] After five years, if the intermediary's average annual loss rate during the preceding five years is less than 15% and no other factors exist that may impair the intermediary's ability to repay its obligations to the SBA, the SBA Administrator may reduce the required balance in the intermediary's Loan Loss Reserve Fund to the intermediary's average annual loss rate during the preceding five years, but not less than 10% of the portfolio.[27] Intermediaries are required to maintain their Loan Loss Reserve Fund until they have repaid all obligations owed to the SBA.

The borrower default rate for the Microloan program is about 12%.[28] Because the Loan Loss Reserve Fund is used to contribute toward the cost of borrower defaults, and is often sufficient to cover the entire cost of such defaults, the SBA's loss rate for intermediary repayment is typically less than 3%.[29]

An intermediary may be suspended or removed from the Microloan program if it fails to comply with a specified list of program performance standards. For example, intermediaries are required to close and fund a minimum of four microloans per year, cover the service territory assigned by the SBA, honor the SBA determined boundaries of neighboring intermediaries and non-lender technical assistance providers, fulfill reporting requirements, maintain a loan currency rate of 85% or more (where loans are no more than 30 days late in scheduled payments), maintain a default rate of 15% or less, and "satisfactorily provide" in-house technical assistance to microloan clients and prospective microloan clients.[30]

Intermediary Marketing, Management, and Technical Training Assistance

As mentioned previously, the SBA provided intermediaries and qualified "non-lending technical assistance providers" $20.0 million in FY2012 to provide Microloan borrowers and Microloan prospective borrowers marketing, management, and technical training assistance.

P.L. 112-175, the Continuing Appropriations Resolution, 2013, which provides appropriations through March 27, 2013, provides the SBA a projected $20.124 million in FY2013 for this purpose.

Intermediaries are eligible to receive a Microloan technical assistance grant "of not more than 25% of the total outstanding balance of loans made to it under this subsection."[31] Grant funds may be used only to provide marketing, management, and technical assistance to microloan borrowers, except that up to 25% of the funds may be used to provide such assistance to prospective Microloan borrowers. Grant funds may also be used to attend training required by the SBA.[32] In most instances, intermediaries must contribute, solely from non-federal sources, an amount equal to 25% of the grant amount.[33] In addition to cash or other direct funding, the contribution may include indirect costs or in-kind contributions paid for under non-federal programs.[34] Intermediaries may expend no more than 25% of the grant funds on third-party contracts for the provision of technical assistance.[35]

Also, as mentioned earlier, P.L. 111-240, the Small Business Jobs Act of 2010, temporarily allowed the SBA to waive, in whole or in part through FY2012, the 25% non-federal share requirement for grants made to Microloan intermediaries for small business marketing, management, and technical assistance under specified circumstances (e.g., the economic conditions affecting the intermediary and the intermediary's performance) for up to a fiscal year.[36]

The SBA does not require Microloan borrowers to participate in the marketing, management, and technical assistance program. However, intermediaries typically require microloan borrowers to participate in the training program as a condition of the receipt of a microloan. Combining loan and intensive training assistance is one of the Microloan program's distinguishing features.

Intermediaries that make at least 25% of their loans to small businesses located in or owned by residents of an Economically Distressed Area (defined as having 40% or more of its residents with an annual income that is at or below the poverty level), or have a portfolio of loans made under the program "that averages not more than $10,000 during the period of the intermediary's participation in the program" are eligible to receive an additional training grant equal to 5% of "the total outstanding balance of loans made to the intermediary."[37] Intermediaries are not required to make a matching contribution as a condition of receiving these additional grant funds.

Non-lending Technical Assistance Providers

Each year, the SBA is authorized to select qualified non-profit, non-lending technical assistance providers to receive grant funds to provide marketing, management, and technical assistance to Microloan borrowers. Any non-profit entity that is not an intermediary may apply for these funds.[38]

The SBA may award up to 55 grants each year to qualified non-lending technical assistance providers to deliver marketing, management, and technical assistance to Microloan borrowers. The grants may be for terms of up to five years and may not exceed $200,000.[39] The nonprofit entity must contribute, solely from non-federal sources, an amount equal to 20% of the grant. In addition to cash or other direct funding, the contribution may include indirect costs or in-kind contributions paid for under non-federal programs.[40]

The SBA stopped awarding these grants at the beginning of FY2005. The SBA determined at that time that the non-lending technical assistance providers duplicated much of what was already being provided by Microloan intermediaries and other SBA entrepreneurial development programs.[41]

Microloan Borrower Eligibility Standards

With one exception, Microloan borrowers must be an eligible, for-profit small business as defined by the Small Business Act. P.L. 105-135, the Small Business Reauthorization Act of 1997, expanded the Microloan program's eligibility to include borrowers establishing a nonprofit childcare business.

Microloan Borrower Program Requirements

Intermediaries are directed by legislative language to provide borrowers "small-scale loans, particularly loans in amounts averaging not more than $10,000."[42] They are also directed, "to the extent practicable ... to maintain a microloan portfolio with an average loan size of not more than $15,000."[43] Microloans for more than $20,000 are allowed "only if such small business concern demonstrates that it is unable to obtain credit elsewhere at comparable interest rates and that it has good prospects for success."[44] The maximum loan amount is $50,000 and no borrower may owe an intermediary more than $50,000 at any one time.[45]

Microloan proceeds may be used only for working capital and acquisition of materials, supplies, furniture, fixtures, and equipment. Loans cannot be made to acquire land or property, and must be repaid within six years.[46] Within these parameters, loan terms vary depending on the loan's size, the planned use of funds, the requirements of the intermediary lender, and the needs of the small business borrower. On loans of more than $7,500, the maximum interest rate that can be charged to the borrower is the interest rate charged by the SBA on the loan to the intermediary, plus 7.75 percentage points. On loans of $7,500 or less, the maximum interest rate that can be charged to the borrower is the interest charged by the SBA on the loan to the intermediary, plus 8.5 percentage points.[47] Rates are negotiated between the borrower and the intermediary, and typically range from 8% to 10%.[48] Each intermediary establishes its own lending and credit requirements. However, borrowers are generally required to provide some type of collateral, and a personal guarantee to repay the loan. The SBA does not review the loan for creditworthiness.[49]

Microloan Program Statistics

In FY2012, the SBA provided 42 loans amounting to $23.9 million to intermediaries, and intermediaries provided 3,973 microloans amounting to $44.7 million to small businesses. The average loan to an intermediary was $568,238, and the average microloan to a small business was $11,255.[50]

The Microloan program is open to all small business entrepreneurs, but targets new and early-stage businesses in "underserved markets, including borrowers with little to no credit history, low-income borrowers, and women and minority entrepreneurs in both rural and urban areas who generally do not qualify for conventional loans, or other, larger SBA guaranteed loans."[51] An analysis conducted by the Urban Institute found that about 9.9% of conventional small business loans are issued to minority-owned small businesses and about 16% of conventional small business loans are issued to women-owned businesses.[52] In FY2012, more than half (57.4%) of the Microloan program's loans went to women-owned or -controlled firms and, of those reporting their race, 43.0% went to minority-owned or -controlled firms.[53] More than three-quarters of all microloan borrowers (79.8%) in FY2012 were located in an urban area. Also, startup companies received about half (51.9%) of all microloans in FY2012.[54] As mentioned previously, the borrower default rate for the Microloan program is about 12%.[55] Because the Loan Loss Reserve Fund is used to contribute toward the cost of borrower defaults, and is often sufficient to cover the entire cost of such defaults, the SBA's loss rate for intermediary repayment is typically less than 3%.[56]

Microloans are often used for more than one purpose. In FY2012, they were most commonly used to finance working capital (65.5%), purchase new equipment (26.0%), and purchase inventory (24.3%).[57]

CONGRESSIONAL ISSUES

Critics of the SBA's Microloan program argue that it is duplicative of other available programs, expensive relative to alternative programs, and subject to administrative shortfalls. The program's advocates argue that it provides assistance that "reaches many who otherwise would not be served by the private sector or even the SBA's 7(a) loan program" and "has provided an important source of capital for low-income women business owners and minority borrowers."[58]

Program Duplication

Critics of the SBA's Microloan program argue that its direct lending program is duplicative of the SBA's 7(a) loan guarantee program and its marketing, management, and technical training assistance grant program is duplicative of the SBA's training assistance provided through Small Business Development Centers, SCORE (Service Corps of Retired Executives), and Women Business Centers. For example, President George W. Bush proposed to eliminate all funding for the Microloan program in his FY2005, FY2006, and FY2007 budget requests to Congress, arguing that "the 7(a) program is capable of serving the same clientele through the Community Express programs for much lower cost to the Government."[59] President Bush also proposed to terminate the Microloan program's marketing, management, and technical assistance grant program in his FY2008 and FY2009 budget requests to Congress.[60]

Critics of the SBA's Microloan program argued in 2007 that about 44% of the SBA's 7(a) program's loan guarantees at that time were for loans under $35,000 (the Microloan program's former loan limit for borrowers), representing more than 17 times the number of loans issued through the SBA's Microloan program.[61] In their view, the 7(a) program had demonstrated that it can service the needs of small businesses targeted by the SBA's Microloan program.[62] They also argued that the SBA's Microloan program's marketing, management, and technical assistance grants program was not necessary because the SBA "already supports a nationwide network of resource partners who provide counseling and training to entrepreneurs, including Small Business Development Centers, Women's Business Centers, and SCORE."[63] They argued that about 94% of Microloan intermediaries are located within 20 miles of a Small Business Development Center, a Women's Business Center, or a SCORE partner.[64]

The program's advocates argue that the SBA's Microloan program is complementary, not duplicative of the SBA's 7(a) loan guarantee program. They assert that microloan borrowers are particularly disadvantaged when seeking access to capital, often having no credit history or lower credit scores than most applicants for the SBA's 7(a) loan guarantee program.[65] In their view, it is important that the SBA has a program whose sole focus is to assist microloan borrowers in starting a microbusiness and have in place intermediaries that "have essential expertise on the needs of this key demographic."[66]

They also argue that the SBA's Microloan marketing, management, and technical assistance grants program is "a crucial element which enables intermediaries to assist microbusiness owners step by step through their development and growth" and "not only increases the likelihood of full repayment of the loan, but augments business survival and success."[67] As mentioned previously, intermediaries typically require Microloan borrowers to participate in the training program as a condition of the receipt of the microloan.

Program Cost

Critics of the SBA's Microloan program argue that it is expensive relative to other SBA programs, costing about $9,685 per small business assisted in FY2011, compared to $1,882 per small business assisted in the SBA's 7(a) loan guarantee program.[68] President George W. Bush cited the program's higher expense when he recommended in his FY2005, FY2006, and FY2007 budget requests to Congress that the program be terminated and when he recommended in his FY2008 and FY2009 budget requests to Congress that the interest rate charged to Microloan intermediaries be increased to make the program "self-financing."[69]

The SBA's Microloan program's advocates argue that the program's higher cost per small business assisted is unavoidable given the relatively unique nature of the program and the special needs of its borrowers. They assert that intermediaries often have to spend a significant amount of time with Microloan borrowers because those borrowers tend to have less experience with the credit application process and a more difficult time documenting their qualifications for assistance than borrowers in the SBA's loan guaranty programs. Also, in their view, raising the interest rate charged to intermediaries to make the program self-financing would reduce the program's cost, but could also defeat the program's purpose. They assert that because microloans are small, it is difficult for intermediaries to generate enough interest income to cover their costs. As a result, if the interest rate charged to intermediaries is increased, they contend that intermediaries would have to pass the increase on to Microloan borrowers. In their view, increasing the program's cost to microloan borrowers "will create an economic hardship for them and make it more difficult for them to grow their businesses" and "lead to fewer jobs created and fewer tax dollars paid."[70]

Program Administration

On December 28, 2009, the SBA's Office of Inspector General released an analysis of the SBA's administration of the Microloan program. It reported a number of deficiencies that it argued needed to be addressed. The analysis was undertaken in response to language in P.L. 111-5, the American Recovery and Reinvestment Act of 2009 (ARRA), directing Offices of Inspector General to perform audits of their respective agencies to determine whether adequate safeguards exist concerning the use of ARRA funds.[71]

Program Oversight

The SBA's Office of Inspector General found that the SBA's oversight of the Microloan program "was not sufficient to ensure effective operation of the Microloan program":

> SBA's oversight is focused on the intermediaries' ability to repay their SBA loans and is limited to a cursory review of quarterly financial reports supported by only one monthly bank statement.... The bank statements are used to simply verify the outstanding balances reported on the intermediaries' quarterly reports. This review process does not allow SBA to analyze the sources and uses of funds ... which is necessary to detect inappropriate fund transfers between the intermediaries' [Microloan Revolving Funds and Loan Loss Reserve Funds] accounts.[72]

The Office of Inspector General's report noted that the SBA only conducts onsite reviews when an intermediary defaults on its SBA loan. It also argued that the program was inadequately staffed, operating at that time "with 6 analysts who oversee more than 160 intermediaries, 460 intermediary loans, and approximately 2,500 microloans per year."[73]

The SBA agreed with the Office of Inspector General that a more detailed review of the financial information provided by intermediaries was appropriate. It now collects three months of bank statements each quarter from intermediaries. It also hired three additional staff members to monitor the program's ARRA funding, and indicated that it will continue to reassess the program's overall staffing needs.[74]

Reliability of the Microloan Program's Performance Data

The SBA's Office of Inspector General found that the SBA's reported Microloan borrower default rate of 12% "appeared low given the high-risk nature of the program."[75] It found that one intermediary made 1,182 microloans valued at over $11 million since 1993 and only reported slightly more than a 1% historical default rate, and 39 other intermediaries that reported that none of their loans had defaulted. It also identified duplicate loan reporting; multiple loans to microloan borrowers in the same amount, indicating the use of revolving lines of credit, which is disallowed by program regulations; and 92 microloan borrowers with outstanding microloan balances exceeding the $35,000 limit. It noted that ARRA "makes clear the importance of data verification" yet "all of the data used by SBA to report on the Microloan program performance is based on unverified information that is self-reported by intermediaries."[76] It concluded that "as a result, SBA cannot ensure that the reported microloan default rates are accurate and comply with the statutory requirement."[77]

In response, the SBA agreed with the Office of Inspector General with the need for accurate program data and indicated that microloan data will be evaluated as part of a "data quality initiative to identify areas for improvement."[78] The SBA also indicated that it will revise its SOPs (standard operating procedures) to "include guidance on data review and procedures for following up with intermediaries to resolve data discrepancies."[79]

Outcome-Oriented Performance Measures

The SBA's Office of Inspector General found that the SBA's program performance is based on the number of microloans funded and small businesses assisted. It argued that these "performance metrics ... do not ensure the ultimate program beneficiaries, the microloan borrowers, are truly assisted by the program" and "without appropriate metrics, SBA cannot ensure the Microloan program is meeting policy goals."[80] It noted that the SBA does not track the number of microloan borrowers who remain in business after receiving a microloan to measure the extent to which the loans contributed to the success of borrowers and does not determine the effect that technical training assistance may have on the success of microloan borrowers and their ability to repay loans.[81] It recommended that the SBA "develop additional performance metrics to measure the program's achievement in assisting microloan borrowers in establishing and maintaining successful small businesses."[82]

In response, the SBA indicated that it has "contracted with the Aspen Institute to advise on appropriate program and performance metrics for both microloans and technical assistance grants."[83] It also indicated that the program metrics developed will be used to assist the agency in measuring the Microloan program's effectiveness.

LEGISLATION

Congress has not considered any bills during the 112th Congress that would affect the Microloan program. However, it did consider several bills during the 111th Congress that would have affected the SBA's Microloan program before passing the Small Business Jobs Act of 2010, which President Obama signed into law (P.L. 111-240) on September 27, 2010.

H.R. 3854, thc Small Business Financing and Investment Act of 2009, was passed by the House by a vote of 389-32, on October 29, 2009.[84] The Senate did not act on the bill. It would have authorized several new SBA programs and changed several existing SBA programs, including the Microloan program. For example, it would have

- increased the Microloan program's loan funding to "such sums as may be necessary" to support $110 million in direct microloans in FY2010 and $110 million in FY2011.[85]
- increased the program's marketing, management, and technical assistance grant funding to $80 million in FY2010 and $80 million in FY2011.
- authorized $20 million ($10 million in FY2010 and $10 million in FY2012) for a new Microloan interest assistance grant program.[86]
- broadened the eligibility requirements for Microloan intermediaries to qualify for lower interest rates.[87]
- increased the program's maximum loan amount to intermediaries during their first year of participation in the program from $750,000 to $1 million, and in later years from an aggregate of $3.5 million to $7 million. The SBA's Administrator would

have been provided discretion to increase the limit to $10 million if such treatment was determined by the SBA Administrator to be appropriate.[88]

- broadened the eligibility requirements for Microloan intermediaries "to help expand access to the Microloan program."[89]
- required the SBA to establish a process under which Microloan intermediaries "provide to the major credit reporting agencies the information about the borrower, both positive and negative, that is relevant to credit reporting, such as the payment activity of the borrower on the loan."[90]
- provided lenders with the authority to offer more flexible loan terms to Microloan borrowers, particularly with longer-term loans or revolving lines of credit, by removing existing requirements that all microloans be "short-term."[91]
- increased the percentage of technical assistance grant funds that an intermediary can spend on prospective borrowers from 25% to 35%, and on the provision of technical assistance through third-party providers from 25% to 35%.[92]
- required the SBA to annually provide the House Committee on Small Business and the Senate Committee on Small Business and Entrepreneurship a detailed, comprehensive report on the Microloan program.[93]

S. 2869, the Small Business Job Creation and Access to Capital Act of 2009, was ordered to be reported by the Senate Committee on Small Business and Entrepreneurship on December 10, 2009. It would have authorized changes to several SBA programs, including the Microloan program. The Senate did not take further action on the bill, but several of its provisions, including those affecting the Microloan program, were later included in P.L. 111-240. For example, it would have

- increased the SBA's Microloan program's maximum loan amount to intermediaries after their first year of participation in the program from $3.5 million to $5 million.[94]
- increased the maximum loan amount to Microloan borrowers from $35,000 to $50,000.[95]

As mentioned previously, P.L. 111-240 the Small Business Jobs Act of 2010, authorizes the Secretary of the Treasury to create a $30 billion SBLF to encourage community banks to provide small business loans ($4 billion was issued), a $1.5 billion State Small Business Credit Initiative, and about $12 billion in tax relief for small businesses. It also includes revenue raising provisions to offset the act's cost, and authorizes a number of changes to the SBA's loan guaranty, export promotion, and contracting programs, including changes to the SBA's Microloan program. For example, it

- authorizes the SBA to increase the Microloan program's loan limit for borrowers from $35,000 to $50,000, and for Microloan intermediaries after their first year of participation in the program from $3.5 million to $5 million.[96]
- temporarily allowed the SBA to waive, in whole or in part through FY2012, the non-federal share requirement for loans to the Microloan program's intermediaries and for grants made to Microloan intermediaries for small business marketing, management, and technical assistance under specified circumstances (e.g., the

economic conditions affecting the intermediary and the intermediary's performance) for up to a fiscal year.[97]

CONCLUSION

During the 111th Congress, congressional debate concerning proposed changes to the SBA's loan guaranty programs, including the Microloan program, centered on the likely impact the changes would have on small business access to capital, job retention, and job creation. As a general proposition, some, including President Obama, argued that economic conditions made it imperative that the SBA be provided additional resources to assist small businesses in acquiring capital necessary to start, continue, or expand operations and create jobs.[98] Others worried about the long-term adverse economic effects of spending programs that increase the federal deficit. They advocated business tax reduction, reform of financial credit market regulation, and federal fiscal restraint as the best means to assist small business economic growth and job creation.[99]

In terms of specific program changes, the provisions considered in H.R. 3854 and S. 2869 and authorized by P.L. 111-240 (allowing the SBA to temporarily waive the Microloan program's non-federal share matching requirements, increasing its loan limit for borrowers from $35,000 to $50,000, and increasing its loan limit for intermediaries after their first year of participation in the program from $3.5 million to $5 million) were all designed to achieve the same goal: to enhance job creation by increasing the ability of Microloan borrowers to obtain credit at affordable rates. Determining how specific changes in federal policy are most likely to enhance job creation is a challenging question. For example, a 2008 Urban Institute study concluded that differences in the term, interest rate, and amount of SBA financing "was not significantly associated with increasing sales or employment among firms receiving SBA financing."[100] However, they also reported that their analysis accounted for less than 10% of the variation in firm performance. The Urban Institute suggested that local economic conditions, local zoning regulations, state and local tax rates, state and local business assistance programs, and the business owner's charisma or business acumen also "may play a role in determining how well a business performs after receipt of SBA financing."[101]

As the Urban Institute study suggests, given the many factors that influence business success, measuring the SBA's Microloan program's effect on job retention and creation is complicated. That task is made even more challenging by the absence of performance-oriented measures that could serve as a guide.

The SBA's Office of Inspector General has recommended that the SBA adopt performance-oriented measures, specifically recommending that the SBA track the number of Microloan borrowers who remain in business after receiving a microloan to measure the extent to which the Microloan program contributed to their ability to stay in business. It has also recommended that the SBA require intermediaries to report the technical assistance provided to each Microloan borrower and "use this data to analyze the effect technical assistance may have on the success of Microloan borrowers and their ability to repay microloans."[102] Other performance-oriented measures that Congress might also consider include requiring the SBA to survey Microloan borrowers to measure the difficulty they experienced in obtaining a loan from the private sector; the ease or difficulty of finding, applying, and obtaining a microloan from an intermediary; and the extent to which the microloan or technical assistance received contributed to their ability to create jobs or expand their scope of operations.

End Notes

[1] U.S. Small Business Administration, "Fiscal Year 2010 Congressional Budget Justification," pp. 29, 30.

[2] Veronique de Rugy, *Why the Small Business Administration's Loan Programs Should Be Abolished*, American Enterprise Institute for Public Policy Research, AEI Working Paper #126, April 13, 2006, at http://www.aei.org/files/ 2006/04/13/20060414_wp126.pdf. Also, see U.S. Government Accountability Office, *Small Business Administration: 7(a) Loan Program Needs Additional Performance Measures*, GAO-08-226T, November 1, 2007, pp. 3, 9-11, at http://www.gao.gov/new.items/d08226t.pdf.

[3] U.S. Congress, House Committee on Small Business, *Full Committee Legislative Hearing on the SBA's Microloan and Trade Programs*, 110th Cong., 1st sess., July 12, 2007, H.Hrg. 110-35 (Washington: GPO, 2007), p. 6.

[4] Christopher Hayes, *An Assessment of the Small Business Administration's Loan and Investment Programs: Survey of Assisted Businesses* (Washington: The Urban Institute, January 2008), p. 5, at http://www.urban.org/UploadedPDF/ 411599_assisted_business_survey.pdf.

[5] The SBA also provided direct loans to small businesses until 1994. For further analysis, see CRS Report R40985, *Small Business: Access to Capital and Job Creation*, by Robert Jay Dilger.

[6] Robert Cull, Asli Demiriguc-Kunt, and Jonathan Morduch, "Microfinance Meets the Market," *Journal of Economic Perspectives*, vol. 23, no. 1 (Winter 2009), pp. 169-172; and U.S. Congress, Senate Committee on Small Business and Entrepreneurship, *Microloan Program Improvement Act of 2001*, report to accompany S. 174, 107th Cong., 1st sess., May 26, 2001, S.Rept. 107-18 (Washington: GPO, 2001). About 3.55 million firms in the United States in 2009 had fewer than five employees. See U.S. Census Bureau, *Statistics of U.S. Businesses: U.S. & States, Totals*, at http://www.census.gov/econ/susb/index.html.

[7] 15 U.S.C. §636 7(m)(1)(A).

[8] U.S. Small Business Administration, Office of Advocacy, *Small Business Economic Indicators for 2003*, August 2004, p. 3; and Brian Headd, "Small Businesses Most Likely to Lead Economic Recovery," *The Small Business Advocate*, vol. 28, no. 6 (July 2009), pp. 1, 2.

[9] For further information and analysis concerning the Small Business Lending Fund see CRS Report R42045, *The Small Business Lending Fund*, by Robert Jay Dilger. For further information and analysis concerning the State Small Business Credit Initiative see CRS Report R42581, *State Small Business Credit Initiative: Implementation and Funding Issues*, by Robert Jay Dilger.

[10] For information and analysis concerning the SBA's 7(a) and 504/CDC programs, see CRS Report R41146, *Small Business Administration 7(a) Loan Guaranty Program*, by Robert Jay Dilger and CRS Report R41184, *Small Business Administration 504/CDC Loan Guaranty Program*, by Robert Jay Dilger.

[11] P.L. 111-240, the Small Business Jobs Act of 2010, increased the loan limit for borrowers from $35,000 to $50,000.

[12] There are no Microloan intermediaries located in Alaska and Utah. U.S. Small Business Administration, "Microloan Program: Partner Identification & Management System Participating Intermediary Microlenders Report," at http://www.sba.gov/sites/default/files/ partner_by_subcat_report_20120705.pdf. An intermediary may not operate in more than one state unless the SBA determines that it would be in the best interests of the small business community for it to operate across state lines. For example, the microloan intermediary located in Washington, Pennsylvania is allowed to service ten West Virginia counties due to its proximity to these counties and the distance to the only other intermediary serving West Virginia, which is located in Charleston, West Virginia. Also, a microloan intermediary located in Laguna Nigel, California, which focuses on the capital needs of disabled veteran-owned businesses, serves many jurisdictions throughout the nation that lack a participating intermediary.

[13] The Obama Administration and the House Committee on Appropriations recommended that the Microloan program receive an appropriation of $3.765 million for FY2012, which was expected to support about $25.0 million in lending to intermediaries. The Senate Committee on Appropriations recommended that the Microloan program receive an appropriation of $3.678 million for FY2012, which was expected to support about $25.0 million in lending to intermediaries. See U.S. Office of Management and Budget, *FY2012, Budget of the United States Government, Appendix*, pp. 1161-1172; U.S. Congress, House Committee on

Appropriations, *Financial Services and General Government Appropriations Bill, 2012*, report to accompany H.R. 2434, 112th Cong., 1st sess., July 7, 2012, H.Rept. 112-136 (Washington: GPO, 2012), p. 67; and U.S. Congress, Senate Committee on Appropriations, *Financial Services and General Government Appropriations Bill, 2012*, report to accompany S. 1573, 112th Cong., 1st sess., September 15, 2011, S.Rept. 112-79 (Washington: GPO, 2011), p. 115.

14 U.S. Office of Management and Budget, *FY2013, Budget of the United States Government, Appendix*, p. 1267. The House Committee on Appropriations recommended that the Microloan program receive an appropriation of $2.844 million for FY2013, which is expected to support about $18.0 million in lending to intermediaries. The Senate Committee on Appropriations recommended that the Microloan program receive an appropriation of $4.0 million for FY2013, which is expected to support about $25.0 million in lending to intermediaries. See U.S. Congress, House Committee on Appropriations, *Financial Services and General Government Appropriations Bill, 2013*, report to accompany H.R. 6020, 112th Cong., 2nd sess., June 26, 2012, H.Rept. 112-550 (Washington: GPO, 2012), p. 78; and U.S. Congress, Senate Committee on Appropriations, *Financial Services and General Government Appropriations Bill, 2013*, report to accompany S. 3301, 112th Cong., 2nd sess., June 14, 2012, S.Rept. 112-177 (Washington: GPO, 2012), p. 115.

15 U.S. Small Business Administration, "Fiscal Year 2013 Congressional Budget Justification and Fiscal Year 2011 Annual Performance Report," p. 15; and P.L. 112-74, the Consolidated Appropriations Act, 2012.

16 U.S. Office of Management and Budget, *FY2013, Budget of the United States Government, Appendix*, p. 1265. The House Committee on Appropriations recommended that the Microloan technical assistance program receive an appropriation of $20.0 million for FY2013. The Senate Committee on Appropriations recommended that the Microloan technical assistance program receive an appropriation of $24.0 million. See U.S. Congress, House Committee on Appropriations, Financial Services and General Government Appropriations Bill, 2013, report to accompany H.R. 6020, 112th Cong., 2nd sess., June 26, 2012, H.Rept. 112-550 (Washington: GPO, 2012), p. 76; and U.S. Congress, Senate Committee on Appropriations, *Financial Services and General Government Appropriations Bill, 2013*, report to accompany S. 3301, 112th Cong., 2nd sess., June 14, 2012, S.Rept. 112-177 (Washington: GPO, 2012), p. 111.

17 U.S. Small Business Administration, Office of Congressional and Legislative Affairs, correspondence with the author, October 16, 2012. The Microloan technical assistance program provided counseling services to 15,900 small businesses in FY2011, 14,916 small businesses in FY2010, and 2,757 in FY2009. See U.S. Small Business Administration, "Fiscal Year 2013 Congressional Budget Justification and Fiscal Year 2011 Annual Performance Report," p. 34.

18 13 C.F.R §120.701; and 13 C.F.R §120.702. P.L. 111-240, the Small Business Jobs Act of 2010, increased the loan limit for borrowers from $35,000 to $50,000.

19 13 C.F.R §120.706. P.L. 111-240, the Small Business Jobs Act of 2010, increased the loan limit for intermediaries after their first year of participation in the program from $3.5 million to $5 million.

20 13 C.F.R §120.706.

21 15 U.S.C. §636 7(m)(3)(F)(iii). In August 2012, the SBA's interest rate to intermediaries was 0.0% if the average loan size in the intermediary's portfolio was under $10,000. The rate was also 0.0% if the average loan size was greater than $10,000. U.S. Small Business Administration, Office of Congressional and Legislative Affairs, correspondence with the author, August 2, 2012.

22 13 C.F.R §120.706. Note: The 15% contribution must be from non-federal sources and may not be borrowed. For purposes of this program, Community Development Block Grants are considered non-federal sources.

23 Ibid.

24 P.L. 111-240, the Small Business Jobs Act of 2010, §1401. Matching Requirements Under Small Business Programs.

25 13 C.F.R §120.709.

26 13 C.F.R §120.710. If the intermediary's average annual loss rate during the preceding five years is less than 15% and no other factors exist that may impair the intermediary's ability to repay its obligations to the SBA, the SBA Administrator may reduce the required balance in the intermediary's Loan Loss Reserve Fund to the intermediary's average annual loss rate during the preceding five years, but not less than 10% of the portfolio.

27 Ibid.

28 U.S. Congress, House Committee on Small Business, *Full Committee Hearings on the Small Business Administration's Microloan Program*, 110th Cong., 1st sess., June 14, 2007, H.Hrg. 110-30 (Washington: GPO, 2007), p. 15. Note: A study released on December 28, 2009 by the U.S. Small Business Administration, Office of the Inspector General, concluded that Microloan intermediaries may be under-reporting the default rate. See U.S. Small Business Administration, Office of the Inspector General, "SBA's Administration of the Microloan

Program under the Recovery Act," December 28, 2009, at http://www.sba.gov/office-of-inspector-general/868/12427.

[29] U.S. Small Business Administration, "2008 Loss Report," p. 10, at http://archive.sba.gov/idc/groups/public/documents/sba_program_office/cfo_2008_loss_ report.pdf; and U.S. Small Business Administration, Office of Congressional and Legislative Affairs, correspondence with the author, August 2, 2012. In FY2011, the Microloan program's intermediary default rate was 2.15%. See U.S. Small Business Administration, "Agency Financial Report, Fiscal Year 2011," p. 8, at http://www.sba.gov/sites/default/files/ Agency%20Financial%20Report%20 FY%20 2011_ 0.pdf. A total of 27 loans to intermediaries have been charged off over the life of the Microloan program, through August 2, 2012. The amount charged off on these 27 loans is $3,985,056.54. This represents 1.11% of total funds disbursed to intermediaries and 3.20% of the current outstanding principal balance of loans to intermediary lenders.

[30] 13 C.F.R §120.716.

[31] 15 U.S.C. §636(m)(4)(A). Note: The SBA's Program for Investment in Microentrepreneurs Act (PRIME) program also provides non-profit organizations grant funding to assist low-income entrepreneurs with training assistance. See, U.S. Small Business Administration, "PRIME Program," at http://www.sba.gov/content/prime-program-0.

[32] 13 C.F.R §120.712.

[33] Ibid. Intermediaries who make at least 50% of their loans to small businesses located in or owned by residents of Economically Distressed Areas are not subject to the 25% contribution requirement. An economically distressed area is a county or equivalent division of local government in which, according to the most recent available data from the U.S. Census Bureau, 40% or more of the residents have an annual income that is at or below the poverty level. See 13 C.F.R §120.701.

[34] 13 C.F.R §120.712. Intermediaries may not borrow their contribution.

[35] Ibid.

[36] P.L. 111-240, the Small Business Jobs Act of 2010, §1401. Matching Requirements Under Small Business Programs.

[37] 13 C.F.R §120.712; and 15 U.S.C. §636(m)(4)(C)(i).

[38] 13 C.F.R §120.714.

[39] Ibid.

[40] Ibid.

[41] U.S. Small Business Administration, Office of Congressional and Legislative Affairs, correspondence with the author, August 2, 2012.

[42] 15 U.S.C. §636(m)(1)(A)(iii)(I).

[43] 15 U.S.C. §636(m)(6)(B).

[44] 15 U.S.C. §636(m)(3)(E).

[45] 13 C.F.R §120.707. P.L. 111-240, the Small Business Jobs Act of 2010, increased the loan limit for borrowers from $35,000 to $50,000.

[46] Ibid.

[47] 15 U.S.C. §636 7(m)(6)(C)(i); and 15 U.S.C. §636 7(m)(6)(C)(ii).

[48] In FY2012, Microloan borrowers were charged, on average, an interest rate of 8.18, compared to 8.45% in FY2011. U.S Small Business Administration, "Nationwide Loan Report, October 1, 2011 through September 30, 2012," October 15, 2012; and U.S Small Business Administration, "Nationwide Loan Report, October 1, 2010 through September 30, 2011," November 2, 2011.

[49] U.S. Small Business Administration, "Microloan Program," at http://www.sba.gov/ content/microloan-program.

[50] U.S. Small Business Administration, Office of Congressional and Legislative Affairs, correspondence with the author, October 16, 2012.

[51] U.S. Small Business Administration, "Microloans Help Small Businesses Start, Grow and Succeed," at http://archive.sba.gov/idc/groups/public/documents/sba_homepage/recovery_ act_microloans.pdf.

[52] Kenneth Temkin, Brett Theodos, with Kerstin Gentsch, *Competitive and Special Competitive Opportunity Gap Analysis of the 7(A) and 504 Programs* (Washington: The Urban Institute, 2008), p. 13, at http://www.urban.org/ UploadedPDF/411596_504_gap_analysis.pdf.

[53] U.S Small Business Administration, "Nationwide Loan Report, October 1, 2011 through September 30, 2012," October 15, 2012.

[54] Ibid.

[55] U.S. Congress, House Committee on Small Business, *Full Committee Hearings on the Small Business Administration's Microloan Program*, 110th Cong., 1st sess., June 14, 2007, H.Hrg. 110-30 (Washington: GPO,

2007), p. 15. Note: A study released on December 28, 2009 by the U.S. Small Business Administration, Office of the Inspector General, concluded that Microloan intermediaries may be under-reporting the default rate. See U.S. Small Business Administration, Office of the Inspector General, "SBA's Administration of the Microloan Program under the Recovery Act," December 28, 2009, at http://www.sba.gov/office-of-inspector-general/868/12427.

[56] U.S. Small Business Administration, "2008 Loss Report," p. 10, at http://archive.sba.gov/idc/groups/public/documents/sba_program_office/cfo_2008_loss_report.pdf; and U.S. Small Business Administration, Office of Congressional and Legislative Affairs, correspondence with the author, August 2, 2012. In FY2011, the Microloan program's intermediary default rate was 2.15%. See U.S. Small Business Administration, "Agency Financial Report, Fiscal Year 2011," p. 8, at http://www.sba.gov/sites/default/files/ Agency%20Financial%20Report%20 FY%202011_0.pdf. A total of 27 loans to intermediaries have been charged off over the life of the Microloan program, through August 2, 2012. The amount charged off on these 27 loans is $3,985,056.54. This represents 1.11% of total funds disbursed to intermediaries and 3.20% of the current outstanding principal balance of loans to intermediary lenders.

[57] U.S Small Business Administration, "Nationwide Loan Report, October 1, 2011 through September 30, 2012," October 15, 2012.

[58] U.S. Congress, House Committee on Small Business, *Full Committee Hearing on the Small Business Administration's Microloan Program*, 110th Cong., 1st sess., June 14, 2007, H.Hrg. 110-30 (Washington: GPO, 2007), pp. 1, 2.

[59] U.S. Office of Management and Budget, *Budget of the United States Government: Fiscal Year 2005*, p. 334, at http://www.gpoaccess.gov/usbudget/fy05/pdf/budget/sba.pdf; U.S. Office of Management and Budget, *Budget of the United States Government: Fiscal Year 2006*, p. 313, at http://www.gpoaccess.gov/usbudget/fy06/pdf/budget/sba.pdf; and U.S. Office of Management and Budget, *Budget of the United States Government: Fiscal Year 2007*, p. 283, at http://www.gpoaccess.gov/ usbudget/fy07/pdf/budget/sba.pdf.

[60] U.S. Office of Management and Budget, *Budget of the United States Government: Fiscal Year 2008*, pp. 139, 140, at http://www.gpoaccess.gov/usbudget/fy08/pdf/budget/sba.pdf; and U.S. Office of Management and Budget, *Budget of the United States Government: Fiscal Year 2009*, p. 130, at http://www.gpoaccess.gov/usbudget/fy09/pdf/budget/sba.pdf. The Bush Administration also proposed to increase the interest rate charged to intermediaries.

[61] U.S. Congress, House Committee on Small Business, *Full Committee Legislative Hearing on the SBA's Microloan and Trade Programs*, 110th Cong., 1st sess., July 12, 2007, H.Hrg. 110-35 (Washington: GPO, 2007), p. 37.

[62] Ibid.

[63] Ibid., pp. 37, 38.

[64] U.S. Congress, House Committee on Small Business, *Full Committee Hearing on the Small Business Administration's Microloan Program*, 110th Cong., 1st sess., June 14, 2007, H.Hrg. 110-30 (Washington: GPO, 2007), p. 7.

[65] U.S. Congress, House Committee on Small Business, *Full Committee Legislative Hearing on the SBA's Microloan and Trade Programs*, 110th Cong., 1st sess., July 12, 2007, H.Hrg. 110-35 (Washington: GPO, 2007), p. 27.

[66] Ibid., p. 7.

[67] Ibid.

[68] U.S. Small Business Administration, "Fiscal Year 2013 Congressional Budget Justification and Fiscal Year 2011 Annual Performance Report," pp. 31, 34.

[69] U.S. Office of Management and Budget, *Budget of the United States Government: Fiscal Year 2008*,pp. 139, 140, at http://www.gpoaccess.gov/usbudget/fy08/pdf/budget/sba.pdf; U.S. Office of Management and Budget, *Budget of the United States Government: Fiscal Year 2009*, p. 130, at http://www.gpoaccess.gov /usbudget/fy09/pdf/budget/sba.pdf; U.S. Congress, House Committee on Small Business, *Full Committee Legislative Hearing on the SBA's Microloan and Trade Programs*, 110th Cong., 1st sess., July 12, 2007, H.Hrg. 110-35 (Washington: GPO, 2007), p. 38; and U.S. Congress, House Committee on Small Business, Subcommittee on Finance and Tax, *Subcommittee Hearing on Improving the SBA's Access to Capital Programs for our Nation's Small Businesses*, 110th Cong., 2nd sess., March 5, 2008, H.Hrg. 110-76 (Washington: GPO, 2008), p. 33.

[70] U.S. Congress, House Committee on Small Business, Subcommittee on Finance and Tax, *Subcommittee Hearing on Improving the SBA's Access to Capital Programs for our Nation's Small Businesses*, 110th Cong., 2nd sess., March 5, 2008, H.Hrg. 110-76 (Washington: GPO, 2008), p. 46.

[71] U.S. Small Business Administration, Office of the Inspector General, "SBA's Administration of the Microloan Program under the Recovery Act," p. 1, at http://www.sba.gov/office-of-inspector-general/868/12427.

[72] Ibid., p. 4.

[73] Ibid.

[74] Ibid., p. 8.

[75] Ibid., p. 4.

[76] Ibid., p. 5.

[77] Ibid.

[78] Ibid., p. 8.

[79] Ibid., p. 9.

[80] Ibid., p. 6.

[81] Ibid.

[82] Ibid., p. 7.

[83] Ibid., p. 9.

[84] H.R. 3854 combined language from eight bills and would have authorized changes to several SBA programs and create several new programs. For further analysis, see CRS Report R41385, *Small Business Legislation During the 111th Congress*, by Robert Jay Dilger and Gary Guenther.

[85] H.R. 3854, the Small Business Financing and Investment Act of 2009, §310. Authorization of Appropriations.

[86] Ibid.

[87] H.R. 3854, the Small Business Financing and Investment Act of 2009, §307. Interest Rates and Loan Size. The interest rate charged to intermediaries is based on the five-year Treasury rate, adjusted to the nearest one-eighth percent, less 1.25%. However, intermediaries that maintain an average loan size of $7,500 or less are charged an interest rate based on the five-year Treasury rate, adjusted to the nearest one-eighth percent, less 2.0%. H.R. 3854 would have enabled more intermediaries to qualify for the lower rate by increasing the required average loan size from $7,500 to $10,000.

[88] U.S. Congress, House Committee on Small Business, Small Business Financing and Investment Act of 2009, report to accompany H.R. 3854, 111th Cong., 1st sess., October 26, 2009, H.Rept. 111-315 (Washington: GPO, 2009), p. 34; and H.R. 3854, the Small Business Financing and Investment Act of 2009, §304. Increased Limit on Intermediary Borrowing.

[89] U.S. Congress, House Committee on Small Business, Small Business Financing and Investment Act of 2009, report to accompany H.R. 3854, 111th Cong., 1st sess., October 26, 2009, H.Rept. 111-315 (Washington: GPO, 2009), p. 34. At that time, intermediaries must have made and serviced short-term, fixed rate loans of not more than $35,000 (now $50,000) to newly established or growing small businesses for at least one year and have at least one year of experience providing technical assistance to its borrowers. Under H.R. 3854, intermediaries would have been required to have at least one year of experience making microloans to startup, newly established, or growing small business concerns, or have a full-time employee who has not less than three years' experience in managing a portfolio of loans to startup, newly established, or growing small business concerns. They would have been required to also have at least one year of experience providing, as an integral part of its microloan program, intensive marketing, management, and technical assistance to its borrowers, or one full-time employee who has not less than one year experience providing, as an integral part of its microloan program, intensive marketing, management, and technical assistance to its borrowers. This change would have allowed an aspiring intermediary with no direct experience in microlending and technical assistance to hire trained employees with considerable, equivalent experience and still qualify to participate in the program.

[90] H.R. 3854, the Small Business Financing and Investment Act of 2009, §301. Microloan Credit Building Initiative. This change was designed to enhance Microloan borrowers' credit scores and their future access to capital. Intermediaries generally opposed the provision, viewing it as an administrative burden. U.S. Congress, House Committee on Small Business, *Small Business Financing and Investment Act of 2009*, report to accompany H.R. 3854, 111th Cong., 1st sess., October 26, 2009, H.Rept. 111-315 (Washington: GPO, 2009), p. 34.

[91] H.R. 3854, the Small Business Financing and Investment Act of 2009, §302. Flexible Credit Terms; and U.S. Congress, House Committee on Small Business, *Small Business Financing and Investment Act of 2009*, report to accompany H.R. 3854, 111th Cong., 1st sess., October 26, 2009, H.Rept. 111-315 (Washington: GPO, 2009), p. 34.

[92] U.S. Congress, House Committee on Small Business, *Small Business Financing and Investment Act of 2009*, report to accompany H.R. 3854, 111th Cong., 1st sess., October 26, 2009, H.Rept. 111-315 (Washington: GPO, 2009), p. 35.

[93] H.R. 3854, the Small Business Financing and Investment Act of 2009, §308. Reporting Requirement. The report was to include the following information: the names and locations of each intermediary participating in the program; the amounts of each loan and each grant provided to each intermediary during the fiscal year and in prior fiscal years; a description of the contributions from non-federal sources; the number and amounts of microloans made by intermediaries to all borrowers and to each of the following: women entrepreneurs and business owners, low-income entrepreneurs and business owners, veteran entrepreneurs and business owners, disabled entrepreneurs and business owners, and minority entrepreneurs and business owners; a description of the marketing, management, and technical assistance provided by each intermediary to all borrowers and to each of the following: women entrepreneurs and business owners, low-income entrepreneurs and business owners, veteran entrepreneurs and business owners, disabled entrepreneurs and business owners, and minority entrepreneurs and business owners; the number of jobs created and retained as a result of microloans and marketing, management, and technical assistance provided by each intermediary; the repayment history of each intermediary; and the number of businesses that achieved success after receipt of a microloan.

[94] S. 2869, the Small Business Job Creation and Access to Capital Act of 2009, §103. Maximum Loan Limits Under Microloan Program.

[95] Ibid.

[96] P.L. 111-240, the Small Business Jobs Act of 2010, §1113. Maximum Loan Limits Under Microloan Program.

[97] P.L. 111-240, the Small Business Jobs Act of 2010, §1401. Matching Requirements Under Small Business Programs.

[98] Representative Nydia Velázquez, Small Business Financing and Investment Act of 2009," House debate, *Congressional Record*, daily edition, vol. 155, no. 159 (October 29, 2009), pp. H12074, H12075; Senator Mary Landrieu, "Statements on Introduced Bills and Joint Resolutions," remarks in the Senate, *Congressional Record*, daily edition, vol. 155, no. 185 (December 10, 2009), p. S12910; and The White House, "Remarks by the President on Job Creation and Economic Growth," December 8, 2009, at http://www.whitehouse.gov/the-press-office/remarkspresident-job-creation-and-economic-growth.

[99] Susan Eckerly, "NFIB Responds to President's Small Business Lending Initiatives," Washington, DC, October 21, 2009, at http://www.nfib.com/press-media/press-media-item?cmsid=50080; and NFIB, "Government Spending," Washington, DC, at http://www.nfib.com/issues-elections/issues-elections-item/cmsid/49051/.

[100] Shelli B. Rossman and Brett Theodos, with Rachel Brash, Megan Gallagher, Christopher Hayes, and Kenneth Temkin, *Key Findings from the Evaluation of the Small Business Administration's Loan and Investment Programs: Executive Summary* (Washington, DC: The Urban Institute, January 2008), p. 58, at http://www.urban.org/ UploadedPDF/ 411602_executive_summary.pdf.

[101] Ibid.

[102] U.S. Small Business Administration, Office of the Inspector General, "SBA's Administration of the Microloan Program under the Recovery Act," pp. 6, 7, at http://www.sba.gov/office-of-inspector-general/868/12427.

INDEX

D

E